Why Current Affairs Needs Social Theory

Why Current Affairs Needs Social Theory

ROB STONES

Bloomsbury Academic
An imprint of Bloomsbury Publishing Plc

B L O O M S B U R Y
LONDON · NEW DELHI · NEW YORK · SYDNEY

Bloomsbury Academic

An imprint of Bloomsbury Publishing Plc

50 Bedford Square	1385 Broadway
London	New York
WC1B 3DP	NY 10018
UK	USA

www.bloomsbury.com

BLOOMSBURY and the Diana logo are trademarks of Bloomsbury Publishing Plc

First published 2015

British Library Cataloguing-in-Publication Data
A catalogue record for this book is available from the British Library.

ISBN: HB: 978-1-7809-3348-1
PB: 978-1-7809-3182-1
ePDF: 978-1-7809-3180-7
ePub: 978-1-7809-3179-1

Library of Congress Cataloging-in-Publication Data
A catalog record for this book is available from the Library of Congress

Typeset by Deanta Global Publishing Services, Chennai, India

For Klong and Pim

Contents

List of Figures

Acknowledgements

I'd like to express my gratitude to the University of Western Sydney for the conditions and resources that allowed me to write *Why Current Affairs Needs Social Theory*. The engagement of colleagues at UWS, audiences at Roskilde University and Loughborough University and former colleagues at the University of Essex all played an important role in the development of the book's perspective and argument. I would also like to thank Trish Greenhalgh for her refreshing confidence in social theory, and for offering valuable comments despite her own pressing deadlines.

I owe a good deal to Emily Drewe at Bloomsbury, for encouraging me to pursue a nascent idea, and helping it to take shape. Mark Richardson, Jyoti Basuita and Caroline Wintersgill at Bloomsbury provided subsequent support and made everything very easy. My brother Mike brought a professional's touch to the diagrams that have become an intrinsic part of my argument.

My deepest appreciation is to my family. To Ja, my wife, for her grace, affection and wisdom, and to our daughter, Klong, and our son, Pim, for their astute interest, and for making life such a great place to be. The book is dedicated, with much love, to Klong and Pim.

The author and publishers wish to thank the following for permission to use copyright material:

Routledge, an imprint of the Taylor and Francis Group, for material from 'Social Theory, Current Affairs, and Thailand's Political Turmoil: Seeing Beyond Reds vs. Yellows' by Rob Stones & Ake Tangsupvattana, published in *Journal of Political Power*, Vol 5:2, 217–238 (2012). The Journal's website can be found at: www.tandfonline.com

John Wiley & Sons for material from 'Social Theory and Current Affairs: A Framework for Intellectual Engagement', published in *The British Journal of Sociology*, Vol 65:2, 293–316 (2014). The Journal's website can be found at: www.lse.ac.uk/BJS/home.aspx

Preface

This is primarily a book for audiences. It is a primer for people who wish to improve the quality of their engagement with news and current affairs. Much like books that are bought with a view to learning a foreign language, I can't guarantee that you will get through the book, or even the first chapter, although I've tried my best to write it in such a way that this will happen. I've no doubt that it will be demanding at times, and this can't be helped; it's in the nature of the beast. I can, however, promise that if you do get through the book, having read it attentively, rising to whatever challenges it poses without losing patience, then you will get a great deal more from news and current affairs accounts than you previously have. You will be better equipped to engage in considered, reasonable, judicious debate about the social and political issues of the day than you previously were.

The book aims to realize this promise by bringing the academic specialism of social theory into a sustained conversation with the ways in which educated, thoughtful, citizens view and read news and current affairs. My motivation as I started writing the book lay in the determination to test out a belief that had for too long remained an intuition. This intuitive belief was that social theory, with its sustained, systematic quest to think deeply about the nature of society and the many different ways in which it ticks along, should be able to make more inroads into public life than it seems to manage. It should have the potential to contribute much more to the quality of public understanding about social and political issues than it does.

Part of social theory's under-performance has to do with the chasm that exists between the language it uses and the language of the public sphere, including the various registers of news and current affairs. These are languages from different worlds, each with their own traditions and history. If social theorists are to carry their thoughts into the public sphere, to persuade citizens that they have something valuable to offer, then ways have to be found to mediate between the two linguistic worlds. The conditions have to be created in which exchange and dialogue is possible.

Social theorists have a particularly heightened awareness of the role that *ideas and preconceptions* play in what we make of social life. That is, a heightened awareness of their influence on the way we see the world, its people and its institutions, in the way social interaction takes place, and in the way we interpret what we encounter in the media. Because of this, theorists spend a lot of time thinking about these ideas and preconceptions, asking themselves how these 'ways of seeing' might affect the quality of our grasp of the social world. They recognize that poor preconceptions, inadequate ways of envisioning the social and political worlds, lead to poor understanding. Our preconceptions – our typified ways of seeing – naturally influence our judgements about how to identify such things as an abuse of power, unfitting behaviour, pitiless decision-making, or the immediate source of suffering. Such judgements are based on generalizing criteria, so that there is much about the skills required to, say, identify a cause of suffering, that can be transposed, carried, from one situation to another. It is important to remember this, that background ways of seeing are routinely transposed from one situation to another. We carry them with us across the borders of different situations and events, and then adapt them to the specific circumstances and details of the case at hand.

The quality of the background, transposable, ways of seeing we bring to these judgements needs to be good if we are to develop genuine understanding about important social events. There is also an onus on knowing how to combine these general preconceptions with the colour and details of varied, individual cases. There needs to be quality at both of these levels. This is as true with respect to how we approach news and current affairs accounts as it is in any other aspect of our social lives. If there is an absence of quality at either of these levels, then our ability to interpret particular news and current affairs accounts will be limited; our judgements about causes, morality and the best ways forward will lack authority.

Social theorists reflect constantly on both levels of quality relevant to understanding news and current affairs. They reflect, that is, on how to improve the general ways of seeing that we carry with us from one situation to another, and on how we should combine these with the details of particular events and processes. Because of the key role played by ways of seeing that are general and transposable, and hence separated at a certain point in the thinking process from the concrete details of real-world situations, social theorists are inevitably and necessarily drawn to concepts and abstractions. The specialist terms and language they develop tends to parallel this. The language reflects a way of thinking that gets used to extracting the general from the detailed particulars of everyday life, of pulling back from the fray. Discussions of distinct political and social issues in the public sphere, on the other hand, tend to be expressed in the language of the everyday worlds of the various institutions that make up societies. The overriding impulse here is not one of abstraction. Rather, it is that of getting down to immediate tasks, making it through the day successfully enough, interacting with flesh-and-blood people, following or breaking written or unwritten rules, striving to achieve broader goals, to solve problems, to help someone out or to give them their comeuppance. Here there is a natural tendency to the concrete, the situational, the empirical in the many small worlds that loom large for us at work, home and in other spheres of life. This is paralleled in significant part in the more overarching public sphere, in the world of social and political issues conveyed by the media in news and current affairs coverage.

The gulf between the two languages needs to be bridged somewhere in the middle. Social theorists can play their part by engaging more directly with the visual, oral and written languages used in the various genres of news and current affairs, working hard at bringing their concepts into contact with the stories that are told in these formats, thinking about forms of expression in which the two worlds can be spoken about in one breath. The citizen-audiences for news and current affairs, for their part, need to be building from the other shore, prepared to bring the familiar and the abstract together in their interpretations.

At present, there is very little dialogue, and the dialogue that does exist is severely impoverished. It is conducted primarily in the realm of numbers – too often cut off from careful reflection on concepts – or in the realm of abstract moral ideas. These are significant areas to be concerned with, but they are a huge distance away from being enough. They need to be combined with, integrated with, and framed by, much deeper ways of thinking about the *in-situ* processes of the social world itself. How should we think about the precise mechanisms at work in the social and political processes that we see on television news? What is an adequate way to link these mechanisms to their consequences? How should we combine a better understanding of such real-world causes and consequences with the abstract thought about morality produced in political and ethical philosophy? And, in the light of these reflections about causes and consequences, and about how action in the midst of such complexities should be judged in moral terms, how can we also find a responsible way to think about remedies, solutions, or of simply making a bad situation a little less so? Another way of couching the last point is to ask: How should we think about strategy and political will in particular circumstances, and about the role that values should play in formulating these?

The intellectual sophistication with which we approach literature and the arts in the public sphere, and which we have latterly begun to show to an understanding of the natural world with the rise of popular science, is missing from public engagement with social and political issues. Adoption of the approach I advocate in *Why Current Affairs Needs Social Theory* could go some way to addressing this deficit. The strategy of the book focuses on improving the quality of the 'ways of seeing' audiences bring to news and current affairs. It begins by setting out just why it is essential for the dramatic surface events and spectacles of current affairs, of the kinds that overwhelmingly populate television news bulletins, to be thought about within their wider context. Events can only be understood once they are envisaged as positioned within this context, which should be thought of as a network of social and material relations in which the events have been produced. It isn't possible to understand how these events have come about, to understand what causal sequences are responsible for producing them, unless an effort is made to think about how they have emerged from a particular set of relations and circumstances that stretch beyond the immediate moments and visual spectacles of the events themselves. The immediate events have a history that is now in the past and, in this age of extended, complex societies, they will have been affected by processes that are also spatially distant. It is necessary to understand these 'absent' or 'invisible' conditions in order to understand why and how the events have come about as they have, and what alternatives are possible. This means we need to develop ways of thinking, ways of seeing, that incorporate these absent conditions if we are to have a better grasp of news and current affairs. Another way of talking about the same thing, of referring to the networks of relations in which events and the people involved in them are embedded, is to talk about the ways in which *social actors* – people and organizations – and their actions are embedded in *social structures*. The key objectives of the book can be summed up as follows. First, it wants to give audiences a firm sense of how to locate news and current affairs events within a context of social structures and processes within which the events make sense. And secondly, it provides the conceptual tools for audiences to be able to judge just how much or how little knowledge of this structural context, and what goes on within it, has been provided by a given current affairs account. In doing these things, it aspires to radically increase audience capacity for genuine understanding and analysis.

This emphasis can be thought of most fruitfully in tandem with the kind of message promoted by Alain de Botton in his recent book *The News: A User's Manual*. As I was completing my own book, I went to listen to de Botton give a lecture on *The News* to 2,500 people in the Concert Hall of Sydney Opera House. Inescapably, I wanted to quell the anxiety that we'd not both written the same book, but more realistically I was intrigued to see how two approaches to roughly the same subject matter, written at roughly the same time, would compare. The lecture was enviably insightful and engaging, and my conclusion was that while these were two very different books, each approach could enrich the other. For while de Botton's eloquent arguments were not directly concerned with social structure, or with the embedding of news events in contexts of relevant social networks, one of his central concerns is with how to get people to care sufficiently about news stories that they start to think seriously about them, and this is also of central importance for my own goals. De Botton writes of the need to expand the ways in which the news is told, venturing to broaden and develop the sensibilities of audiences. In search of these ends, he says, news stories should look to adopt some of the techniques of art and literature, including travel literature, whose neglect would be misguided. Journalists should seek out sensory, visual, empathetic ways of exciting our deeper interest in people and places, and their news organizations should encourage them to be unafraid of taking a distinctive perspective, of expressing a response with an individual voice and personality. Writing about world news, he declares that much less harm would be caused by such intrusions into neutrality than by those 'reporters who, by their implicit denial of ever having a response to anything foreign, fatally undermine our desire to add to our knowledge of the world'.[1]

De Botton draws on George Eliot, the author of *Middlemarch*, that masterpiece of empathy with large lives lived in hidden, prosaic places, traversed and fettered by the large forces of history. He argues that writers such as Eliot have the ability to help us imagine what it feels like to be caught up in news events: to be a human being in the midst of war, famine and dictatorship, or to be at the receiving end of human rights' abuses, or to be caught in the net of poverty, exploitation or corruption, or to find oneself at the mercy of a socio-natural catastrophe of the many kinds that continue to escape our capacity for prediction. Art, in its widest sense, said Eliot, is capable of helping us by 'amplifying experience and extending our contact with our fellow-men beyond the bounds of our personal lot'. It stretches our imagination to the lives of others, extending our sympathies and our sensibilities: '. . . a picture of human life such as a great artist can give, surprises even the trivial and the selfish into that attention to what is apart from themselves, which may be called the raw material of moral sentiment'.[2]

This concern to awaken audiences to 'the planet's less obtrusive beauty and tragedy', to get audiences to pay close attention to at least some of the news, some of the time, about others we don't naturally have an interest in, is not something I address explicitly in this book. In this, my argument needs to be complemented by de Botton's writing. However, the concern is there implicitly, and quite centrally, in my argument's key insistence. For the central contention of the book is that it isn't possible to truly understand the experience and fate of individuals if one fails to grasp the network of relations in which those lives are enmeshed, which impose their demands, rewards and sanctions on those individuals, and which provide the substance of everything they care about.[3] What is true for individuals is also true for the organizations and institutions in which they live their lives. To truly understand what is happening in news and current affairs events, to understand what has brought about these situations and predicaments, to be able to identify, who, if anyone, is responsible, and to responsibly suggest how things might change for the better, one needs the capacity to envisage the events as embedded in their relevant structural context. This capacity can provide imaginative empathy with added weight, with the ballast that grounds an individual within communities, social contexts and concrete networks of relations.[4] Caring about the substance of news and current affairs, and about those caught up in its forces, can be brought about both by the expansion of sensibility aided by art and literature and by the depth of comprehension allowed by situating events within the social co-ordinates which have made them what they are. Social theory complements the literary and artistic imagination. It enables us to explore the causes of events in specific times and places; to think seriously about moral responsibility within complex networks of social relations; and to engage with issues of what can be done, feasibly and responsibly, from a position that has a considerable grasp of what it does and doesn't know.

The arguments of the book are informed by the writings of a distinguished array of social thinkers. I have introduced some of these writers directly within the main text. However, for the sake of fluency and readability, in the body of the text I focus more on explaining the theoretical ideas and concepts relevant to the argument rather than spending too much time discussing their provenance. This gives readers the option of following the argument itself without having its flow disrupted by too many scholarly interruptions. On the other hand, I've used endnotes, numbered in the text, to reference all the theorists whose ideas are referred to, and to comment on these ideas where appropriate. This means that the book can also be read, with the aid of the endnotes, as an introduction to the underlying history and landscape of social theory, and also as a guide to which aspects of the work of given theorists are applicable to which aspects of real-world situations. References in the endnotes are both to short, introductory material and to more complex writings for those wanting to venture deeper into particular issues. For the introductory material, I've drawn heavily on my edited collection, *Key Sociological Thinkers*, which is a series of accessible 5,000-word chapters on prominent theorists written by leading commentators on their work.[5]

As will become clear in the course of *Why Current Affairs Needs Social Theory*, I approach the work of social theorists in an ecumenical spirit, wanting to draw from as many approaches as seem to offer insights into whatever problem is at hand. Any theorist, however, will have their own set of predilections, and will automatically gravitate towards some abstract concepts and approaches rather than others. In my case, these are around ideas of social structure, agency, time, space, power, culture, norms and ethics, and my leanings towards these can be partly explained by the fact that I've found these notions the most useful for the topics and questions I've grappled with, and attempted to shed some light on, during my own intellectual life. Such reasons will also have figured in other theorists' attraction to different concepts and ideas. As will also be seen in the course of the book, many seemingly disparate approaches are in fact compatible with each other, and my first instinct is always to look for ways of combining approaches so as to have the most powerful set of concepts to hand in seeking greater clarity about whatever part of the social world is beckoning.

1

What we should look for in television news

Spectacle and excitement

Something that frustrates many viewers of television news bulletins is the emphasis on spectacle and excitement over and above explanation and understanding. How many times have we watched an item on the evening news and come away shocked and perturbed, but none the wiser about the events covered? Hard-boiled, unquestionably courageous, professional journalists – often motivated above everything else by high public principles – are sent hither and thither across a region of the globe to pick up and run with the latest story, quickly attempting to understand the basic gist of what's been going on in order to be able to put together a 2- or 3-minute package. Some of these journalists will, in fact, have been covering a region for years on end and will have an in-depth background knowledge of their subject matter. Others have a more rudimentary knowledge, but have alternative skills valued by their networks, fluency perhaps, or screen presence. Even in the former case, one has a sense that the exigencies of the television news format radically constrain and channel the quality of information journalists are able to convey. Social theory can do little to directly affect many of the institutional, commercial, logistical and other pressures that create these constraints. It can, however, shed a good deal of light on the quality of the news and current affairs diet we are ultimately provided with. It can offer intellectual resources to strengthen the powers of interpretation and assessment available to audiences and to journalists, who may or may not have the autonomy to make use of them in their professional lives.

For the news channels themselves, conveying knowledge often seems to be less important than getting journalists and the cameras to where the action is, and, even more important, to have their journalists be seen to be where the action is. Sometimes it does matter where journalists are, when the authority we accord to what they tell us requires that we know they've witnessed something first hand, or that their presence *in situ* can in other ways assure us of the authority of their message. However, on many occasions it is by no means self-evident that their presence provides them with any special authority. At the extreme, we've all seen the rather forlorn, vaguely comic, pictures of a reporter, who is unable for one reason or another to be in the country he or she is talking about, speaking from just across the border in a neighbouring country, or from that second country's capital city. The message is that they aren't exactly where the action is, which is implied to matter in and of itself, but they're pretty close. The unspoken assumption is that to unlock the secrets of a news story, to really grasp the essence of what is going on, one has to be there or thereabouts. News authenticity consequently means having feet on the ground, a familiar face speaking to camera, preferably out of breath and dishevelled, with the story's ambient noises palpably present, whether these are the sounds of vehicles, the clamour of people scurrying, scuffling, marching, calling out their demands or their insults, or plaintively pleading for their plight to be recognized. There may also be the resonant rattle of gunfire, explosive reverberations from mortars, bombs and other killing devices, and, of course, the sights and the sounds of hardship, suffering and grief, often very hard to watch, all providing audiences back home with the vicarious sense-experience of being there. Sometimes, tragically, the journalists themselves become the victims.

Visually evocative background settings, also, are a deep-seated part of the news package. Settings are invoked in familiar tableaux: the desolate, boarded up shops and homes of an American mid-western automobile town; listless clusters of distracted men, at home in the middle of the day, set against billowing washing lines and the surrounding moorland of a Yorkshire mining village; the sight of saffron-robed monks on dusty tracks, standing out in sculpted relief against lush green tropical vegetation, as they demonstrate against the military junta in Burma; the intermittent lighting up of the sky in Baghdad, Belgrade or some other city, as it is attacked from the air; and the white and variously stained, sun-drenched, flat-roofed dwellings, palm trees, fences and checkpoints in Gaza or the West Bank. With the right treatment, such images can capture the imagination; they can potentially give a greater sense of what it feels like to suffer certain experiences, to be able to stand in the shoes of the people at the heart of a story.

But in reality, sounds, settings and suffering by themselves, and as palpable and intense as they are, are not enough to sustain anything more than a generic sense of fellow-feeling, coupled with a sense of having seen the same thing many times before. The fragmented, disembedded nature of what we are shown, and the speed with which one story flows into another, leaves us feeling disorientated, dizzy. Or it does if we continue to pay attention and try to make sense of it. History comes across as cyclical and unchangeable – what goes around comes around – and this typically engenders fatalism, an overwhelming sense that it would be futile to try and change the course of this interminable wheel of inevitable and homologous events.

There are *two key, related reasons* for these feelings of vertigo and fatalism. The *first* is the absence of co-ordinates to provide viewers with a sense of orientation, so that they can understand how the events on camera are related to the conditions and processes that surround those events, that led up to them, that played major roles in causing them to happen. This is the absence of what I will refer to throughout the book as a suitable *contextual field*. By this I mean the provision of contextualizing markers that would somehow manage to offer an adequate-enough map of the primary institutional and individual actors, networks, forces, pressures, dynamics and histories that are relevant to the moments of action we witness on our screens. Many aspects of this contextual field will not be visible in the action, in the events on screen, but without them the events would not have happened. They are the necessary conditions of existence of the events on camera, but for the most part their existence is elsewhere. These are conditions such as the decisions of corporate managements to close car factories or coal mines that are deemed to be uneconomic. They are sequences of networked conditions such as those created by the Burmese military dictatorship in the trade deals it negotiated with influential foreign powers, creating the financial conditions for its own survival, which, in turn, allowed it to continue its abuse of human rights and to curtail the freedom of speech of political dissenters. It is only the final stages of this latter sequence – the protests against these abuses and curtailments – that we see on camera. These influences on the events captured by television news might be at the other end of the city or on the other side of the globe, and so they are absent spatially from the events we see, but their various effects are transmitted to where the action is, and to what the action is. They thus have a presence in the events that are shown to us, even though they are not visible.

A key question to ask of any news story is consequently: What is its *relevant* contextual field? That is, in thinking about the what, where, when, who and how of the events that are spoken about or are captured on camera, we need to understand that there is more to understanding each of these things than what we see before our eyes. In the course of the book I shall argue that audiences need to initially try and map what they can of this field on the basis of the raw material provided in the story itself. The journalists producing the stories will be more or less helpful in facilitating and guiding such a process. The mapping needs to have a geographical, spatial dimension, providing a basic orientation as to how current institutions, individuals and forces – wielding variable powers – zone in from near and far to contribute their bit to the events in the field of vision. The mapping also needs a historical, temporal dimension, because the contextual field relevant to any event – the field relevant to the production of that event – will have its own history, and at its most palpable this history will have conveyed into the present such things as technology, infrastructure, hierarchies of power, distributions of wealth and so on. It will also have conveyed less tangible, but just as powerful, cultural elements such as memories, values, affiliations and grievances.

Precisely which parts of the contextual field will be relevant to a particular story will depend on that story's focus and claims, and we will return to this point through the book. The raw material that television news stories provide for mapping the contextual field will vary a good deal, both in terms of what a story actually covers and in terms of the degree of detail and precision with which it covers it. It is important for audiences to be highly attuned to this variability.

The *second* reason for the sense of dizziness and hopelessness news often conveys is that the absence of a contextual field is typically compounded by an additional absence. This is the lack of a genuine, empathetic engagement with the experience of the people that news accounts focus upon. Social theory calls this the 'hermeneutic' engagement.[1] Such engagement has the potential to add ballast to the spinning-top of news, to slow it down, to allow one to focus for more than a split second on those involved. It requires imaginative sympathy with the characters in focus, such that concerted effort is made to understand something of their cultural worldviews, including such things as what they most care about in life,[2] what their memories, sensibilities and mental scars are, what they wish for – or wished for – and how any of these affect the ways in which they experience the events in focus. If it's the case that news can't provide any of this, and shouldn't be expected to, then we should be cognizant of this. Its absence should be emblazoned in lights within the interpretative schemes we bring to our readings; we would need to fully and clearly recognize the relative poverty of such accounts when compared to the enriching accounts of interior lives captured in other genres, from in-depth oral histories to the great novels of world literature.

If it is the case that there is a relative dearth of empathy and imaginative sympathy in television news, then a further element that is key to the uprooted quality of news follows from this. For without focused engagement on the subjectivity of the social actors who appear in news stories, it is logically impossible to look at the ways in which that subjectivity is inhabited by the socio-structural context in which it lives, and which it constantly negotiates. It is not possible to situate these interior worlds in relation to such things as the objective social networks of roles, duties and obligations that impinge upon them. It would be difficult to over-emphasize this point, as it means that we can't anchor the subjective viewpoints of actors in their own sense of the dynamic nexus of social forces, power relations, expectations, pressures, potential sanctions and rewards, risks and dangers that provides them with their context. Subjective viewpoints are indeed 'subjective' and part of subjectivity is a potential to look at things differently from the ways society expects, and to resist social injunctions to do things in a particular way. However, while actors are not entirely determined by social situation, their relationship to their social context is far from being completely arbitrary or wilful. Subjective points of view, and the socialization processes that help to produce them, are not formed in a vacuum, but in relation to a particular contextual field. What actors feel, do and say can only be understood once they are placed within this context.

We consequently need to know how the contextual field 'out-there' enters 'in-here', how it is internalized in the minds of the subjects of the news stories, how it gets under the skin of the people and institutions that appear on the television screen. We need to know how it articulates with their ideals, values and cultural orientations. To do this we need empathy complemented by a sense of how those we empathize with experience the social relations or structures of the contextual field in which they are positioned. This means that a cultural, 'hermeneutic' engagement needs to be complemented by an awareness of how the subjectivity of those actors is grounded in, anchored in, a set of socio-structural relations provided by the relevant contextual field. We could refer to this as a 'hermeneutic-structural' engagement.[3]

This should affect how we approach news stories. If we feel that stories should be designed to elicit empathy, then we need to make a distinction between a kind of disembodied, universal empathy for all human beings and a more grounded, fleshed-out attempt to understand what it feels like to be a particular person in a particular time and place. More context is required for viewers to gain an adequate level of understanding about how it feels to be the person in the lens of the camera at that place at that time, rather than how it feels to be any person caught up in a roughly equivalent generic set of circumstances. Insisting upon the significance of the specificity of events means that one can situate particular people, with their unique names and biographies, within the push and pull of the specific what, where and when of the forces and dynamics within the story at hand. The universal, disembodied kind of empathy doesn't really require us to know something about a person's everyday concerns, who they care about, what their worries are and what lies ahead of them in the coming weeks and months. The more grounded, embodied kind of empathy does require these things, and it is then a small step to want to understand more about the social structures and relations which have conspired to make that person's life one dominated by fear, insecurity, poverty, ill-health or loneliness. For a journalist, or a viewer, to understand what everyday life feels like for this person, and also to have insights into whether things could conceivably be otherwise, and if so then how this might come about, then a good deal of background, situating context is required.

These points have direct implications for the feelings of fatalism and hopelessness induced by television news. For, as with situated actors, if engaged viewers are to be able to look for ways of improving a situation, are to be able to reflect upon whether resistance, protests, changes in consciousness or innovative policies are likely to make a positive difference, then they need to be able to objectively position actors within a mapping of the relevant contextual field. They also need to understand how these structural things look, subjectively, for the variously positioned people within this field. Part of this will involve understanding how things look from the perspective of those without power and part of this will mean understanding how they look for those with power. These are essential prerequisites for thinking responsibly about political strategy. So, the first reason for vertigo and fatalism is the lack of *a contextual field* in which to place a news story, and the second reason is the lack of *a hermeneutic-structural* engagement with the people that television news tells us about.

It would clearly be asking a lot of television news if we were to demand that it tries to fully address both of these issues. Only a moment's reflection is required to see that it is probably unfair and inappropriate to criticize television news for not being entirely satisfactory in its treatment of these matters. But should it do more than it does? At this point I want to leave the question hanging as a potentially fruitful quandary about just how much we should expect from television news, or from any other genre of news and current affairs for that matter. It is surely possible to expect too much. In part this is why I want to place much of the onus of my claims for social theory on the greater depth of awareness it could provide for audiences. In later chapters I will focus on the tools which social theory can provide to enable audiences to do more with what is given to them. For the moment, however, I will use the framework I've introduced as a backdrop against which to say more about what television news actually does provide and the various ways in which this is objectively limited.

Amusing ourselves to death

Nearly 30 years ago, Neil Postman, a professor of communication arts and sciences at New York University, composed an argument about the limitations of television as a source of education that helps to explain why the landscape of television news is as it is. Postman didn't confine his argument just to television's news output, but he definitively included television news within his compass. He was concerned to focus on all kinds of nominally serious television. His argument can usefully be read as an explanation for television's preoccupation with spectacle and excitement, and its propensity to present an interminable litany of potentially interchangeable events. Equally, it illuminates why television channels would be likely to resist any suggestion that television news should provide more of the kinds of context, specificity and structural-hermeneutics essential to raise reporting to a higher level. The argument also sheds more light on the characteristics of television news we've already mentioned. It should be noted that Postman's argument is directed most evidently at commercial television, and that there will be some important differences, and perhaps more hope for optimism, when one looks at public service broadcasting.[4] There will also, however, be significant similarities.

Writing in the US context, Postman's book, entitled *Amusing Ourselves to Death,* focused on how the values of entertainment had increasingly encroached upon the world of news and current affairs.[5] This, he argued, was a phenomenon closely linked to the significance accorded to ratings and advertising revenues. Given the importance of these revenues to news channels, it was clear that the media was increasingly reluctant to make demands on its audience lest they vote with their feet, switching to another channel or switching off. This had major implications for the capacity of television to promote quality news and current affairs programmes with a view to educating audiences. If keeping the audience away from other channels were to be the primary goal then this had a knock-on effect on the kind of programming that could be tolerated.

Postman took the implications of this seriously, and trenchantly criticized the idea of news as entertainment. He broadened the critique to cover television's more general advancement of a philosophy of education based on simply pleasing and entertaining the audience. Those in today's higher education world who embrace the results of student satisfaction surveys without the hint of qualification would well heed his reasoning. Even by the mid-1980s there had already been a rapid dissolution of education organized 'around the slow moving printed word, and the equally rapid emergence of a new education based on the speed-of-light electronic image'.[6] Postman felt it was necessary to face up to the consequences of this, and particularly to what he called the three commandments that form the philosophy of education associated with television. Each of these commandments has a bearing on the ability of television to provide sufficient background context for a story to be understood, both in terms of information and in terms of how to conceptualize that information.

The first of these commandments was said to be, 'thou shalt have no prerequisites', meaning that the idea of building up of a body of knowledge over time, constructing edifices of understanding brick by brick, could not be countenanced except at the most minimal of levels. This commandment fed into television's mission to 'exclude no viewer for any reason, at any time'. The second commandment was captured as 'thou shalt induce no perplexity', lest the intellectual demands made encourage the viewer to switch to another channel:

> This means that there must be nothing that has to be remembered, studied, applied or, worst of all, endured. It is assumed that any information, story or idea can be made immediately accessible, since the contentment, not the growth, of the learner is paramount.[7]

The third commandment, which Postman believes is the most formidable, is 'thou shalt avoid exposition like the ten plagues visited upon Egypt'. Taken together, these commandments, says Postman, mean that television teaching always takes the form of storytelling, conducted through dynamic images and supported by music, and it gives short shrift to serious, rigorous and sustained '[a]rguments, hypotheses, discussions, reasons, refutations or any of the traditional instruments of reasoned discourse'. The name we properly give, says Postman, to education without *prerequisites*, *perplexity* or *exposition*, is entertainment.[8]

Postman's arguments are made with the United States of 30 years ago in mind, but they are generalizing arguments. Whether it is always like this, and if it is, then whether it will always have to be like this, should be open questions. And it is equally worth asking if some countries or some media organizations have managed to confront these challenges more adequately than others and also if there has been any movement and change over time. In any event, Postman's observations have enough truth in them to be worthy of serious reflection.

Seeing beyond the immediate spectacle

The very idea of asking audiences to approach news stories with the notion of a contextual field in mind is a statement of the need for prerequisites – *conceptual prerequisites*. It is to insist on the idea of the contextual field as a conceptual prerequisite for understanding, one that provides the background categories with which audiences can interpret whatever exposition is made available. The contextual field is designed to direct audiences to look for the positional markers in a story required to situate events within an appropriate context.

In writing about the Israeli–Palestinian conflict, academics Greg Philo and Mike Berry, associated with the Glasgow University Media Group, work implicitly with something akin to the idea of a contextual field. They criticize the failure of television news in the United Kingdom to provide the informational raw material that could populate a contextual field. What they say reinforces Postman's points by illustrating the extent to which television news avoids the exposition, and the potential perplexity, that would be required to sufficiently place news events in a meaningful context. They argue, specifically, for the inclusion of more historical context. Surely, they say, viewers should be told that 'when Israel was created in 1948, a large number of Palestinians were displaced from their homes and became refugees', and that 'many of these people then went to live on the West Bank of the Jordan, in East Jerusalem and in Gaza, all of which were subsequently occupied by Israel in the war of 1967. The Palestinians subsequently lived under Israeli military control which they bitterly contested. . .'.[9] They later note the BBC's failure to properly explain the ongoing nature of the military occupation imposed by Israel on the Palestinians, quoting radio references to 'building' in East Jerusalem, wondering 'if BBC journalists will ever run out of euphemisms for describing this'.[10] They poke fun at the idea that there isn't enough time in a short bulletin to unpack what 'building' might mean:

> This vague description conveys very little of what is at stake. Actually what the Israelis were doing was putting houses for their own people in a city which they had taken by force. It does not take long to say this.[11]

Any mention of Israel and Palestine, of course, immediately raises the spectre of ideological perspective, of the side from which a story is being told, and what this means for standards of objectivity. Suffice to say that from whatever perspective a story is being told, the issues of context and specificity remain the same, and are always critical for questions of the status and adequacy of an account. The ability to assess the status and adequacy of any news account from any perspective is key to the argument of this book.

The kind of historical information that Philo and Berry suggest could easily be included in news stories is still really quite rudimentary. It is certainly much less than the sum total of information we would ideally like citizen viewers to possess as they carry out the work of forming their opinions. Television news would have to change quite radically in order to provide enough of the kind of positioning and specificity required for the formation of well-informed, politically educated citizens. The truth, for now, is that television news stories very often end up being virtually interchangeable, one with the other, with the sounds, the commentary and the images of a story from Syria appearing to be very much like one from Iraq or Egypt. This is precisely because the stories are too free-floating; they lack a grounding in their context. They are presented without provision of that background knowledge that would allow us to understand the nature of their positioning, and to grasp enough of the detailed processes that have led to things ending up this way. We are told almost nothing about such things as the various *causes* of the news event, about why the news event has happened now rather than last week or last year, about the relative strength of the various forces involved, or of what kinds of solutions would be possible within this context and the odds for or against these happening. Instead of specific contexts and processes, clearly conveyed, we have the same journalists in different places, wearing roughly the same clothes, ducking and diving, exuding the same urgency and spirit, implying or openly stating their moral condemnation of one side or the other and displaying what comes across as genuine, unaffected concern for the plight of the suffering. It is often only the visual backdrops and the names of leaders or groupings that provide some cues to geographical context. Social critics have referred disparagingly to these tendencies of news bulletins as a preoccupation with 'hot live action' or the 'bang bang stuff', deriding the way in which the preference for the dramatic moment or spectacle – with one of that station's own journalists in its midst – crowds out any space for the provision of the context and the causal explanation required for real understanding.

Excessive expectations of television news

But this brings us back to the question of what we should expect from television news. Perhaps its job is simply – but vitally – to alert us when something newsworthy is happening. It tells us the bare bones. We certainly shouldn't expect it to deliver all the intellectual raw material necessary for effective citizenship. We need to balance a concern that we get the best out of television news with an acceptance that there will always be limits to what it can provide. Television news alone will be more or less adequate as a source depending upon the degree of depth a viewer requires on a particular subject. For getting a greater depth on a subject, we need to conceive of informed citizens reading across genres of news and current affairs, and supplementing this, where necessary, with recourse to the arts, humanities and natural sciences. Television news can be complemented by news, feature and opinion pieces in broadsheet newspapers or magazines; by documentary films; by long pieces in periodicals such as the *New York Review of Books* or the *London Review of Books;* by fiction or drama in its many forms; or by academic journal articles and books. The home pages of television channels such as the BBC, Al Jazeera, or the ABC in Australia, or those of broadsheet newspapers across the globe, now provide an invaluable resource for 'reading across' stories and genres, filling in gaps by following trails of links to further stories from within and outside that organization. Video links are combined with the written word, and timelines and background summaries can be found on most topics. All of this can be supplemented, of course, by a constant flow of alerts, notifications and feeds, more or less tailored to an individual's preoccupations. There is still, of course, the issue of trust and the essential checking and double-checking of the veracity of facts and information, something that is quite rightly close to the heart and the integrity of traditional journalism.

These webs of information can provide more of the information we would ideally want citizens to possess. By themselves, however, they wouldn't provide the 'ways of seeing' necessary to make adequate sense of the information, or to develop an appropriate response to it. For this we would need to return to the question of how to marshal and make sense of all the information. This requires guidance from social theory – from the stocks of systematic reflections on social phenomena – as to how to conceptualize social entities and processes and how to link these concepts to the many fragments of empirical evidence that assail us.

I have begun to argue that the place to anchor this conceptualization is within a contextual field. We start by identifying the contextual field relevant to the story at hand and to the key arguments or concerns of the account.

If the story were about power, then in order to provide the relevant context, we would want an idea as to who was wielding the decisive influence and authority, what interests and values were informing the use of it and what kinds of interests and values were held by those suffering from it, or resisting it. Further, we would want to ask how much power these latter, weaker, groups had, and whether all of these groups had reasonable claims to legitimacy. Once we had made some inroads into these still very basic questions then – if we were interested in remedies, solutions – we could begin to surmise, and even begin to explore, whether it would be possible for some alliance of groups to put a stop to illegitimate uses of power. Alternatively, we might decide that fatalism is indeed the necessarily appropriate response. All this involves a form of mental mapping, and I will say more about this in the next chapter. For now, the important message is that the world of social theory is a world in which more demanding questions can be asked about the raw material of news and current affairs. It is a world in which it is important to draw attention to the lack of relevant context and specificity in a news story, and to try and work through which ways of thinking, and what kinds of background information are most relevant to the events that a news story is covering.

Media frames and audience skills

How a story is told can help or hinder the intuitive propensity of audiences to place events within a contextual field. A set of fascinating experiments bearing on this point were carried out in the 1980s and published in the early 1990s by Shanto Iyengar, then professor of Communication Studies at the University of California, Los Angeles. His research noted that when poverty was covered in the news, which was rarely, it tended to be covered in what he called an *episodic frame*. This meant it only talked about a specific incident, cut off from its structural context and typically presented from a human-interest angle. In his experiments, three examples of news stories presented in episodic frames – which according to Iyengar amounted to 66 per cent of all news stories on poverty – were shown to audiences.[12] One was a report on the high cost of heating, which described a particularly harsh winter in the upper Midwest, focusing on two families who were unable to pay their heating bills. A second, entitled 'Homeless', focused on two black teenagers living on the streets of New York City and a white couple living in their car in San Diego. And a third story described the financial difficulties facing the family of an unemployed car worker in Ohio. The participants in the experiment were asked to watch these kinds of news stories, with Iyengar correctly hypothesizing that their episodic framing would influence the viewers to hold the poor people themselves responsible for their predicament. This was even more so in cases such as the story involving the black teenagers, because of deeply rooted cultural preconceptions – background categories – about race and welfare issues.[13] This latter observation says a good deal about the importance of the predispositions that audiences bring with them to their interpretation of news texts, something which I will return to shortly.

These reactions, of blaming individuals, contrasted with responses to stories that used what Iyengar called a *thematic frame*, a frame that placed poverty in a broader context, documenting an increase in national poverty, marked reductions in the scope of federal social welfare programmes, and the implications for poverty of the management and regulation of the federal budget deficit. When this broader thematic frame was used, pointing towards socio-structural factors making a difference, responsibility for the plight of individuals tended to be attributed, instead, towards government and society: 'poverty was depicted in terms of collective or societal outcomes and trends'.[14] I see this sketching out of a broader thematic frame as an important part of what it means to provide a more adequate contextual field for news stories, which means positioning them in relation to the wider socio-structural environment, rather than treating the stories as somehow free-floating, emerging out of thin air.

The forces and dynamics of the immediate socio-structural environment in which people experience poverty have an objective reality, and one that will involve all kinds of local features mixing in with more national and global dimensions. Because of this, it is important to both embrace and go beyond the broad, macro, contours of the kind of thematic frame identified by Iyengar. More can be said about this thematic frame, and its implications for macro-, meso- and micro-issues, and much of the rest of the book will be devoted to doing this through an elaboration of how we approach the contextual field. The meso-level issue is at the heart of my argument. It's necessary to zoom in to this middle ground, to identify all the most relevant contextual forces encroaching on, constraining and so on, the lives of the various subjects of the kinds of news stories drawn upon by Iyengar. The macro – national and global – forces will still be present in their effect, at this middle ground, but they will have local manifestations. Zooming in, attempting to map something of all of the most important contextual structures impinging on lived lives, is required if we are to try and grasp the nature of the objective forces these people are subject to. It is also important, however, to understand how these *objective* factors put their stamp on the people's *subjective* experience, on their inner realities. It will hopefully become clearer and clearer as the book proceeds, that this interplay between objective forces and subjective experience lies at the heart of what takes place in the events news stories cover, whether or not news stories pay attention to them. Dynamics, forces and subjective experiences differ from place to place, situation to situation, and if these fail to be understood by journalists, or it they grasp them but fail to convey them in their news bulletins, then the essential texture of those people's reality will be lost. News stories will end up simply presenting generic, empty stereotypes of conflict, the last story interchangeable with the next and the next interchangeable with the last.

Iyengar's findings reveal how the framing of news by those who produce it has effects on audiences that are 'unnoticed'. The experiments demonstrate that audience responses are profoundly affected by producers' decisions to frame stories in episodic or thematic ways, and they also show that viewers were unaware of these effects. This points to the profound ability of textual 'framings' to elicit certain responses from people. These effects will be particularly pronounced when the viewers in question are not primed to take some critical distance from the news stories they are exposed to. This is not a straightforward matter of general levels of education; Iyengar's audiences tended to be more educated, more affluent and more politically engaged than one would have found in a representative sample of the American electorate. Rather, it is a matter of drawing attention to the critical tools – the background preconceptions and categories intuitively drawn on in responding to stories – that are brought to the interpretation of news stories, and to ask what can be done to cultivate and educate these.

These categories and preconceptions, which have been elucidated by the phenomenological tradition in social theory,[15] have the same basic structure as the more general sets of background understandings we bring to our interpretations of plays, films and political dramas, and more broadly to all our interactions in everyday life. They determine how we intuitively think about things. Given the significance of news to democratic citizenship, and the significance of the quality of background capacities to the interpretation of news, it's clear that it should be an intrinsic part of education to heighten awareness of what they are, how they work and whether we think they are adequate to the task. Iyengar was able to point to background preconceptions among his sample, triggered particularly by episodic accounts, in which exposure to actors possessing certain combinations of race, gender, age and marital status (i.e. black adult single mothers) was automatically translated into assumptions of individual responsibility, without any sense of a need for an understanding of social forces and pressures. This lack of ability to think in categories of *social structure*, and of individuals being embedded within social structures, is of key importance. It points to something deficient in the quality, durability and resilience of the background understandings that Iyengar's viewers brought to their interpretation of sociopolitical issues.

The notion of social structure is difficult to pin down once and for all, making sure none of its characteristics have been left out of a definition or characterization. It can be usefully thought of as all those elements – such as the structured distribution of resources and the structured organization of social interactions, with all their hierarchies, rules, rewards, sanctions and expectations – that provide the context within which individual and institutional actors do whatever they do. Because of this, for my purposes, it can often be thought of as synonymous with the contextual field. Where someone is positioned within social structures, either at birth or at a later point, will have a profound effect on their subsequent life chances. The aspects of social structure most written about and discussed in both academic and non-academic literature are those related to political power, class and occupation, gender, race, nationality, ethnicity, language, religion, disability, sexuality and access to housing and services, including education and health services. The social structural context presents actors with a variety of constraints, depending upon where they are situated within it, and it can also, of course, provide opportunities, empowerment and so on, the character and extent of which also depend upon one's situation. Notions such as status and stigma, and of differential levels of cultural capital[16] (to do with levels of education; manners of speech, dress, gesture, comportment; aesthetic tastes; cultural knowledge; and so on), overlap with the categories just mentioned, and are often derived from them in various ways. All are deeply embedded as structural categories that provide the possibilities available to individuals, and which imprint themselves on who they are.

Emphasizing social structure means moving away from accounts of the world that place all the emphasis on individual actors, blaming them entirely for everything that befalls them, or praising their efforts and talents, and these alone, when they succeed in some way. What individuals experience, how they act in the world, and with what degrees of success or frustration, will certainly depend to a degree on their own agency, but it will also depend to a huge extent on the socio-structural cards they have been dealt, and on the cards they continue to be dealt as they navigate their way through life. There are many things in their lives, and the context of their lives, that people can neither control nor influence.

Media frames and social-theoretical frames

As long as audiences are unaware of the mechanisms at work in news stories, and so are unable to protect themselves from their effects, power is well and truly lodged in media accounts and how they are framed. The idea of 'media frames' is used widely by academics in contemporary media and communications studies to indicate the perspectives and categories through which people read news stories, and through which they are constructed in the first place. Iyengar's experiments demonstrated the ability of frames to manipulate the sample audiences of that time, place and culture, albeit that much of this was probably unintentional on the part of journalists. We should be concerned by the vulnerability of audiences that such studies imply, and by the relatively low level of current affairs literacy that this entails. Iyengar's use of the idea of media frames is ultimately very broad brush, with the episodic frame representing a more individualistic, free-floating, presentation of events and the thematic frame broadly representing a more structural presentation. I want to develop and deepen a form of audience literacy that takes Iyengar's thematic, structural, frame as just the starting point for its readings.

Before moving on to explore the structural terrain as such, developing the conceptual language of the contextual field, it is necessary to provide a stronger sense of what we might call the 'relative autonomy' of the media frame itself. This is the independent power of the media text, with its particular perspective, rhetorically conveyed through such things as the content, emotion and force of its language, and through the spectacle and the connotations of its visual images. The media text is able to convey a great deal about the world in a way that will be more or less impressionistic and rhetorical, and which can leave the audience feeling they know much more than has been expressly stated, argued for or substantiated. It can suggest a sense of individual responsibility for poverty or of structural responsibility for poverty through a variety of techniques that would stand up more or less well to rigorous scrutiny on the basis of social theory. It's important to be able to analyse this 'rhetoric of the text', and in order to do so it is useful to adopt additional concepts from the wider media frames' literature to add to the ideas of the thematic and episodic dimensions of frames. These additional concepts allow more to be said about the character and content of any news and current affairs text, and to develop a more sophisticated sense of how audiences are guided to particular points of view. They provide scaffolding on the basis of which each text can be treated in its own terms, with analysis focusing on the ways in which it functions as 'a form of rhetoric . . . persuading us – the readers, the viewers – that something happened'.[17] Analyses focus on the precise ways 'in which news stories work *as stories*; the way they generate a narrative, with protagonists, whose motives and actions assign causation and responsibility'.[18]

I will focus on a set of concepts that are highly influential among media frame researchers within media and communications studies, establishing themselves as an orthodoxy of sorts. These were introduced in a seminal article published in the 1990s by Robert M. Entman, then professor of communication studies, journalism and political science at Northwestern University, Illinois. Entman noted four main operations performed by the framing of news, namely: (i) the defining of problems; (ii) the diagnosis of causes; (iii) the making of moral judgements; and (iv) the suggestion of remedies.[19] These operations can have a major effect on how news is told, and thus on the shape taken by the news of the day is relayed into homes across the nation and beyond. One can summarize by saying that the frame approach focuses on those processes of selection, emphasis, rhetoric and form by which texts, crucially, 'define problems, diagnose causes, make moral judgements, and suggest remedies'.[20] As frames are a way of selecting, categorizing and organizing the information available in a story, politicians of different stripes inevitably attempt to get their own 'frames' on each of these four operations accepted by journalists, while journalists may insist on their own frames, which might overlap with those of the politicians or be entirely different. In turn, audiences either accept the frame presented to them in the news or come to some kind of more or less conscious negotiation between a news frame and their own preconceived perspective and values.

Entman's characterization of these four main operations carried out by news texts is remarkably close to the key preoccupations of social theorists who are concerned with the status and adequacy of knowledge claims about processes within the social and political world.[21] The reason for this similarity is not hard to see, as both sets of analysts are concerned with the same phenomena and with presenting plausible, convincing accounts about those phenomena. The difference is that the focus of analysis in the media frames' literature is on the ways in which the rhetoric of the text persuades, while social theorists are concerned with the status and satisfactoriness of media representations of, and judgements about, social reality. However, social theorists have to pay close attention to both sets of interests. For in order for social theorists to be able to make judgements on the status and adequacy of media accounts of reality, they first need to be able to grasp the rhetoric of news texts, excavating or recovering the claims that have been made, making explicit what is often left as a message that is only partially stated or vaguely implied, but which leaves a powerful impression that such and such is the case.

At this point in the analysis – as one sees how problems have been defined, causes diagnosed, moral judgements made and remedies suggested within the news text – that social theory indicates a further moment. This is the moment when the analysis of how the media has framed reality gives way to an analysis of whether the media has framed reality in an adequate manner. This is the moment when the social-theory frame takes over. Thinking about events as embedded within a contextual field is a key part of this stage, providing a set of benchmarks against which to reflect upon the character and adequacy of the reality conveyed by a news text. Put another way, the purpose of this book is to present *social-theoretical frames* through which audiences can critically interrogate news *media frames*, keeping a particular eye on the extent to which they over-simplify and misrepresent social relations.

Social-theoretical frames situate events within contextual fields; they are attuned to the structural positioning of actors within networks of social relations. As we shall see in future chapters, they provide clear conceptualization of the entities, relations and processes that *exist in* the social world, that populate it. However, social-theoretical frames are not only about what exists in the social world but also about providing protocols for gaining systematic *knowledge about* what exists, both in general and in a particular place and time. They offer guidelines on how to ascertain the quality of the knowledge provided by a media text, and on how to judge the adequacy of that knowledge when compared to the claims the text makes for it.[22] Drawing on social theory to approach news and current affairs entails a project of expressly cultivating and refining the usually tacit, taken-for-granted ways of seeing employed by current affairs audiences, so they become better equipped for the task at hand. Such a project is shamelessly pedagogic in its intent, and it is resolutely, patiently committed to the long haul. It is about audiences, citizens, having a greater capacity to minimize manipulation and set their own agenda. It is also about asking journalists to think about the intellectual agenda they bring to telling news and current affairs, and to interrogate the room for manoeuvre within the sets of constraints they work within.

But this is to get ahead of ourselves. In the next chapter I will go on to outline the key concepts of the contextual field and how these can be drawn on to judge the quality of knowledge contained in media accounts. Before that, however, it's important to say a little more about the role played by the idea of the contextual field in my argument. I will do this through reference to a critique of journalism and news made by the celebrated French sociologist and public intellectual, the late Pierre Bourdieu, whose account begins to articulate how social theory can identify those areas of social context that need to be included in a news story if it is to be rendered more meaningful. Bourdieu was talking about the same phenomenon as that captured by the discussion of 'episodic frames', or 'bang bang stuff', when he wrote of the 'demagogic simplification of television news coverage'.[23] He argued that the lack of context reduces news events to the level of the absurd, rendering them so cut off from their antecedents and their consequences that it is impossible to make any sense of them. The result is a series of flash photos, a fragmented, deracinated, de-historicized, 'litany of events with no beginning and no real end'.[24] We could add that the events have no real beginning in that they suddenly appear on our screens without warning, and seemingly out of nowhere as we have usually been unaware that the antagonisms, conflicts or other dynamics in this or that part of the world have been bubbling away under the surface for months or perhaps years. But the events also have no real beginning in the sense that once they have appeared on our screens, there is very little provision, even then, of the relevant historical background, of antecedents, required to situate them and with which to begin to develop an understanding of what is happening, and why. Likewise, the events have no real ending as the stories just disappear at some point from our screens, more often than not without any clear sense of resolution.

Lacking historical context, a proper sense of the factors that have helped to bring about the present events-in-focus, or any account of the dynamic forces and pressures that make up the current strategic terrain, it is impossible to think cogently about how to address the issues being reported. Without adequate contextualization there can be no real appreciation, for example, of the probable consequences of intervention by agencies of goodwill, whoever these might be. Bourdieu recognized the importance for genuine understanding of embedding events within their appropriate contextual field. He wrote of the need for news and current affairs coverage to reinsert events back into the 'networks of relevant relationships' in which they are actually embedded. That is, there must be an attempt to 'make events (say, an outbreak of violence in a high school) really understandable' by reinserting 'them in a network of relevant relationships (such as the family structure, which is tied to the job market, itself tied to government hiring policies, and so on)'.[25]

From the perspective of systematic knowledge it's important to take very seriously the adjective 'relevant' that Bourdieu attaches to 'networks of relationships'. The aspects of a news event that are somehow 'relevant', the bits of information relating to the event that can be appropriately labelled as 'relevant', will depend on *the character* of the news story. There is a difference, for example, between a story that makes an argument that includes causal claims and one that is entirely descriptive, simply evoking a spectacle through words or images. If a current affairs documentary were to make a causal claim about an outbreak of violence in a high school, then the precise character of this claim would determine what was 'relevant' to substantiating it. Let's say the claim, to follow Bourdieu's lead, was that the violence was directly linked to tension in local households, that this, in turn, was due to lack of employment in the vicinity, and that this, in its turn, was due to cutbacks in public expenditure or the withdrawal of state subsidies, which had led to a large locally based employer closing down its operations. The claims about this causal chain would then determine the precise forms, contours and sites of the contextual field relevant to these claims. This would not prevent the same documentary from describing the outbreak of violence itself in some detail, from taking an interest in the history and organization of the school, or in the characters and idiosyncrasies of some of the teachers, or of various people's descriptions about what happened on the day in question. But many of these things would be irrelevancies in relation to the causal claims unless they happened to shed some light on whether the causes of the violence were indeed what the documentary claims they were.

Outline of chapters

Bourdieu's account adeptly begins the process of indicating how social theory can be used to shed critical light on current affairs accounts. However, his suggestions are still fairly rudimentary. In the next chapter I will begin to flesh out and elaborate upon the concepts required to look in detail at the social entities, relations and processes of news accounts. For more is needed if we are to adequately address the kinds of questions and claims in Bourdieu's example of high school violence, and of the analogous questions and claims that appear in virtually all news and current affairs accounts. I will start by outlining the core elements of the central idea of a *contextual field*, with a concentration on the key *objective factors* audiences should mentally sketch in when mapping the relevant contextual field of a story they are interested in.

Some of the exposition of concepts in this chapter will be quite abstract, and I make no apologies for this, as it is a necessary step in the argument. However, it is important that the clarification sustains the level of engagement with real lives and particular dilemmas that I want to be carried through into readings of current affairs. To try and achieve this, I interweave two sets of illustrative examples into the account. The first is an imaginative example drawn from the work of the political theorist Iris Marion Young, which focuses on the socially structured predicament of a young single mother, Sandy, starting its narrative from the point at which she needs to move out of her rented central-city apartment building in an American city because a developer has bought the building and plans to convert it into condominiums. This discussion illustrates how Sandy, as a social actor directly involved at ground level, *experiences the objective character of the contextual field* that she is faced with.

The sections that come after Sandy's story, told from the position of an involved actor, look at academic media analyses of stories told from the perspective of externally positioned journalists. Specifically, I will focus on journalistic coverage of transport policy in Denmark at the turn of the new millennium, and of news coverage in Sweden, in 2011, of the mistreatment of elderly people in private health care. The contrast between these accounts and Sandy's story should also ideally draw attention to the contrasting kinds of knowledge that are likely to be produced from the two situated perspectives – involved and external – and where the blind spots are likely to be. However, my emphasis in this section is on the ways academic media analysis tends to focus much more on the language, rhetoric and so on of the journalistic text and much less on what it manages to say about the objective characteristics of the contextual field as such. My purpose is to indicate that it is not only audiences and journalists that need social theory, but also academic media scholars. It is to insist that while we do certainly need the sophisticated analyses of media texts, with their emphasis on discourses and media frames, we also need the tools to look beyond these discourses, to analyse what current affairs texts tells us about the characteristics of the events they are writing about, including what they tell us about the relevant networks of relations that have produced those events. The analysis of the journalistic accounts also, importantly, allows us to see the limitations of the ways in which journalists perceived the contextual fields relevant to their stories.

There is just enough in the academic analyses of the media accounts of the two cases to allow us to glimpse some of the limitations of the way in which journalists do engage with the contextual fields relevant to their stories. Chapter 2 can thus also begin to clarify social theory's role in pointing to the limitations of the frames journalists tend to employ. It can thus begin the process of revealing more about the ways in which these frames fail – to return to Bourdieu's locution – to adequately reinsert events back into the 'networks of relevant relationships' in which they are actually embedded, and within which they would be understandable. The two case studies from Scandinavia reinforce one's common-sense knowledge that the frames typically employed in the presentation of, and in the audience reception of, news events tend to contain vague, thin and overly rhetorical ways of apprehending the social world. They show that these 'ways of seeing' lack the conceptual granularity necessary to guide specific pieces of information into their appropriate place within relevant networks of relations. Without this conceptual granularity, and the provision of the relevant historical and socio-structural context it enables, it isn't possible to make sufficient sense of the fragments of information that circulate around a topic. The chapter will begin the process of providing audiences (and journalists) with concepts that can allow them – as far as the content of particular news accounts permits – to embed events carefully within a suitable contextual field.

Chapter 3 will take the argument a step further by providing a detailed account and analysis of an episode from the Danish political drama, *Borgen*. The purpose of this analysis is twofold. The first intention is to use the genre of political drama, in which there is a range of devices for the representation and exploration of interior lives engaged with the immanent political context, as a benchmark against which to mark the weakness of this *subjective* dimension in the vast majority of news and current affairs accounts. The exposition of the ways in which, in one episode of *Borgen*, the contextual field is subjectively internalized and responded to by individuals and organizations complements the exposition of objective elements in Chapter 2. It enables us to introduce the additional concepts necessary to think systematically about the ways in which actors internalize the contextual field, the effects it has on them and the predicaments it presents. It will also allow us, later in the book, to make reference back to the relative depth of treatment of the interior life in this drama, as a means of highlighting the poverty of such treatment in specific news, documentary or radio texts.

The second purpose of this focus on the *Borgen* episode is to demonstrate that audiences already have interpretative skills that are much more sophisticated than they are likely to give themselves credit for. Audiences already routinely position key actors within broader contextual fields. They already mobilize, in nascent form, many of the concepts social theory suggests should be brought to the interpretation of events and processes within those fields. We should take heart from the fact that there are segments of the television audience who, without reaching for the channel switcher, routinely deal with exposition and perplexity, to use Postman's terms, and do so on the basis of their own stocks of typified knowledge which provide the necessary conditions, or prerequisites, for interpretation and understanding. And as audiences already deploy quite sophisticated skills of interpretation when they engage with drama series it is not a great leap to ask them to deploy similar skills when it comes to their reception of news and current affairs, and for them to demand this of others. Greater awareness that these skills are, to a great extent, already there, can embolden, encourage and facilitate their transfer. None of this is to take away from my case that a serious explicit engagement with the concepts of social theory can appreciably refine and enhance these skills.

In Chapters 4 and 5 I will directly apply the ideas introduced in the opening chapters, and illustrated in the discussion of *Borgen,* to items from news and current affairs. For the analyses of all the examples in Chapter 4 I will adopt a particular method, which is to examine single items from the perspective of a reader or viewer who has no previous knowledge of the issue at hand. Their interpretation of this item consequently places a great deal of weight on the abstract typifications of concepts, fields and so on that can be transposed from situation to situation. The knowledge that audiences come away with from a single news item on an unfamiliar topic will hence be a combined product of two elements: of their transposable background knowledge and of the information provided by the single current affairs item at hand. A typology of types of knowledge is introduced in order to enhance audience abilities to assess the status and adequacy of the account provided by a current affairs item. The first three illustrative examples in the chapter will focus on the concept of 'interdependence', and will cover the following issues: an Israeli high court ruling in July 2011 ordering the destruction of settlers' homes in the West Bank, reported in the British *Independent* newspaper; a debate in the US Senate from June 2013, reported in the *Washington Post*, on the Immigration Reform Bill, which would give 11 million illegal immigrants the chance to become citizens; and an Agence France-Presse account, reported in the *Bangkok Post*, on the Burmese government's seemingly blithe decision to extend the house arrest of Aung San Suu Kyi in August 2009 in the face of international pressure to condemn its litany of human rights' infringements. Parallels are then drawn between the interdependencies at play in this latter example and those not far from the surface of events in reports of demonstrators on the streets of the Ukranian capital of Kiev in December 2013. The final illustrative example in Chapter 4 switches the focus to the need to be aware of the rhetoric of the text within the media frame, and analyses an *Independent* report covering renewed popular street protests across Egypt in July 2011, concentrating primarily on the demonstrations in Tahrir Square, Cairo, just after the fall of President Hosni Mubarak and his replacement by an interim military council.

The final substantive chapter, Chapter 5, is divided into two main parts. In the first I examine two current affairs pieces whose coverage is much broader in scope than those previously analysed, covering larger sets of social relations, with a greater spatial and historical span. Attention is drawn to the *plural character* of causation within these pieces, and to the ways in which these pluralistic, spacious, stories with a large historical or geographical sweep, are typically made up of particular kinds of patchworks of varying types of knowledge. The first analysis focuses on a newspaper feature from the *Guardian Weekly* that argues that key aspects of Germany's recent economic success have been dependent on a deeper, more embedded set of structural preconditions, and the second analysis examines the script of a BBC radio broadcast, written and presented by Fergal Keane, situating the Rwandan genocide of 1994 in its historical and political context.

In the second half of the chapter the theme of plurality is continued, approaching two sets of news and current affairs accounts on very different issues with a view to foregrounding the complexity of relevant causal forces at work within their respective fields. The two issues focused on are the violent clashes on Bangkok's streets in May 2010 and the anger caused by the poor treatment of patients in a UK National Health Service hospital run by the Mid-Staffordshire Trust between 2005 and 2009. For each issue, attention is given to a number of different accounts, each with its own angle of vision on the events in question. Attention is accordingly given to the skills audiences require in order to make creative connections *between different items* of news and current affairs, either from within the same genre or from different genres. The theme of making connections between different items is a natural corollary of the recognition of the patchwork quality of the knowledge provided in a single item. Audiences are at the heart of this, as the implication is that the audience reception and interpretation of single texts needs to be integrated into a slowly evolving stock of knowledge – derived from a range of texts – about the same issue, and about the same complex of questions with respect to that issue.

Both of the issues focused upon involve a good deal of complexity, and the ideal for audiences is to be able to creatively combine sources in such a way that they would be able to address those key areas identified in the media frames literature. To remind ourselves, these are: ascertaining the appropriate definition of the situation or problem-to-be-explained; identifying the relevant causes of that situation; identifying moral judgements made with respect to this causation (and we should want to seriously probe and evaluate these judgements); and formulating strategies to improve or remedy the situation. In attempting to put together responses to each of these dimensions audiences have two broad options. They could take their cue from particular current affairs accounts, subjecting the assumptions of those accounts to critical analysis, or they could develop their own hunches, explanations and judgements, and seek to substantiate or falsify these through adding to their stocks of knowledge through further reading and viewing. The chapter shows that it is no straightforward matter to be able to combine the information provided by different sources in a way that is able to adequately address the four dimensions of stories identified by the media frames approach. It is also shown, however, that the problems are by no means insurmountable, and that the more audiences exercise the skills necessary to the task, the more fluent and effective they will become in doing so. So, audiences can indeed be empowered, even when it comes to extremely complex cases, by close reflection on the relationships between the four different elements of media frames with respect to the substantive details of the current affairs story at hand. The guidance of the four elements, combined together and focused on the relevant contextual field, can indeed help audiences to decide on the extent to which they have been offered appropriate and sufficient knowledge by any one account. Such awareness provides the grounds on which it is then possible to identify the relevant additional knowledge available in complementary sources and genres.

It might well be that journalists already have a greater intellectual grasp of what is necessary to position events within contextual fields so as to provide a greater depth of understanding, but that they are prevented from acting upon this because of institutional and other constraints. I am not in a position to make a clear judgement on this. It might also well be the case that audiences, especially those among them who are experts on particular issues, have a better intellectual grasp than I sometimes assume. What I can say is that social theory is an invaluable intellectual resource that can, without a doubt, fortify and refine those categories used by journalists and by audiences to address the many issues that fall within the remit of the four dimensions outlined in the media frames literature. The concepts of social theory offer a fuller, more cultivated basis on which to: explain the *causes* of a *problem* or *phenomenon-in-need-of-explanation*; provide a grounded sense of what the likely consequences would be of a proposed solution or *remedy*; and identify the relevant context against which to make *moral judgements*. Each of these categories needs to be located within a contextual field relevant to the issue in focus, and carefully unpacked. The appropriate weight of detail and degree of precision necessary to grasp the relevant who, what, how, and so on, of processes related to a particular news story will vary. What is appropriate will be determined, as noted, by the degree of relevance of the detail to the claims the story makes, or to any alternative aspirations it might have. Journalists and audiences need to be more alert to what these claims and aspirations are, as they can creep into reports while backs are turned, often surprising their authors. Claims can stealthily burrow their way into reports in countless ways, through narrative, description, argument or rhetorical implication.

Conclusion

A social-theoretical frame elaborated along the lines I've sketched in can provide audiences with the ability to be more methodical and systematic in their reading of news accounts; at the same time it can provide journalists with similar abilities that could ideally be put to use in the construction of news stories. It has the potential to equip audiences with a heightened alertness and sensitivity towards the adequacy or inadequacy of the relevant details provided by a news story about the events it covers. Chapters 2 and 3 will outline this social-theoretical frame, and the contextual field which is its object of analysis, and Chapters 4 and 5 will then explore, through the analysis of a series of varied news and current affairs texts, how this set of conceptual tools can help journalists and audiences to raise the bar as they strive to make sense of news and current affairs events.

2

Contextual fields and social theory

Introduction

In the last chapter we established the need for co-ordinates that can provide an adequate degree of orientation to audiences for news and current affairs. Such co-ordinates can allow audiences to have more than a disembedded, superficial understanding of the events presented to them, enabling them to grasp more of the conditions, meanings and processes that surround those events, that led up to them, that played major roles in causing them to happen. In the terms I've introduced, this is the need for a suitable *contextual field*, a mapping of the primary institutional and individual actors, networks, forces, pressures and dynamics relevant to the key events a current affairs account is focused upon.

In this chapter I will begin to flesh out the idea of contextual fields, indicating how they can guide us to be on the lookout for certain things when viewing or reading a current affairs account. In the first part of this chapter I will make some very general, and therefore inevitably quite abstract, points about contextual fields, indicating that they have certain features that are applicable in all places and at all times. Seen in this way the features have a generalized status. However, this is combined with more specific qualities. Contextual fields take on particular forms and shapes in different times and places, and so to truly understand a set of news events one needs to combine knowledge of the generalizable features they possess with an ability to grasp the specific colours and tones of particular times and places. The fact that the general features have to be complemented by the hues, tones and shades specific to localities of time and place means being alert to these particularities of context, to the unique qualities of particular events. It means that when we approach a particular news event, we need to be sensitive to how much we probably don't yet know, to the kinds of things we need to learn, and to the fact that there will always be a good deal we'll never know. All this means that even when the general, abstract aspects of contextual fields are known, there is still a lot of work to be done in interpreting particular news and current affairs stories. This should never be forgotten. Having said this, however, the general, abstract categories can take us a long way.

That contextual fields do possess general features is useful because it means that the knowledge we build up about these is transposable from situation to situation, news story to news story. This means we don't always have to start entirely anew when a fresh news story breaks. In order to develop the best set of generalizable, transposable tools for thinking about all news stories, in any place at any time, I will take the discussion of contextual fields, and the concepts that populate it, as far as I can at an abstract level. This will involve the introduction and elucidation of some key concepts of social theory, whose true value will only emerge slowly over time as we apply them to news events and stories in a range of different circumstances. I will try to present the abstract concepts as clearly and succinctly as possible in this section, and then, as the book proceeds, to gradually demonstrate how they can be used in a variety of different ways with respect to a variety of different real-world circumstances and news events, combining the general with the local tones and shades of particular stories. As noted, it is the combination of the two – the general and the detailed particular – that will determine whether the knowledge that audiences are provided with is strong or weak, adequate or inadequate with respect to the claims of a given story.

In fact, audiences already possess relatively complex understandings of the generalizable characteristics of *contextual fields*, which is a highly encouraging sign for this venture. As viewers or readers approach a text of some kind, their initial orientation will be provided by their pre-existing stocks of generalized, typified, notions of how to position and understand what is going on. The next chapter will draw out this point further in indicating that, at the very least, the audiences for high-quality political drama on television employ sophisticated understandings of contextual fields, which they bring to their interpretation of unfolding events. It is debatable, however, whether the same audiences currently employ the same quality of interpretation when they consume television news. In any case, audience understandings and competencies are usually intuitive, tacit, and are rarely, if at all, made explicit, and I want to argue for the importance of making them explicit. This would allow these routine skills and interpretations to be compared to the most adequate forms of understanding available. If the comparison reveals that the general background understandings audiences bring to news and current affairs items are overly gauche or naïve then those understandings need to be subjected to constructive critique, as a means to improve them. The setting out of theoretically informed generic categories and forms of social understanding in this chapter, and in following chapters, rests on this chain of reasoning. That is, it rests on recognition of the key role played by background understandings of contextual fields in audience interpretation of news events, and of the corresponding importance of the quality of those understandings.

So, let us start with the general understanding of contextual fields. How should one identify the basic contextual features relevant to grasping the key issues, puzzles or dilemmas of a story? Contextual fields, as we've noted, involve structured networks of relations or configurations of forces, and it's important to be able to think of these as having an *objective* existence. By 'objective' here, I simply mean aspects of the social context that have a real existence. So, for example, the fact that the objectively existing social field can facilitate or empower actors in what they want to do, or can constrain or prevent them from doing what they want to do, suggests that the contextual field has objective qualities above and beyond the wishes of the actor-in-focus. If social actors are not to get their fingers burned then they need to take these objective qualities seriously.

To talk about the social context having an 'objective' existence doesn't mean that aspects of social life we typically think of as subjective – such as the world views, ideologies, cultural perspectives and personal moral and emotional orientations of individuals – aren't included in contextual fields. They are, of course. The social context and the processes that go on within it continue to be reproduced minute by minute, hour by hour, and there are people out there to help reproduce these processes, people who are subjectively interpreting their situation in order to act within it. Social processes rely on human subjects, even if they involve much more than this. The processes within the contextual field, and the other characteristics of the field – both subjective and objective, human and non-human, material and cultural, with all their many interweavings and entanglements – all have an *objective existence*.[1] This is an **ontological** point – a point about the nature of the entities and relations that exist in the world (see **box 1**, below). Social theorists concern themselves with conceptualizing these entities and relations in a systematic fashion, developing powerful illuminating ways to think about such elements of the world as time, space, agency, structure, the body, technology, meaning, culture and so on. We require concepts that are up to the job if we are to be able to think satisfactorily and accurately about the world, but we also need to remember that these relatively abstract concepts can only do half of the job. For we also need to include the detail of specific processes in particular places if we are to capture the full-bodied character of social life. We need to be able to see the different shapes taken on by the conceptualized entities in varying situations if we are to grasp reality in its detailed complexity. If social life was a paint-by-numbers canvas, then the concepts would provide the topography of empty shapes, white and numbered, and the rich and messy detail of everyday life would be equivalent to the paint box of many colours. The key difference is that everything isn't as static in social life, with general concepts and unique situations interweaving with each other in all kinds of ways. In order to truly find out about what is going on in particular places within this objective reality, one needs to do a good deal of further work, involving the moments of methodological and epistemological objectivity (see box 1, also) that I will now describe.

Box 1 Three valuable meanings of 'Objectivity'

[1] ONTOLOGICAL OBJECTIVITY
(a commitment to the reality of the world, *and* to the conceptualization of the kinds of entities and relations existing within it)

Objectivity, here, indicates a commitment to the independent existence or reality of events, and to particular conceptualizations of this reality. These conceptualizations are of the constituents of the contextual field relevant to an event, and of the processes within this field. Both objective and subjective elements (see next row) are included in ontological objectivity. Concepts of these elements only grasp half of the story of the reality of events, as the real-world shapes taken by actual processes and events will vary from situation to situation. Finding out about these detailed processes will involve a good deal of further work, including the moments of (2) and (3).

[2] METHODOLOGICAL OBJECTIVITY
(investigates what is in the world with a focus on 'objective elements')

Objective elements, here, refers to a way of bracketing out reference to the interior worlds of actors (subjective elements). Knowledge of these elements can be gained from an 'external perspective'. Objective elements are to be distinguished from subjective elements (see Chapter 3).

[3] EPISTEMOLOGICAL OBJECTIVITY
(evaluating the quality of knowledge claims about the world)

Objectivity here refers to the validity or invalidity, the adequacy or inadequacy, of knowledge claims. This includes the need to assess the adequacy of the detailed evidence provided to back up claims about the particular shapes taken by conceptualized independent reality (i.e. 1 – ontological objectivity) in specific situations.

There is an important **methodological** point to be made about how to best reflect upon and investigate the relations between a news event and the contextual field that provides it with meaning. Here it is extremely useful to be able to discriminate, analytically, between two broad aspects of this reality when considering how to initially approach a particular issue and its contextual field. On the one hand, attaining knowledge of some aspects of the contextual field doesn't require detailed reference to the interior worlds of actors, and I will refer to these as *objective elements* (see **box 2**, below). I will focus on these in the present chapter. On the other hand these are to be distinguished from questions about the contextual field that do require detailed reference to the interior worlds of actors. I will refer to the latter as *subjective elements*, and I will focus on these areas of the contextual field in Chapter 3.

Claims to possess knowledge of either subjective or objective elements, or of the ways in which they are intertwined in a given story, can be more or less valid or invalid. Some knowledge claims will be well substantiated in terms of evidence, and others will be less well substantiated or just plain wrong, relying on empty rhetoric, flimsy or inaccurate evidence and so on. This means that claims to knowledge can be more or less 'objective' in a third sense. This is an **epistemological** point – a point about assessing the quality of the knowledge one has about the entities and relations that exist in the world. Knowledge of a more objective kind, in the epistemological sense, will be substantiated by a good deal of evidence commensurate with the claims that have been made. These three types of objectivity can each be distinguished from the kind of anodyne, misguided, conception of objectivity as a neutral 'view from nowhere' that dominates and eviscerates so much of news and current affairs.[2]

Knowledge claims **[3]** *about* the processes taking place within contextual fields **[1]** can thus be objective, in that it is quite possible to try and identify the existing dominant characteristics of these processes at a given point in time. There will be characterizations of these that focus methodologically [2] on objective elements, characterizations that focus on subjective elements, and those that combine the two. Whatever the methodological focus, the knowledge acquired can be better or worse, more or less accurate, and we should be able to make disciplined and informed judgements in these respects.

In initially orienting oneself to the relevant *objective elements* of the contextual field included in a particular news or current affairs account, it will be useful to try and identify the presence or absence of some or all of the following basic repertoire of objective elements:

Box 2   Objective factors in the contextual field

- the *key actors* involved, both individual and collective;

- when and where to locate key actors, processes and events (issues of time/history and space/geography);

- the most important *duties, obligations, sets of expectations, values and goals* that are formally or informally attached to an actor's position (the formal aspects of these are akin to a job description);

- The various kinds of *resources and powers* actors have at their disposal, the effectiveness with which they can deploy them, and the various kinds of constraints that their immediate positioning imposes on their use.

- The social relations of *interdependence* that link key actors to each other and to non-key actors, providing conditions of existence for each other's activities and for degrees of control. These relations include various kinds of hierarchy, power dependence and other kinds of interdependence, including those based on resources, technology, logistics and communication.

- The shared *cultural or ideological affiliations* between actors, or alternatively, objectively existing relations of ideological antagonism and conflict.

- The *forces, pressures, constraints and sanctions* that actors impose, or could impose, on each other as a result of these powers, relations and interdependencies.

The presence and significance of these factors within a news event will vary, depending upon the event. Choosing which to focus on will be a matter of judgement and purpose. It is important to the scheme I'm proposing that it is possible to approach these objective elements of the social context from two, different, primary perspectives. The first is by looking at the contextual field – the structural context – from the perspective of an *external observer*, and the second is by looking at it from the viewpoint of the *involved actor*, an actor positioned within that contextual field. These two different vantage points will give rise to different fields of vision; they will inevitably draw differing aspects of the contextual field into view, simply because of the position of the viewer. This will be a central point in the present chapter. If audiences are to examine the status and quality of an account they must first ask themselves from whose perspective that account is being told.

In what follows, I will clarify each of the points listed in Box 2, building up the discussion in three parts. In the first part, saying more about the generalizing, abstract, level, I will explore what is involved in mentally 'mapping out' the contextual field for a news story. I deal here with the basic stocks of knowledge about objective features that should guide the interpretation and assessment of news events and stories. Their primary content is conceptual, involving an understanding of how to think about, how to conceptualize, the elements contained in the above-mentioned points. The conceptual shapes provided, for example, by ideas of what social actors are, and how they function, or of the kinds of power interdependencies that exist between actors, and how these work, are the basis on which we can make sense of evidence. Fragments of evidence need to be pinned onto conceptual shapes before they will make sense, even in those instances when unexpected and unforeseen evidence means that the conceptual shapes themselves need to be attenuated. Evidence without conceptual shape is meaningless. The basic shapes of the contextual field that are brought to the interpretations of events are inherent in any attempt to make sense of any news event. The quality of these sense-making conceptualizations is thus of paramount importance to the quality of the final understanding.

I will follow this account of the general characteristics of the contextual field with a particular example, with its own hues, colours and tones. This section will demonstrate how these general aspects of the contextual field can be employed in the interpretation of a particular set of circumstances. The story is one of a young single mother, Sandy, facing a particular contextual field as she searches for somewhere to live in a contemporary American city. This story will be told from Sandy's viewpoint, the viewpoint of *the involved actor*. This means I will draw attention to her (hermeneutic-structural)[3] subjective frame of meaning, which, of course, is the perspective through which she experiences and negotiates her predicament. However, the *thematic focus* of the section will be less on how Sandy is dealing with the situation within her inner world and thoughts – which is something we will spend more time on in Chapter 3 – and more on how she experiences the *objective character of the contextual field* that she is faced with. I will indicate how the view of the contextual field used in Sandy's understanding corresponds to various elements of the basic objective repertoire as indicated in Box 2. It is important to recognize both the typical strengths and the typical limitations of this kind of perspective. Audiences should adopt this perspective, this way of seeing, when a current affairs account makes claims that imply knowledge of how the structural terrain looks from the viewpoint of the people in the thick of it.

In the third and final section of the chapter I will change perspective. Specifically, I will recount the findings of two in-depth analyses undertaken by media scholars of particular news events in Denmark and Sweden, respectively. One of these two sets of media analyses focused on the coverage of transport policy in Denmark at the turn of the new millennium, and the other on the Swedish news coverage in 2011 of the mistreatment of elderly people in private health care.

I want to draw attention, here, to both the strengths and the limitations of current academic media analysis. My account of these cases is meant to indicate that the limitations are readily apparent in even high-quality research whose ostensible focus in on practical policy fields. I will, first, point to the sophisticated ways in which academic media analysts shed light on the language, rhetoric and so on of journalistic texts. I will then indicate that the concentration on the 'rhetoric of the text' is accompanied by a lack of focus on what news and current affairs texts manage to say about the objective characteristics of the contextual field as such. I want to insist that, on the one hand, we need the sophisticated analyses of media texts, with their emphasis on discourses and media frames. But, on the other hand, we need social theory to help us to look beyond these discourses, to analyse what current affairs texts tell us about the characteristics of the events they are writing about, including what they tell us about the relevant networks of relations that have produced those events.

There is just enough, however, in the academic analyses of the media accounts of the two cases to allow us to glimpse some of the limitations of the way in which journalists engage with the contextual fields relevant to their stories. The two case studies do suggest some of the intricacies and subtleties involved in journalistic presentation and, in the first case, in audience reception and interpretation. However, despite the analyses being focused on news accounts from a plurality of sources and genres – each focused on the particular domestic issues mentioned – the findings suggest that journalists worked with quite simplistic frames, with little sense of mapping an appropriate contextual field. It seems they did very little to position the actors and events they were covering within a contextual field, provided little in the way of evidential detail and lacked any real hermeneutic engagement with the perspectives of involved actors on the objective character of the contextual field that confronted them. Similarly, audiences tended to work with a very thin background conception of the contextual field. An inevitable consequence of a thin, simplistic, notion of the contextual field is a corresponding dearth of attention given to any of the objective factors within this field, that is, to the kinds of objective factors whose generalized features are outlined in the box on page 32.

If Sandy's viewpoint stands for the perspective of many of the people who are interviewed on the streets and in the homes of news and documentary events, the external viewpoint stands for the typical perspective of the journalist or the academic, looking in from the outside. We will see later that one of the strengths of this latter viewpoint, when it is sufficiently focused on key objective factors within the contextual field, is in generating 'ways of seeing' directed more towards the larger, broader, scale. As always, it will be important to explore, and to make explicit, exactly what these kinds of accounts provide, and what they do not. One aspect of particular importance for us not to lose sight of is how the external perspective – a typically broader, but more distanced, way of seeing – should relate to situated, more immersed, points of view. One way of thinking about this is to ask how pictures taken with a wide-angled lens from up on the hilltop should combine with those taken close-up, from within the midst and heat of the battle.

The contextual field: General and transposable concepts

When approaching a news and current affairs story about an unfamiliar topic, it is useful to begin by 'mapping' as many as possible of the key objective factors derived from the general, abstract level, to get an initial sense of what is involved in the story's particular contextual field, even when this has to be carried out in an impressionistic and rudimentary manner. A rough template for such a mapping is represented in graphic form in **Figure 2.1**. This diagram is useful to keep in mind while thinking about contextual fields in general.

The black circular nodes represent collective and individual actors, and are also meant to bring to mind their immediate power resources and capabilities. It is essential to acquire a grasp of the positioning of each of the key actors in relation to the other relevant actors. One consequence of this is that it is usually necessary to identify precisely which actor one is focusing on at any one time. This individual or institutional actor, who faces a particular context

Legend:

● Individual and collective actors

Ⓐ Actor-in-focus

──── Networked links with other agents

↑ Large historical and socio-structural forces

Position-practice relations

Large historical and socio-structural forces

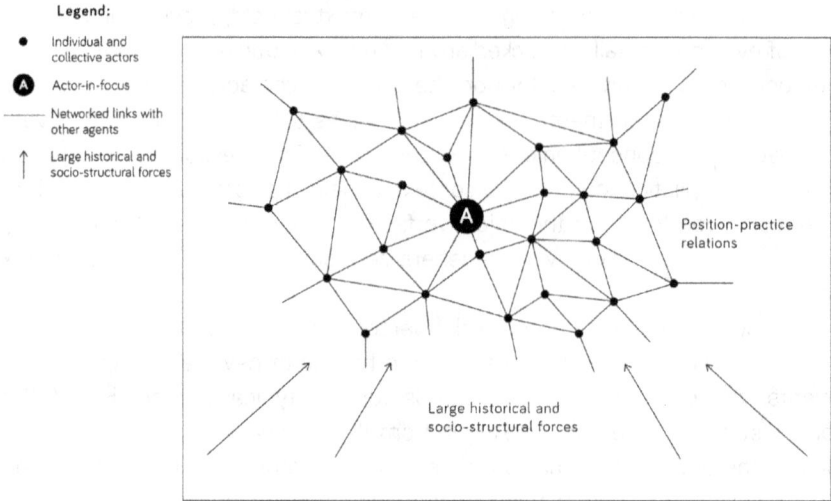

FIGURE 2.1 *A contextual field.*

at a particular time, and so has a specific relationship to that world, should be thought of as *the actor-in-focus*. This is in order to differentiate that actor from all the other actors who are implicated in producing and reproducing the social structure that is the context for that actor-in-focus. Without this simple discipline, commentators and casual conversationalists alike often slide inadvertently into giving too much power to social actors over social structures. The slide begins with the recognition that when social structures get reproduced or undermined then it is usually because social actors have brought this about. There is often a leap from this observation to the truism that if all the actors got together then they could change many of the structures. However, this is a very general, highly abstract, and entirely conditional statement about structures and actors. It is not a statement about particular actors in particular situations. It is a short, but misleading, step from such aspirational ruminations to the *non sequitur* that a particular actor, no matter how they are positioned, has the power to change, resist or undermine a particular structure. They often don't have this power. Think, for example, about the situation of an individual or collective actor (the actors-in-focus) facing a contextual terrain in which the dominant ideological and cultural affiliations of key actors are in conflict with their own. For these actors-in-focus the characteristics of the ideologies and cultural formations that face them will often possess objective qualities of obstacle and constraint. Keeping track of the actors-in-focus and their positioning helps to keep feet firmly on the ground.

The positioning of actors in relation to one another can be formulated in several different ways, depending upon the definition of the situation most relevant to the problem being explored by an account, or the claims being made within the account. Actors and their practices can be positioned in relation to each other in a number of different ways, and along a number of different dimensions. These can include their positioning in relation to each other: in geographical terms; in terms of time, including chronological sequence or simultaneity; in terms of shared cultural or ideological affiliations, or, alternatively, connections through relations of ideological antagonism and conflict; or in terms of lines of communication, regular face-to-face meetings and so on. However, when considering current affairs it will typically be most useful *to begin* by thinking about the black, networked lines linking actors as indicating *relations of dependence and interdependence* with respect both to power resources and to obligations and duties attached to social position. Actors rely on other actors to provide them with resources of various kinds, from finance through material and technological objects and artefacts to information. The resources provided by actors to other actors can also take the form of granting them permission to do something, or of giving them the authority to command others to do something. Actors also often depend on others to follow their commands, but also to simply do the 'right thing' without always having to ask them to do so, and without peering over their shoulders.

These interdependencies will usually be embedded in broader hierarchical systems, which can be internal to organizations or can reflect the relations between organizations. These hierarchies need to be identified when they are germane to a current affairs account, but it must also be kept in mind that their levels of integration will vary, with some hierarchies functioning efficiently and effectively in their own terms, while others don't function well at all.

It will be quite easy to superimpose the other aspects of mutual positioning – with respect to geography, time, cultural and ideological affinity, quality and frequency of communication and so on – onto this key dimension, and to think about the ways in which the various factors interweave with each other. Mutually beneficial power interdependencies, for example, will very often lead to the downplaying of ideological or cultural differences. This is not always the case, however, and like all general concepts, care must be taken in applying them to particular situations. Nationalist, religious or moral zeal, for example, will often refuse to bend to the demands of those who might withhold resources of one kind or another. On the other hand, as we shall indicate in a moment, such zeal can often be met by negative sanctions, by the withholding of resources that are necessary to sustain practices that the unyielding party also holds dear. Things get interesting in such configurations, and such configurations are frequent.

An initial primary focus on the black, networked lines as indicating a relation of dependence and interdependence regarding power resources has the virtue of indicating in quite concrete terms what actors have to gain and to lose if that relation breaks down. One can quickly see how the current set of social relations in which actors are embedded could have their conditions of existence undermined, or significantly altered, by a disturbance of relations of interdependence. Taking this as the primary focus for the black, networked lines also draws direct attention to the sources of an actor's current power resources, so that one gets a keen sense of how power resources of various kinds can be expanded, or potentially diminished, through shifts in networks of relations and 'alliances'. It is useful to remember that when actors join together in resource alliances they will often, as a consequence, have more power to alter the structural terrain than when they act alone. The extent to which this is true will also depend, naturally, on how much power they command on their own, and how much additional power the alliance gives them. The goals and objectives of actors will almost invariably be pursued within configurations of the kind indicated by the configured lines.

Social theorists refer to the duties and obligations an organization expects its personnel to fulfil as 'normative expectations', or norms. These *norms* can be more or less formal or informal, and more or less clear cut. Individuals in their various roles will have to make judgements as to what would and would not be acceptable in a given situation. The sociologist, Erving Goffman, wrote very insightfully and entertainingly about the tacit mutual knowledge and subtle skills we employ in judging what is appropriate behaviour in a variety of social contexts.[4] When, for example, is it appropriate to hold hands with someone else, and where, when, and with whom, would holding hands be a transgression of acceptable behaviour, a transgression of the social norms prevailing in that particular kind of context? Does the age, gender or race of each of those holding hands make a difference? What degree of embarrassment or discomfort would be produced by the transgression of the prevailing social norms? There are also strict norms about whom we are allowed to approach socially, and where and when we are allowed to do so. Such norms around 'access' can be policed by controls over entry to certain kinds of buildings, or they can be more informal, so that it is a matter of courtesy not to follow your doctor around the supermarket, reciting a string of ailments and symptoms. In public places, we are traditionally allowed to ask a stranger for the time, directions, or, in the old days, for a match, but there will be fairly strict time and other rules about the nature of even these permissible interactions, and one would need to rely on special skills or characteristics in order not to very quickly come up against the limits of what seems normal and acceptable.

The point of this excursion is to emphasize the significance of norms in social life as a prelude to highlighting the formidable role they play in sustaining relations of interdependence between key actors – nodal points in Figure 2.1 – within a contextual field. There will typically be normative expectations on either side about the conditions under which the interdependence should be continued, and the potential cost of transgressing such norms will be either tacitly or explicitly understood. For power structures to be sustained, resting as they typically do on networks of interdependence, actors within the organizations at each end of the chain will need to be 'doing the right thing'. For an involved actor looking outwards from their position within a contextual field, the behaviours expected of them – as duty, obligation, appropriate action – by others within the relevant networks of relations will often be experienced as an objective set of imperatives. The dynamic force of these external expectations will be quite correctly understood as forming objective structural demands and constraints. A simple, and increasingly widespread, example of this would be where the failure to meet certain targets attached to one's working role leads to the sanction of demotion and an unfavourable change in contract. For an organization, the failure to meet profit or performance targets and related sets of external normative expectations can, in some circumstances, lead to loss of general confidence, financial calamity, or both.

Power relations and norms usually work hand in hand, and their various combinations are part of the objective social relations of any contextual field. Normative expectations are very often the form in which power expresses itself. At the more macro level of international relations, sets of expectations will commonly be attached as conditions to be met if aid, finance, trading agreements, or the provision of military hardware and support, are to be continued. In using the contextual field as a guide to the analysis of current affairs texts, these general considerations need to be drawn to mind and sized up when texts are concerned with the constraints and opportunities facing particular actors, which they very often are. These conceptualizations can, for example, focus our attention on how much of a situated actor's perception of the strategic field, if any of it, has been considered by a particular journalistic account.

In order to avoid thinking of social structures as too 'thing-like', too fixed and impersonal, it is essential that the networks of the contextual field – representing the social-structural context – be thought of as contexts that are always partially in motion at any moment. All kinds of situated practices are involved in maintaining, repairing, consciously running down, damaging, improving, and otherwise variously changing, existing social structures. Social structures, contextual fields, will always have social actors within them, undertaking practices of more or less import. Because of this, any sense of social structures as fundamentally intractable, which they undoubtedly often are to a particular actor-in-focus, needs to be leavened with questions of 'to whom?', 'due to what?', 'within what time frame?', and so on.

Large socio-structural forces, and other kinds of forces, active in the social practices of the past, can leave significant marks on the form and content of the contextual field of the present. The four thick arrows pushing into the current network of positioned relations in Figure 2.1 indicate this legacy, and its provenance in past times. This inherited presence can exist in objective crystallized forms – in current power resources and hierarchies, and in laws, bureaucratic and informal rules, technologies and architecture – within current contextual fields. These crystallized forms provide the inherited social terrain inhabited by current organizational actors. Such organizational actors can include, of course, governments and states, transnational corporations engaged in production, services and so on, and cultural and normative institutions such as educational and legal bodies. The individuals who work within these organizations, no matter how powerful they are, will have to manoeuvre within and negotiate the weight of the past – the inherited sedimentations of past practices. These individuals may eventually change the structures they inherited, in turn leaving a new set of sedimentations for those who come after them. But at least initially they will inherit circumstances that are not of their own making.[5]

There is a lot that could be said about the junction between the past and the present. It is especially important to be continually aware of the various ways in which the practices and constructions of the past can *colonize the future*, so that long before it arrives, it is already populated, less empty, more constraining than is routinely supposed.[6] This is a general point that needs to be combined with knowledge of specific histories, and is an observation to remember in analysing any news story. It's a simple but often overlooked truth that one can't simply will completely new worlds into existence when there are all kinds of impediments in the way, all sorts of legacies from the past that make some things impossible, others difficult, and yet others very dangerous. The temptation to campaign for an ideal future based on a moral vision abstracted from any knowledge of historical inheritance lodged in current arrangements risks all kinds of unintended consequences, including opening a Pandora's box of potential schisms, subdued animosities and latent grievances.

Other insights into the junctions between the past and the present can usefully be gleaned from the writings of the American sociologist C. Wright Mills, and especially from his slim, perennial volume, *The Sociological Imagination*, which has excited and illuminated successive generations of sociology students.[7] Mills noted that an understanding of the power and significance on social life of large social structures and forces inherited from the past will be magnified many times once one grasps how profoundly they influence the biographies of the men and women who live within the folds and creases they leave on the objective landscape. On a subjective level, the individual actors who populate the social structures inherited from the past will themselves have also been socialized by inherited practices within various social institutions, including families and schools, which function, among other things, to prepare new generations for their future. And, of course, this doesn't stop in adulthood, with later jobs and roles continuing to socialize, and to lay the ground more or less intentionally or randomly, and more or less effectively, for subsequent, ever changing, roles. Both the objective and the subjective factors will combine to make up the terrain that faces any one actor at a particular juncture. Interwoven together – with the subjective inhabiting and informing the objective, and vice versa – they will present themselves to that actor with the immense force of often intractable social structures, forever pressing on their lives and pushing them to do this or that, or to suffer the consequences. Our understanding of people's lives is given much greater depth once we understand how these large historical forces and social structures surround, inhabit and mark them, and provide the scope of whatever opportunities they have. What may seem like entirely 'private troubles', Mills famously argued, are greatly illuminated once one looks for how they intersect with 'public issues'.[8]

The impact of past practices on the present events covered by news is not the only dimension that is rendered invisible without a grasp of the broader contextual field. For relevant contextual fields do not only stretch back into the past, but also stretch out in space. Both journalists and audiences hence also need to be able to position events in relation to the spatially extended networks of relationships that have combined to produce them. The networks represented in Figure 2.1 will naturally be variable in terms of the spatial distance between the actors represented by the black nodes, and these distances may span local, regional and globalized contexts. Part of the represented frame may belong, spatially, to micro contexts – say, relations within a department of a business company or a ministry of state – or to middle-level contexts, but part of them may also be part of networks that span the globe. International financial networks, for example, reach from afar right into the heart of local city, town and household contexts. The remittances home from international migrants would be another example from a list of such 'stretched' chains of interaction, an example that now, in the age of globalization, points to a major phenomenon. Such remittances are likely to be between family members, who are stretched between households in different parts of the globe, each engaged in their different micro- and middle-scale (meso) networks. Extended chains now play a part in countless numbers of news stories.

It is important to be subtle in thinking about the relationship between these spatial dimensions and the past, historical – temporally prior – practices we have just been discussing. A remittance could be sent back home to the Philippines, to family members in Manila or Cebu City, or in more remote rural area such as, say, the landlocked Bukidnon province of Northern Mindanao, from a maid working in Hong Kong. The process clearly involves a spatially extended network, but also a temporally extended one, as there will be a time-lag between the work done in Hong Kong and the resultant pay being received, and then spent on food, schooling, or something else, by a family member in the Philippines.[9] It is not only that the two connected practices are geographically far apart but also that one practice happens prior to another. Likewise, with the global financial crisis, the production of certain indicators – signalling a widening trade gap, an expanded money supply or an increase in national debt – will have a pre-history leading up to the release of those figures. Furthermore, the release of the figures themselves will then be prior in time to the response of credit rating agencies such as the Fitch Group, Moody's or Standard and Poor's deciding whether or not the indicators merit, say, relegating Greece, Ireland or Portugal to 'junk' status, or stripping France or Austria of their triple-A rating. It can be important, therefore, to remember that the distinction between the past that is absent from the television screen and the spatial distance, which is also absent, is usually only an *analytical* distinction, as the absent practices are often *both* spatially distant and in the past, to a greater or lesser degree. Accordingly, depending on the current affairs story and the claims being investigated, it will often be important to recognize both dimensions at the same time. It is perhaps best to think of relevant contextual fields as encompassing various combinations of narrow and extended spatial stretches intermingled with shallow and deep temporal stretches.

All of this means that, in Figure 2.1, the large black arrows coming up into the networked contextual field from below could represent both *spatially* distant and *historical,* past, socio-structural connections and influences. It also means that the representation is imprecise in another way. For they are represented as being one step removed from the immanent micro- and meso-level networks whose interdependencies are spelt out through the black interconnecting lines. In reality, the impacts and pressures of spatially distant connections are often experienced *directly* by locally situated individuals and institutions. Such is the case in the examples I've given, where the thoughts and actions of individuals at a local level are impacted by situated actions far away. It is as pertinent to keep this thought in mind when observing a scene of a Filipina grandmother preparing breakfast for her migrant daughter's child as when reading about the officials of an Irish ministry meeting to discuss the implications for spending plans of an overnight reduction in the government's credit rating. These palpable micro events are directly marked by the large social-structural workings of the system of international migration and the international financial system. In order to represent these external pressures accurately within a particular example, the arrows in Figure 2.1 would ideally be represented as connecting directly with the black nodes in the centre of the field.

The combined notions of the social-theoretical frame and the contextual field it brings into view can embrace and help to consolidate all of these insights, while adding further tiers of analytical precision. One of these further tiers is the development of the idea of *networks of relevant relations*, which is able to combine the immediate micro situation, the middle-level network of interdependencies it is located within, and distant but consequential forces, all within the one field of vision. The most general level of a contextual field, as represented in Figure 2.1, is a form of 'typification', in the sense we spoke of earlier. That is, it represents background knowledge of typical 'kinds of situation', which we can invoke in meeting new current affairs stories. Strictly speaking, however, it is a cluster, a gathering-together, of a range of different typifications – of actors, relations, forces and so on, which at this level of generality represent only the scaffolding or the skeleton for the real flesh-and-blood entities and processes we want to grasp. It is one of the roles of social theory to adequately conceptualize and refine these typifications, working out which features possessed at this abstract, general, level are most important to keep in mind when bringing them into contact with the real world. It is the ability to move between a sophisticated grasp of this abstract background knowledge and unique real-world processes and events that is key. The quality of our understanding of news events is dependent upon a combination of how adequately we can hone and refine our various abstract typifications of *various entities and processes*; how adequately we can indicate *their relations to each other* within a contextual field; and how adequately we can flesh out these more or less abstract notions with *the detail, texture and colour* they possess in specific situations.

In the greater scheme of things, the initial criteria I've listed for the contextual field provide parameters that are really quite basic, and it is revealing – especially when we consider the rigour and sophistication we routinely expect from the natural sciences – that making explicit such a frame of understanding for the social world, and setting it as a standard for news and current affairs, seems rather alien, almost too demanding. If I am right that this is more than a passing thought, then a positive message to take from it is that the schooling of audiences to even a minimal level of theoretical competence in the reading of news and current affairs could radically improve the quality of social and political debate.

A *general* understanding of contextual fields provides the basis for viewers of, say, a news story, to think about what kind of map they could create from what they have been told in the news account they have just seen and heard. It provides a basis for then reflecting upon the implications and productive uses of such a mapping, as we will do in case studies throughout the book. A general knowledge of what is involved in the idea of a contextual field establishes a durable foundation in that it provides viewers with the capacity to draw on it selectively, sketching out a series of more specific, limited, contextual fields relevant to whatever the story is at hand. The metaphor of mapping is an especially useful one in thinking about the idea of contextual fields when it is combined with a sense of interlinking networks. It puts into wider perspective any particular set of actors, individual or collective, and starkly reveals the inadequacies of attributing responsibility in overly individualistic or atomistic ways, ways that make no reference to this broader context.

The threat of homelessness: Viewing the contextual field from within

In this section, as noted above, I will recount and explore the predicament of a young single mother of two young children, Sandy, who faces a specific, fleshed-out contextual field as she searches for somewhere to live in a contemporary American city. The story will be told from Sandy's viewpoint, looking at how she experiences the *objective character of the contextual field* she is faced with. I'll make a point of drawing out relevant elements from the basic repertoire of objective elements of the contextual field described within the box on page 32.

Sandy's story is taken from a major contribution to political theory, *Responsibility for Justice*, a brilliant exposition of the implications for moral reasoning of taking social structures seriously.[10] Its author, Iris Marion Young, for many years Professor of Political Science at the University of Chicago, creates the imaginative example of Sandy's predicament, extending it over a period of lived time, in order to explore the moral issues involved in the interaction between an individual and an inherited set of social structures. I will draw on Young's deliberations about Sandy's situation, as the agent-in-focus, in order to indicate how the abstract notion of the contextual field should be brought into contact with the detail, texture and colour of the lived experiences of particular individuals. In focusing on Sandy's positioning in relation to those objective factors within fields that have been captured in box 2, we will be interested in looking at the world from her own situated viewpoint.[11]

In Young's narrative, Sandy needs to move out of her rented central-city apartment building in an American city because a developer has bought the building and plans to convert it into condominiums. This is an objective, external force that Sandy needs to respond to, whatever her own views on the matter. The force is intractable from Sandy's perspective, and it affects her, out of the blue, simply because of her positioning within this contextual field of rented apartments and property development. Sandy's first feeling is that maybe this isn't a bad thing as the rent was quite high, and the building was poorly maintained and falling apart. It is apparent here that the character of Sandy's initial perception of the situation, and the positive, optimistic gloss she puts on this, makes a difference to how she experiences her position. This highlights the power of people's internal frame of meaning on the ways they internalize external forces and situations. Understanding how Sandy feels at this point means understanding both the external forces and her internal values and dispositions.

In the previous chapter we noted the additional weight and significance provided to stories when knowledge of the internal worlds of actors is included. Social theory, following the classical German sociologist Max Weber, typically refers to attempts to understand the internal perspective of social actors as the method of *verstehen*, and as we've already noted, it is often also referred to as the 'hermeneutic method'.[12] However, as we've also noted, this is not always combined with an insistence on including the actor's internalization of the external structural context in the picture, and it is this structural aspect that I want to concentrate on, to thematize, in the current chapter. The relatively recent social-theoretical approach of structuration theory – a synthesis of the fruits of several traditions of social theory – has made much of this structural aspect within the internal world of actors.[13] In Sandy's case we need to think of the ways in which the contextual field 'out-there' is experienced by her as presenting an objective terrain which is for the most part intractable, and which she must try to manoeuver within, and to negotiate, as best she can. Her sense of what she might do, the dilemmas she feels she faces and the kinds of choices she feels are available to her, where there are any at all, revolve around her knowledge of her situation, her knowledge of the relevant contextual field. This is a particular kind of knowledge. It is situational knowledge, knowledge of the immediate social terrain in which she must act, choose, decide and so on, in the awareness that she must live with the consequences, positive and negative.

From the point at which Sandy accepts her immediate fate and begins to look for a new place to live, she is faced with a whole series of specific objective external factors that she needs to take account of. These external factors enter into Sandy's internal world, and what results is a negotiated compromise between what she would ideally want and what the external world will allow. She works as a sales clerk in a suburban mall and has been taking two buses from her current residence in order to reach work, which has meant a total commuting time of 3 hours each day. Her ideal is to travel less and so to find an apartment closer to where she works, but not for the last time she soon finds that there are many aspects of the contextual field that she was unaware of. As she looks in the newspapers and online for rental apartments nearer to her work, and also on a bus route, she is shocked at the rents for one- and two-bedroom apartments:

Sandy learns that there are few rental apartments close to her workplace – most of the residential property near the mall is single-family houses. The few apartments nearby are very expensive. Most suburban apartments in her price range are located on the other side of the city from her job: there are also some in the city but few that she can afford which she judges decent and in a neighbourhood where she feels her children will be safe. In either case, the bus transportation to work is long and arduous, so she decides that she must devote some of the money she hoped would pay the rent to make car payments. She applies for a housing subsidy programme and is told that the waiting time is about two years.[14]

Surprises such as this are not unusual for limited, finite human beings whose lives are carried on in complex modern societies; social theorists have come to reflect upon this in terms of our inevitable ignorance of large swathes of our situated 'conditions of action'. The greater the extent of the conditions of action that we are ignorant of, that are 'unacknowledged', the more likely we are to come across *unexpected obstacles*, or to make decisions that lead to *unintended consequences*.[15] The significance of the newly acquired knowledge for Sandy is clearly not a detached, intellectual, inquisitiveness[16], or a product of mild curiosity. Rather, it is a direct consequence of her objective, flesh and blood, positioning within the relevant contextual field. The knowledge impinges profoundly on her life and the lives of her children, and she is radically constrained by her lack of power. Structural constraints manifest themselves with respect to her positioning in relation to financial resources, transport, time, qualifications, working conditions, and her role as a mother of young children. The various ways in which she is positioned, socially, and the variety of interdependencies that come along with these, mean that she already has a series of duties and obligations to meet, at home and at work, in order to satisfy her own and other people's expectations of appropriate behaviour. Intertwining with, and often in tension with, the internal pressures she experiences as a result of her own personal values, external expectations impose their own sets of constraints as Sandy internalizes the threat of sanctions, potentially disastrous, that would accompany her failure to adequately fulfil various obligations.

Faced with the powerful objective constraints, pressures, forces and dynamics imposing themselves on her from the external context, including the date of the eviction order closing in on her, Sandy makes a decision. This is a decision whose reasoning could only be grasped on the basis of her understanding of context, and her positioning within it. She settles on a one-bedroom apartment that is a 45-minute drive from the shopping mall where she works. It is smaller than she hoped for, but this has had to be a trade-off given the limited resources at her disposal and the money she has had to pay out for the car. The two children will sleep in the bedroom and she will sleep on a foldout bed in the living room. She has had to forfeit the hope of getting an apartment with such amenities as a washer or dryer in the building, and there is no playground for the children. Ultimately, however, although she sees no other option but to rent this apartment, she has a further shock when she realizes that she will be required to deposit 3 months' rent to secure the apartment. This is 3 months' rent that she doesn't have, having used all her savings for a down payment on the car. Her lack of knowledgeability combines with her lack of resources to leave her unable to rent this apartment, or any other apartment, given that this is a standard landlord policy. She consequently faces the prospect of homelessness.[17] None of these are consequences she envisaged in the first flush of optimism with which she confronted the initial news that her existing apartment building had been bought by a developer.

Giving breadth and depth to the contextual field, Young makes it clear that a whole series of different institutional actors have contributed to the structural context that confronts Sandy's 'personal' choice. These actors are both public and private institutions, and are located at the different socio-spatial levels of nation, state, city and locality, all of which influence the supply and price of rental housing. They include:

> the federal Reserve Bank, Congress, executive agencies, and the courts; national housing industry organizations, such as the National Association of Home Builders and the Institute for Real Estate Management; national tenants' advocacy associations; municipal councils and local zoning boards; local housing industry organizations; local tenants associations; and individual professional and amateur landlords.[18]

The various decisions of these institutional actors, working over time and in networks of connection with each other, have interacted with the operations of the market 'to influence rents and the supply of affordable housing.'[19] This means that the current structural context at any one time is only the most immediate layer of the relevant contextual field. This immediate layer will have been produced, caused, over a historical medium term through the combination of the situated decisions and actions of this plurality of actors. Each of these actors will have been working according to their own variously structured sets of cultural rules and expectations. This fleshes out in a further concrete example the point already made that contextual fields have both historical depth and geographical stretch.

It is worth noting that in moving outwards from Sandy's immediate predicament to this broader contextual field, naming the most salient private and public institutions specific to this field, we have taken an external observer's point of view. Many of these institutional actors will have been unknown to Sandy, lying outside her field of vision even as they contributed to her predicament. In this situation, an external observer's point of view that is also aware of the situated actor's point of view is a precondition for being able to identify which parts of the relevant contextual field Sandy knows about and which remain 'unacknowledged conditions of action'. The same point applies to the identification of unintended consequences of action. It is equally worth noting that while Young introduces these additional institutional actors, all contributing to the objective qualities of the contextual field facing Sandy, the attention she pays to their analysis is inevitably more limited than that she pays to Sandy's own situation. She looks at them as an external observer, from the outside, and paints them in with broad brushstrokes. All accounts, to a greater or lesser extent, contain this kind of movement between micro-detail and sweeping summary, and the latter is very often from the viewpoint of an entirely external observer.

Young notes that Sandy's position is shared by many people with 'diverse attributes, life histories, and goals'.[20] All these people are structurally positioned in situations that are the systematic, largely unintended, outcome of the actions of multiple different actors, all for the most part abiding by the rules of society. For example, it is an unintended structural outcome, created by uncoordinated decisions by many different actors, that the median asking rent for a two-bedroom apartment in the United States 'in 2004 was $974, far out of reach of the 40 per cent of renters with incomes less than $20,000.' Not wanting to lay the blame in any simple way on particular actors in this causal chain, Young does want to say that it is surely a structurally unjust situation that has left 'only one in eighty subsidized apartment units . . . located in an area with strong job growth', and in which one-fifth are 'located in areas whose employment opportunities are declining'.[21]

An essential part of Young's argument is that 'moral judgement' – which we should remind ourselves is one of the key journalistic frames identified by the academic literature – needs to be thought about with respect to two different levels. One of these is the common-sense attribution of moral judgements with respect to how people treat each other in more or less direct dealings with one another. The other involves making moral judgements about structural contexts that no one necessarily intended, but which systematically deny opportunities to some people while systematically providing them to others. Sandy's vulnerability to housing deprivation is a *structural position* shared by many people, a generalized set of relations that 'position people prior to their interactions, and condition expectations and possibilities of interaction'.[22] This is not the place to pursue this argument in the detail it deserves, and I must refer the reader to Young's own extended and persuasive argument. However, it is important to say that the moral judgements made in news and current affairs pieces should try to find ways of paying more attention to structural networks, and to the layered ways in which they are created and sustained, if they are not to focus their concern only at the circumscribed level of direct interaction. This is not to diminish the significance of moral behaviour and judgements with respect to people's direct dealings with each other. However, it is to point out that this is a highly restricted domain, and to insist that many moral issues require a close engagement with structured contextual fields. In terms of particular news events, this means that moral judgements need also to be made with attention to the causal configurations that have produced them, over more or less extended periods; this involves structural wrongs of many different kinds. Embedding events and stories within contextual fields is clearly a necessary condition of possibility for being able to do this.

Transport policy and the mistreatment of the elderly: Limitations in the frames of both journalists and audiences

Two detailed academic case studies of news coverage on transport policy in Denmark and the mistreatment of the elderly in Sweden are insightful for what they reveal about the strengths and the limitations of current academic media analysis. They also hint at the limitations of the journalistic frames in both cases, and, in the Danish case, of the limitations of the frames employed by audiences.[23] In both cases journalists are, for the most part, taking an external observer's perspective on events. Also, where one would hope for an appropriate contextual field within which to position the events-in-focus within the news stories, there is, in fact, very little of substance. And with a generally empty contextual field comes, by definition, a corresponding deficiency of attention to any of those objective factors within the field that, from an insider's situated perspective, were so pervasive within the account of Sandy's predicament.

Both cases deal with news stories focusing on specific policy issues – transport policy and the mistreatment of the elderly in private care homes – presented by national and local media in a range of genres, debating values lodged in quite circumscribed everyday concerns within national boundaries. One might expect such coverage to exhibit a significant concern with specific details and context, homing in on causes and possible solutions in a complex field of dynamic forces, constraints and opportunities. Given this, the fact that the level of specificity and context provided turns out to be very limited is particularly revealing.

The first of these studies, focused on Danish transport policy, suggests a lack of specificity within the news accounts, the absence of real engagement with situated processes. It also reveals a similar deficit of involvement on the part of audiences, who turn out to be interested only in details that relate directly to their own experience. The field of vision of the audience is as restricted as their interest in details, with only rhetorical notice paid to the contextual field of key actors in the political realm, or to the concerns of anyone with alternative values.

The second study, concerning the mistreatment of the elderly in Swedish nursing homes, also betrays the news media's lack of engagement with the details of situated processes. At the same time, it reveals a similar restriction of the scope of vision. Part of this involves the adoption of a narrow view that excludes relevant key actors and processes from the picture, consigning key aspects of the contextual field to darkness. The other part entails taking only the most passing, surface-level, interest in those most prominent actors and processes that are included within the range of attention. However, the researchers from Gothenburg University who analysed these news accounts point to aspects of the socio-historical context that explains a great deal about why the various news media in Sweden at this time converged on such a narrow point of view. Providing such contextualized, historically contingent, reasons for the shape of news gives cause for optimism and works against fatalism, as it suggests that such constriction isn't inevitable, that work can be done to resist it. Similar points can be made about the quality of audience involvement and reception in the Danish case, which, likewise, need not be thought of as forever destined to operate at these disappointing levels.

The first of these studies was part of a larger project funded by the Danish parliament, designed to investigate democracy and power.[24] The study aimed to gain insight into the relationship between the presentation of news within the media and citizens' use of this for political purposes in everyday life. They chose traffic and transport policy as the primary areas to explore. The main debates here were around traffic congestion, the extent to which the provision of proposed new motorways would be sufficient, the environmental costs of this, and possible alternatives including an expansion of the rail network. The political background to the study was a great deal of dissatisfaction among many citizens about the direction of policy, with a strong feeling that the views of ordinary people were being ignored. The researchers, Kim Christian Schrøder and Louise Phillips of Roskilde University, focused on the media coverage – three national television channels, one regional television channel, one radio programme, four national daily broadsheet newspapers, two national tabloid newspapers, one local broadsheet newspaper and one local free newspaper – during one week in which an inter-party transport agreement was reached in January 2001 between the Social-Democratic/Social Liberal government and three right-wing opposition parties. They complemented this with seven focus group interviews in which citizens spoke specifically about this transport policy and also about traffic and transport issues in general.

Using these methods, the researchers identified two 'orders of discourse', or culturally inherited ways of talking about something, through which *both* the media and viewers discussed the transport issues.[25] It's important to note in what follows that the main emphasis of the researchers is on the language, rhetoric and discourse of the texts, and on the discursive frames of the audiences, rather than on what is known about the objective characteristics of the relevant contextual field. As noted above, I have no doubt that we need the sophisticated analyses of media texts provided by these studies, with their emphasis on discourses and media frames, and so it is important to include strong examples of such work here. However, in reading these accounts, one should note that they lack a concerted focus on the world that media and audience discourses are purporting to grasp. There is little attempt to engage with the characteristics of the events themselves, or with the characteristics of the relevant networks of relations through which those events have been produced.

The two discourses identified by the researchers consisted of the same cluster of six 'interpretive repertories' but with different weightings in the importance and significance given to particular repertoires. The joint use of these six categories indicated a two-way process between media and citizens, in which interpretation and dialogue took place within this broadly shared discursive frame. The authors of the study believe their findings accord with the dominant view within communications analysis that the media can be seen to set the public agenda of topics, and to have autonomy over the particular ways in which stories are told. However, they insist that the dynamics work both ways, with the news stories being told in such a way that they would dovetail with the framework of perceptions and ways of seeing already existing among the culture of citizen viewers.[26]

It is striking, however, that the two groups – the news media and the citizen viewers – differed in the ways they drew on the shared discourses, giving more emphasis to some aspects than to others.[27] The news media primarily emphasized two 'orders of discourse', one of which, given great weight in the media, is categorized by the researchers under the heading of 'Parliamentary democracy in action'. This is a discourse that celebrates the workings of parliamentary democracy and presents it in an overwhelmingly positive light. The second category, given only slightly less emphasis in the media, is labelled, 'Populism: citizens against "the system"', which is perhaps the clearest point of contact between the frame of the journalists and that of the audience. The citizen-audience, by way of contrast with the media, places very little emphasis on 'Parliamentary democracy in action', and instead places a good deal of weight on the much more cynical, disaffected category of 'Parliamentary democracy: politics as "dirty deals"'. Two other categories are emphasized by the viewer-readers, and one of these is 'Politics in daily life: negotiation of individual responsibility', which speaks for itself, while the other, interestingly, is shared with the news media, and is 'Populism: citizens against "the system"'.[28]

The case brings out well the importance of the audiences' frame, and hence the benefits that could be derived from a pedagogy cultivating this frame by means of social theory's conceptually disciplined perspective. However, Schrøder and Phillips identify a difference within their audience grouping that suggests, perhaps predictably, that some groups would be more immediately open to such pedagogy than others. That is, some uses of the media divide along educational lines, so that those with a relatively short education express a lack of interest in in-depth background knowledge, wishing to gain just an overview of what is in the news on a daily basis, 'without unnecessary and irrelevant details'.[29] Those with a relatively long education, by way of contrast, see themselves 'as socially engaged citizens to whom it matters to be well-informed, which means both to have a broad overview, but also to immerse themselves in the background and context of the political and cultural stories on the news agenda'.[30] Both groups are characterized by the authors of the study as generally well informed about social, political and cultural matters, and to possess 'extensive *knowledge repertoires* which they can draw on in their appropriation and contextualization of the information offered by the media' (original emphasis). Both groups are also said to be able to respond with a certain critical distance to media representations of events, although those with a longer education are judged to possess this capacity to a considerably greater degree than those with a short education.[31]

It is important to acknowledge the extent to which Schrøder and Phillips believe that the audiences they've studied are skilled and knowledgeable.[32] But while one can see what they mean by this, it also seems to be an extremely generous assessment. While we have noted the need to adjust, downwards, our expectations of what television news texts can provide, we also need to adjust upwards what we should demand of audiences in their engagement with the media. In this case of Danish transport policy, Schrøder and Phillips' research findings suggest that both media presentation and audience reception were strikingly limited. Significant elements of the presentational frames shared by the various media remained at an overly vague level of abstraction. Statements indicating the indifferent and intractable workings of 'the system', positioned as working against the wishes of 'the people', were too imprecise to allow audiences any possibility of identifying the precise practices at issue, which would be necessary to be able to reinsert them within a network of relevant relationships.[33] Greater knowledge about causation is needed in order to really understand the contours of the problem, and to begin to think reasonably about possible solutions. Similar points can be made about the media's use of *the populist repertoire*, which sets the system against the people in a blanket manner, serving to discredit politicians and the political system without drilling down into specifics. One effect of this was to 'invite political actors to follow popular moods rather than political vision and rational argument'.[34]

On the audience's side, while it is true, as we have just noted, that some of the material they had to work with was restricted, audience responses were also limited by the character of the discursive frames and interpretive repertoires they brought to bear on the texts. For example, discussion within the focus group criticizing the distribution of resources between different regions and different forms of transport was, according to Schrøder and Phillips, 'attributed to the political system as such', seen as emanating from 'the very essence of politics', as being 'inherent' within the system.[35] 'Dirty politics' and 'the system' were seen as responsible for the perceived shortcomings and policy failures. Audiences felt empowered in their role as 'the people', a collective actor that was presented by the media and by themselves (in focus group discussions) as understanding transport issues from the ground up, as being in touch with the real world. By way of contrast, the politicians were portrayed as elitist and disconnected from everyday life. However, the audience's feeling of empowerment came at a cost. The cost lay in the retreat into moral absolutes that accompanied the binary opposition they worked with, a binary divide that took the form of an impersonal us versus them. Audiences sought refuge in 'indignation and consternation', including in some cases 'the use of extreme-case formulations, such as "crazy", "every single morning", and "chaos"', to recount stories of traffic conditions.[36] Such expressive, cathartic, ways of interpreting and discussing media texts are no doubt healthy at one level, but they indicate a distinctive deficit regarding specificity of appropriate knowledge. This, again, reveals a lack of precision that means audiences are deflected from any interest in identifying the particular practices at issue and their positioning within a relevant network of relations. The limitations of audience response consequently reinforce those of media presentation.

The second study, carried out by Monika Djerf-Pierre and colleagues from Gothenburg University in Sweden, doesn't include an audience dimension, concentrating solely on the media presentation of the issues. The specific case involved a private health care corporation, Carema, which in 2011 was accused of mistreating the elderly in its nursing homes. Disclosures in a number of media outlets resulted in a national scandal, 'where the news media exposure to a large extent came to deal with questions of responsibility and accountability'.[37] The researchers note that the story followed the typical pattern of a news wave or attention cycle whereby an initial report was subject to 'social amplification' through the media, and over time the story evolved in various ways. An initial emphasis on employees and relatives in the nursing homes, who came forward with accounts of offences and misconduct, gave way to a subsequent phase in which 'the problems were blamed on the operating management of the nursing home, and on the corporate culture (the heavy emphasis on cost-cutting and the downsizing of staff) of Carema.'[38]

The study of Djerf-Pierre et al. is based on a corpus of 156 news items that were part of an intensive period of news coverage of the Carema case. The analysis examined the main national coverage, including news, editorials and opinion pieces in two newspapers – the daily 'prestige' liberal newspaper *Dagens Nyheter*, and the daily social democratic tabloid *Aftonbladet* – and the daily national news on both public service television (*Rapport*) and commercial television (*Nyheterna*).[39] The analysis of these items focused on the degrees of effectiveness with which journalists engaged in what the authors of the study refer to as 'accountability interviews' with politicians and others in relation to policy failures. The authors draw on the academic media frames literature to look at questions of accountability with respect to the social problem at issue. Their particular interest, within this, is on causes and solutions, which we have already encountered as key preoccupations of the media frames approach, but also on issues of responsibility. Responsibility is, of course, closely connected to questions of causation and also to the making of moral judgements, and is a natural corollary of concerns over accountability. It is worth noting that when thinking of responsibility one would intuitively think about the particular people or institutional actors who could be identified as responsible for an action or series of actions, as opposed to impersonal systems or structures, and the focus on holding politicians and officials to account fits with this common-sense notion.

The broader social context for the events emphasized by the researchers is that of new public management regimes, a social landscape in which there is a diminishing role for politics in favour of market mechanisms.[40] Against this background the authors were particularly interested in whether journalists now neglected 'political' accountability in favour of other forms of accountability, particularly those associated with the commercial and market worlds that were now an intrinsic part of the processes being investigated. The researchers found that issues of political responsibility were indeed downgraded, being replaced at the apex of interest by a concern with the administrative and professional responsibilities of the management of Carema.

Within this hierarchy of emphasis, Djerf-Pierre and her co-researchers draw attention to the significance of the values embedded in different media frames and the consequent necessity of bringing these to the foreground of awareness. As with the analysis in the Danish case, it is evident that the theoretical tools of media analysis employed by Djerf-Pierre and her colleagues are not primarily directed at the character of the news events and the contextual fields in which they have been produced. Rather, the balance of their concerns is weighted towards the nature of the discursive, media, frames employed by the journalists. The researchers identified three broad social perspectives that framed how political accountability was construed in the news reports. These were: *a new public management frame,* derived from neo-liberal political discourse, with freedom of choice an overriding value and health care for profit seen as 'inherently good'; *an anti-marketization frame –* evident only in some opinion pieces, and in a one-hour-long documentary on Carema (*Dokument Inifrån*) emphasizing the resources and power of international health care corporations in the wake of the potential move to privatization – which was alert to the dangers of capitalism, and viewed the profit motive that accompanied privatization as a threat to quality of care; and *a greed frame,* which focused on the greed of top-level managers at Carema and the corporations behind it (Ambea, Triton, KKR). Translating the latter case into the language of the media frames perspective, the authors of the study write that the message given by the news stories adopting this frame was that '[T]he real cause of the problems at Carema is the personal greed among top-level managers, and the solution (albeit not stated clearly) is public condemnation of such immoral behaviour, thus effectively de-politicizing the problem'.[41] Journalism in the Carema case is said to have 'primarily operated within the new public management frame, supplemented by the greed frame', with issues of political accountability muddled or obscured in the new public management frame and 'lost altogether' in the greed frame, 'making it a moral issue instead of a political problem.'[42]

The researchers combine this media frames' approach with a second research perspective, that of closely analysing the discourses and practices of the journalists using one or other of the frames. This combination brings the approach very close to that used in the Danish study, combining as it does both relatively broad discursive frames and the more localized interpretative practices employed by the journalists as they conduct interviews with key actors. The research question posed by Monika Djerf-Pierre and her colleagues on the basis of this approach is quite precise. They ask how journalistic interviews are used 'in *positioning actors as responsible* and *asking politicians to justify* their decisions and actions (or non-actions).' (original emphasis).[43] There is a clear implication that we are here in the realm of moral judgement, with the justifications offered by politicians as they are held to account being evaluated by journalists and audiences as either 'satisfactory or not'.[44] In the event, the lack, within the journalistic frames, of relevant categories of political–civil society relations, and of historical context in relation to this, meant the journalists were unable to find a way to hold politicians to account for the mistreatment of the elderly.

One of the key arguments of Djerf-Pierre et al. is that the account told from within the more politicized anti-marketization frame indicates that it is not only the current Conservative-led government that should be held accountable for endorsing and legitimizing the marketization of social services, but also the Social Democrats, 'who approved of the market orientation of the public sector when they were in government in the 1990s'.[45] These are the kinds of relevant networks of social relations that Bourdieu was talking about, stretching away from immediate events. These are networks whose causal impact arrives here from other sites in geographical space – from the 'somewhere else', which are the halls, rooms and chambers of political parties and government, to the 'immediately here' moments of mistreatment in the nursing homes – and from the shallow temporal past of the 1990s.

The journalists found themselves unable to hold these politicians to account because the frames they were working with were inadequate. In our terms, the frames were too narrow to bring into view some of the most relevant networks of causal relations, while they also lacked the appropriate historical depth. As a consequence, as we shall see, they failed to adequately position politicians within a contextual field that would have helped to explain the news events-in-focus. The researchers state very clearly that the 'journalists had incredible difficulties in finding a position from which they could hold politicians to account'. They argue that this was because the news media had 'gone native', working entirely from within the new public management frame, with the corporate greed frame a subsidiary perspective within this. This meant that their notion of context simply mirrored this frame, and so excluded politicians' past and current responsibility for creating and legitimizing this system.

As Djerf-Pierre et al. put it, 'the responsibility of the politicians was narrowed down to their role as purchasers of services (managers of bid contracts) and as suppliers of the regulatory framework for agencies doing the quality control'.[46] Even within the broad parameters of the public management frame, however, journalists could still have explored the relevant networks of relations and held the politicians to task for not being able to manage these aspects satisfactorily. The authors argue that they didn't do this because they were in the grip of a hegemonic neo-liberal ideology and an elite consensus that simply assumed that marketization and the new public management was the most appropriate way of organizing welfare services. There was an unstated and unexamined belief that this method would be effective, almost automatically, barring some kind of malfeasance extrinsic to the institutional arrangements. The effect of these presumptions was to render redundant, by ideological fiat, any concern with the relevant political dimensions of the contextual field. It was this that prevented journalists from asking more detailed, specific, questions about the regulatory mechanisms or the workings of the system – questions, as the authors point out, one can readily find prompts to in the academic literature on new public management and political accountability – such as whether 'it is reasonable to expect local politicians to have the purchasing know-how, the resources and capacity to handle complex bids, and if the existing quality-control arrangements are effective enough to monitor the providers (and at what cost it is achieved)'.[47]

In the event, it is argued, the journalists could only fulfil their duty, as the fourth estate, to hold power to account by taking the populist route of the 'greed frame'. But just as we have seen in the Danish transport case, the retreat into populism tends to come at the cost of specificity, with a retreat into moral absolutism, and with emotionally heightened news discourses appealing to outrage, indignation, and an inadequately contextualized empathy.[48] The authors conclude, as they must, that the political accountability work carried out by journalists, and presented in the news items analysed, was 'weak, vague and restricted'. As with the Danish study, the problems were ultimately 'construed as a moral scandal instead of a policy failure'.[49] We are left with the impression that the journalists' exploration of the objective contextual field in both of these studies is extremely thin, even for those elements that have been embraced by their perspective. As a consequence, the kinds of objective concepts outlined in box 2 will have had very little bearing on the accounts they provided.

Conclusion

It will become ever clearer as we proceed that the balance of the academic media analyses we've looked at here is weighted towards the level of the media text. That is, it is weighted towards the media frames of journalists and the framing of the news texts themselves. The point is clearly not an absence of any concern with the objective realities that are the raw material of news accounts. Such concern is plain to see. Rather, it is that the main focus is not on the characteristics of the contextual field. It is not on: the relation between conceptualization and evidence; the character and status of the knowledge acquired or missing from view; or on the evaluation of the validity or adequacy of the knowledge, judgements and strategy derived from within a media frame. These elements, where they are broached, remain intuitive and unsystematic. Moreover, when compared to the benchmark of the social-theoretical frame on the contextual field that we've begun to build up, focusing in this chapter on its 'objective' features, the *journalistic* frames suggested by these two case studies seem badly wanting. It is clear, also, that in order for citizen-audiences to have more effective critical distance and insight into what is and isn't offered by these frames, they would need more sophistication than that revealed in the Danish research. In the next chapter, Danish production values and Danish audiences fight back. I draw here on an episode from the first-rate Danish political drama, *Borgen*, to demonstrate the sophisticated skills it demands of audiences, and to indicate that interpreting the drama's storylines means employing many of the general concepts of the contextual field and then applying them *in situ* to the local tones, colours and details of particular events and processes. I will also use the chapter to complement the general account of the *objective elements* of the contextual field introduced in the current chapter with a more fine-grained exposition of the *subjective elements* that should also be conceptualized and deployed.

3

What we do when we make sense of *Borgen*

Introduction: The interpretative skills of the audience

In this chapter I will continue to explore how the idea of the contextual field can be used to illuminate the meaning of events and processes represented in media texts. I will draw on an episode of the Danish political drama, *Borgen*, to demonstrate how, in order to follow the storyline, audiences do in fact already employ many of the general concepts of the contextual field. Audiences require these general, abstract concepts in order to make sense of the dramatic events offered to them. They draw on them incrementally as the plot unfolds, slowly but surely combining them with the hues, shades and details of the specifics of this particular story, with these particular characters, in this time and place. Through this combination of general ideas and local detail, audiences begin to build up stocks of quite specific background knowledge as an episode progresses, remembering what has already happened in the episode, and potentially from previous episodes, and keeping this quietly in mind. As the episode continues they then, at the appropriate points, refer back to these past moments in order to make sense of new moments in the unfolding of the narrative. Sophisticated skills of interpretation are employed, for the most part intuitively rather than consciously, as many of the general concepts of the contextual field are applied *in situ* to the local tones, colours and details of particular events and processes. The optimistic lesson to be drawn from this is that such audiences already exhibit many of the capacities and skills I am advocating. The challenge is simply to make these more explicit, to refine them further and to apply them to news and current affairs as well as to complex political dramas.

As viewers are not players within the sequence of events, and so are not positioned within the contextual field as Sandy was in the previous chapter, they are always attempting to follow what is going on from within their position as external observers. They will be alert to those relevant *objective factors in the contextual field* (see Chapter 2, page 32) that can be identified from the vantage point of an entirely external observer. By *entirely* external I mean to indicate someone who both isn't involved in the field of action *and* doesn't make any attempt to understand how involved, situated, actors experience that field. However, much in the *Borgen* storyline does in fact rest on viewers also being able to identify with the situated position of the characters within the story, attempting to take their viewpoint and to see the world through their eyes. So, viewers will never be entirely external in the sense I've suggested. There is a link here with objective factors, as being able to take the perspective of involved actors means that viewers will also be alert to the various different ways in which the contextual field presents itself to these characters as an objective contextual terrain. This is an *objective contextual terrain confronting different characters in different ways*. The terrain inevitably confronts the characters in different ways as they are situated in different positions within the contextual field that provides the arena for the episode's unfolding events. The objective terrain confronted Sandy in particular ways because she, likewise, was facing it from a distinctive position, and attempted to negotiate that position in the best way she could, all the time facing the loss of her rented apartment. In *Borgen*, the contextual terrain also presents itself to the characters *in situ* as a specific field of pressures, constraints, risks, possibilities and potential negative and positive sanctions. Their knowledge about some of this terrain will be fairly accurate and well informed, whereas their knowledge about other aspects of it will be murky or non-existent.

Viewers of the *Borgen* episode need to grasp the essentials of all of this in order to understand the various dilemmas around which the plot revolves. Competent audiences of *Borgen* need to be able to understand a good deal about the *subjective ways* in which characters perceive the objective circumstances in which they find themselves. For when *Borgen's* characters experience the powerful objectivity of the contextual terrain that faces them, they do so from within a particular, culturally inflected frame of meaning. That is, from within a deep layer of subjectivity and culture that guides and moulds how they apprehend, perceive and feel about the pressures, duties, obligations, expectations, opportunities and dilemmas that confront them. This is to point to the situated subjective component of their apprehension of their objective context. I think of this moment as the actors' analysis of context, or *context analysis*.[1] As a situated actor's (or in the case of drama, a situated character's) analysis of their contextual field will be deeply affected by both the nuances of their objective position and their cultural and individual perspective on this, there will almost always be a gap between how they experience a situation and the sense of this grasped by a viewer. A viewer, as an external observer, can never totally inhabit the body and perspective of an actor who is in the midst of either a political drama or a news event. In terms of knowledge of the objective characteristics of the relevant context, the characters involved in a drama and the people involved in a news event can know more about their context than the audience, but they can also know less. It is important to remember this, and to be prepared to think about its implications in situations where a grasp of context is significant.

But there is also a further moment of subjectivity involved in how situated actors *process and respond to* their own analysis of the objective context, with its various networks, pressures and dynamics. If the first moment is concerned with how they analyse their contextual field, this second moment is concerned with the process by which they combine that analysis of context with other aspects of their subjectivity as they come to act in a particular way. Such actions may be rationally calculated, emotionally detached, consciously aware and decisive, or they may be devoid of rational calculation, fuelled by emotion, completely intuitive, and hesitant. Alternatively, they may possess various intermediate combinations of these or other characteristics. Further, their actions may be driven more by their perception of immediate external powers, forces and constraints or, alternatively, by the more enduring aspects of who they are as an individual, or as a collective actor, including their values, ethical orientations and principles, both personal and professional. Such identities include a sense of their own history and integrity, and their loyalties, commitments, tastes, ambitions, ideals, virtues and so on. These are aspects internal to an actor that social theorists have got used to calling *habitus*, and we will return to this important conception later in the chapter.[2]

Sometimes, the combination of external pressures and goal-directed personal or collective ambition can lead to values, ethics and loyalties being subordinated, and sometimes, perhaps less often, the confrontation between external pressures and personal ideals can lead to ambitions being forfeited for the sake of ethical commitments. This is an aspect of actors' interior lives in which they decide, more or less consciously, how to conduct themselves, and consequently it is useful for viewers to try and grasp what is happening within this process. The viewers thus need to engage in an analysis of how the situated actor's conduct comes to be what it is: how they reconcile their perception of context with what they'd like to achieve, and with how they'd ideally like to behave. It can be seen immediately here how it is very useful to differentiate **between** attempting to grasp the contextual field confronting an actor (*context analysis*) **and** attempting to grasp the process by which an actor combines their sense of this contextual field with deliberations or judgements about how to act (*conduct analysis*). The precise role an actor's analysis of context plays in their subsequent actions can vary a great deal, and can be more or less at the forefront of an actor's mind as they act. It is important to try and be alert to this when attempting to diagnose motive and rationale for a character's actions. I will say more about this process later.

In any case, we do want to know how characters move from their perceptions and understandings about the contextual field into acting in particular ways at particular junctures – moving from context to conduct. Why actors do what they do – the kinds of actions that will be at the heart of any episode of any drama as well as being central to most news and current affairs events – can involve a whole range of subjective internal processes of impulse, emotion, reasoning, choice and decision-making, within which objective features 'out-there' in the contextual field are both internalized *and* responded to in the form of actions. Consequently, in addition to continuing to direct attention to the objective elements with the contextual field in what follows, I will also provide a more fine-grained exposition of concepts that can illuminate *both* of the important subjective dimensions of actors' orientations to the contextual field.

The episode I will focus on is that of 'State Visit', the 6th episode of the first series of *Borgen*. Let me start by making a very general point about the character of the background knowledge audiences bring to their understanding of a text. A viewer who watches the whole of the episode of 'State Visit', from beginning to the end, will, at any one point in the episode, be able to relate the current onscreen events to everything that has come before. There will be an intuitive, interpretative, tacking backwards and forwards, between the knowledge of what has happened thus far and knowledge of what is happening right now. This is an interpretative movement from the part to the whole, and from the whole to the part, in what theorists call a 'hermeneutic circle'.[3] This means that someone who comes to the episode half way through, or keeps coming in and out of a room where the episode is playing, will build up a poorer, more fragmented and disconnected, sense of the whole, and this will inevitably affect the quality of their interpretation. When a viewer attentively watches the whole of an episode, she will relate to the later scenes within that episode in a way that is analogous to how the viewer of a single news bulletin will relate to that report when she already has a good deal of background knowledge about the issue being presented. This news' viewer is able to place the episodic vignettes presented to her within a single bulletin into some kind of context – into broader, deeper, historical, social and narrative contexts – so that what is happening on the screen, being seen and being heard at the moment, makes greater sense than it would do to someone without any background knowledge. The greater the background knowledge, naturally assuming that it is relevant to the issue at hand, then the more equipped the audience member will be to grasp the essentials of what is going on.

The assiduous viewer of the *whole* series of *Borgen* is correspondingly that much better equipped again than a viewer who has only seen the 'State

Visit' episode. The viewer of the whole series knows the main protagonist, the Danish Prime Minister, Birgitte Nyborg, well enough to know that it is important to her to be an ethical, principled, politician. Her dilemmas typically involve ethical principle. However, her ethical character is not one that is committed to pure ideals separated from any real-life context. For Birgitte is a realist as well as an idealist. A recurring theme is how to reconcile high moral ideals with the need to be pragmatic in situations that demand principled responsibility in a context of limited powers. Understanding this dilemma means that the viewer recognizes not only the moral principles but also the *in-situ* nuances of the power relations facing the prime minister. Understanding these, in turn, means being able to draw on abstract, general, conceptions of power relations within contextual fields, and to visualize how feasible Birgitte's ethical and policy ideals, and those of her party, look when situated within such a strategic or contextual field inhabited by organizations and other entities possessing distinctive powers and significance. We shall see that an attentive, competent, viewer of 'State Visit' is routinely able to grasp a good deal both about the relevant objective nexus of power relations and about the various interdependencies that make up the structural context of action. Such a viewer is also able to grasp a good deal about Birgitte's character, about what moves and animates her, and thus about what to expect from her as a social actor.

These are impressive levels of background knowledge for audiences to deploy, levels that wait there, lying dormant, until the appropriate moment. We usually take for granted these levels of skill and dexterity required from viewers in order for them to follow a story by drawing the appropriate aspects of stored knowledge to the fore at just the right moment. However, it is necessary to positively reflect upon what is involved in this dexterity if we are to fully grasp its importance. For the essential point is that the majority of *Borgen's* viewers automatically, intuitively, call on these skills as a matter of course. In developing a critical pedagogy for audiences of news and current affairs we are asking such audiences to cultivate something akin to the skills used in reading a political drama such as *Borgen*, but to apply them *self-consciously* to current affairs, and to hone them to a fine critical point. The difficulties will lie not in audience incapacity to rise to these heights of interpretation – as such skills are already part of the cultural competence of viewers of drama and other stories, albeit developed to different levels depending on the complexity and demands of their favoured genres and sub-genres. The difficulties will lie in changing ingrained, inured habits, somewhat ironically unaccustomed to news and current affairs programmes making the kinds of demands on their interpretative skills that are commonplace in other genres.

With television news there has typically been a tacit compromise between producers and audiences that the latter aren't to be stretched. The absence of any protocols signalling that audiences for news stories should ground their reception of such stories within the kind of carefully defined context – the relevant networks of relations – routinely required for political or crime drama has had consequences. The culture of audience reception presumed by this is one that is passive and prosaic. It means that audiences – who are also, of course, citizens with democratic rights and responsibilities – routinely accept that it is normal and natural to respond submissively, without the resources of a critical frame, to a news culture pervaded by the power of rhetorically inflected, but relatively empty, opinion and argument. There seems to be little appreciation of, or at least very little articulacy about, how far this falls short of a response that would be more appropriate, one grounded in the robust analysis of forces, relations and dilemmas embedded in context. The challenge that faces us is one of heightening reflexivity and awareness about these issues; there is a need to improve the standards we set ourselves in the reception of news and current affairs accounts.

By looking more closely at what a political drama such as *Borgen* requires from its audience we can create a more detailed picture of the kinds of things that, at a minimum, should be required from audiences for its non-fiction equivalents. I will show that audiences bring a *general* understanding of contextual fields and their significance to their understanding of the dilemma that confronts Birgitte in 'State Visit', and will distinguish between different aspects of such general understandings. I will also show how audiences necessarily combine and interlace these general understandings with knowledge of *particular details* about *this* story in *this* time and *this* place. This process of interlacing is extremely skilled, and shouldn't be taken for granted, but neither, I am insisting, should it be thought of as something beyond the capacity of audiences for news and current affairs.

Subjective factors in the contextual field

In the last chapter I set out a basic repertoire of objective elements around which to focus the subsequent discussion. The broad picture of the contextual field introduced there was focused around just a few key conceptual themes that appear in the sociological literature as power, social structure, agency, time and space. The detail provided in box 2, 'Objective Factors in the Contextual Field', on page 32 elaborated on one or other aspect of these themes, and on the ways in which they interweave. It provided an objective context allowing us to 'embed and root' events, avoiding the seemingly free-floating presentation of events in news reports that Bourdieu and others have complained about. In order to be able to systematically map out the contextual field relevant to a particular account it is necessary to also think about subjective issues. Thus, in this chapter I want to complement the previous discussion by focusing now on subjective factors, and these are outlined in **box 3**, below. Accordingly, in the description and analysis of 'State Visit' that follows, it will be fruitful to try and identify as many of these subjective elements as possible, and then to carry this knowledge through into the analysis of current affairs texts in the chapters that follow. In order to build on the discussion above, I indicate in brackets which aspects can usefully be thought of as most immediately relevant to the analysis of an actor's *context*, or, alternatively, to the analysis of an actor's *conduct*. It should always be remembered, however, that an actor's analysis of their context necessarily informs their conduct, as decisions about how to act are almost always made with knowledge of context in mind. In understanding *Borgen*, audiences necessarily carry out the following tasks:

Box 3 Subjective factors in the contextual field

- identifying the knowledge key actors have of the contextual terrain in which they act, including their knowledge of externally imposed pressures, obligations and constraints; the opportunities afforded by the external terrain; and the likely consequences of particular courses of action (*context analysis* - I will discuss these towards the end of this chapter under the label of 'situational knowledge')[4];

- identifying how much this knowledge of the contextual field includes knowledge of the subjectivity of the individual and collective actors who populate that terrain (*context analysis*);

- ascertaining what the embedded cultural stocks of knowledge, cultural orientations, subjective values, moral principles and ideal goals of key actors are (I will discuss these towards the end of this chapter under the useful labels of 'general dispositions' or 'habitus'.)[5] These cultural dimensions affect how context is perceived, but they will also work through into informing an actor's conduct (This means they are relevant to both *context and conduct analysis*.) A further step in looking at this factor would be an awareness of how aspects of habitus were initially moulded and formed;

- ascertaining which of the forces, pressures and potential sanctions on a key actor's behaviour – emanating from the contextual field – are experienced as benign and helpful and which are experienced as unsympathetic and unwanted (*relevant to context and conduct analysis*);

(Continued)

Box 3   (Continued)

- ascertaining which of the forces, pressures and potential sanctions on a key actor's behaviour are perceived as intractable within a given time period, and which are perceived as potentially malleable or temporary (*relevant to context and conduct analysis*);

- interpreting how a key actor, in coming to conduct themselves in a particular way, 'orders their concerns' into some kind of hierarchy[6] in order to deal realistically with the inevitable tensions between their ideal values and goals and the compromises and negotiations demanded by the contextual terrain in which they are positioned. Which values are they prepared to compromise and subordinate, and which values do they prioritize in acting as they do? (*conduct analysis*)

There is a difference, however, between the last chapter and the present one, as the practice of identifying these subjective elements does not need to be performed without also thinking about the objective dimensions of the contextual field. The fact that we've already been introduced to the objective dimensions in Chapter 2 means that the two dimensions can be looked at together, with an eye trained on how they interact and interweave with each other. The nuances of this social-theoretical approach to the contextual field, with its clear interweaving of explicitly defined objective and subjective elements, should be contrasted with the broad-brush categories of *media frames*. It should be thought of as a benchmark against which to judge the imprecise categories of the latter, which are self-consciously designed to draw attention to the rhetoric of the text, rather than to assess its substance.

The social-theoretical frame
and the contextual field

The ethos of a *social-theoretical frame* is one of precision when thinking about the four main operations that the *media frame* literature suggests are performed by news, namely: (i) the definition of the problems to be addressed; (ii) the diagnosis of causes; (iii) the making of moral judgements; and (iv) the suggestion of remedies or solutions.[7] A social-theoretical frame on the contextual field allows one to locate problems within a specific terrain of actors, powers, pressures and forces, and to think of *causation* in these terms, situating identifiable actors within a particular network of relations. Possible *solutions and remedies*, including pragmatic compromises, can most adequately be reflected upon once they have been located in these networks of relations, with as clear a sense as possible as to what the consequences of proffered courses of action are likely to be given the configuration of forces.

Moral judgements, likewise, are best approached once the actions being judged are positioned within the contextual field. This is the case whether one is thinking about the moral deliberations of *involved actors-in-situ*, or one is making a moral judgement as an *external observer*, who may or may not be attempting to understand the viewpoint of the actor *in-situ*. Moral judgements are best approached in this way because the pursuit of 'pure' moral principles, without heed to circumstance, can lead to disastrous consequences in many situations. Such 'pure' principles therefore often need to be trimmed or attenuated in order to avoid unwanted negative outcomes. The renowned German sociologist, Max Weber, long ago made a key distinction between the 'pure' ethics and politics of conviction, and the ethics and politics of responsibility. In the latter case, the need to cut and trim pure principles in order to avoid unacceptable dangers and risks is brought to the fore.[8] At the same time, the sustained presence of principled conviction acts as a fortification against the narrow, callous pursuit of self-interest. Both principled conviction and responsibility about *in-situ* circumstances are necessary. We shall see that the prime minister in the *Borgen* episode is faced with a moral conflict framed by these kinds of concerns as a direct result of the particular context in which she finds herself.

Let me say a little more about the second aspect of social-theoretical frames, that of causation, before we move to the direct analysis of the 'State Visit' episode. Given that we are deepening media frame analysis through a more elaborate, conceptually refined, grasp of the mechanisms of causation, we need to be careful about how we think about what causation is and how we gather evidence about it. That is, it's important to begin to be self-conscious and reflective about what we should look for in order to demonstrate that precise combinations of objective and subjective factors have been involved in producing a particular outcome. Examples of outcomes that could be useful to keep in mind range from physical clashes on the streets of a capital city, through the nightmare of genocide, to a seemingly mundane political decision on trade or human rights. In this and future chapters we will sometimes be interested in *single causation*, where just one social force or process has played a particularly powerful role in bringing something about.[9] We meet an example focused around single causation at the beginning of the next chapter. That case involves a High Court decision instructing the Israeli Government to arrange the bulldozing of Israeli settlements on the West Bank within 45 days of its judgement. The focus here is on the effects it makes sense to attribute directly to this court order, and so the account can be usefully thought of as focusing on single causation. This is so notwithstanding the reality that many other factors and social entities will clearly be involved in the processes relevant to the carrying out of this order, or in the failure to carry it out.

Another possible example of single causation might be if we wanted to look at the impact of the decisions of international financial institutions, rather than any other set of institutions, on political events in, say, Greece, in the wake of the global financial crisis. We might want to try and trace the impact of their decisions on different moments in Greek politics. Of course, we are actually talking about more than one financial institution, so already, in this sense, we should be couching our discussion in terms of *plural causation* unless we have a good overriding reason for treating all financial institutions as one causal entity. At other times, however, we will be interested in conceptually more complex plural causation, where our focus is on a number of quite different kinds of actors, sets of relations and processes that have come together to produce a set of events. The conception of the contextual field, with its various interlocking networks, and its temporal depth, makes it more natural, and easier than it otherwise would be, to think of social causation in terms of many contributors, each adding something to a consequence or outcome that gradually emerges. This is the strategy to be adopted in this chapter in looking at the configuration of forces in the 'State Visit' episode.

This emphasis on identifying the practical-institutional pressures exerted within a configuration of forces at any one time, and on following through the processes affected by these, needs to be complemented with an additional awareness of the potent role that cultural ideas and values can play. Cultural ideas can travel across different contextual fields in a way that can be less 'anchored' in the immediate situation than other ways in which the external is internalized by actors. Two key types of such roles played by cultural forces appear in this book. The first type of such cultural influence is where a distinctive set of ideas is seen to play a significant role in the production of the form taken by the forces, pressures, obligations and duties experienced by actors. The onus here is on recognizing the significance of the history by which this configuration of forces came to be suffused and animated with a certain set of ideas, and to try and grasp how this history is working within the present. We have already seen this type in Chapter 2, where we noted the deep impact of neo-liberal financial ideology on the practices of the Danish system of care for the elderly. And we will meet this form again in Chapter 5 when looking at the Mid-Staffordshire case in the National Health Service of the United Kingdom. In these cases, the cultural habitus of relevant institutions has been moulded over time according to the texture and priorities of this ideology. The consequence is that the subjective dispositions of actors within the institutions now take it for granted that neo-liberal forms of financial criteria have a dominant position within their hierarchy of concerns.

The second type of such cultural influence will be seen at work in Chapter 5 in looking at recent events in Thailand. The emphasis here is on symbolically channelled rituals that speak to disparate groupings with the effect that they transform diversity, disunity, and even antagonism, into powerful forms of social solidarity. In the Thai case the symbolism is focused around tropes of nationalism, religion and monarchy, but these are historically and societally specific, so the key meanings can differ from place to place, and from historical period to historical period.[10] This power of cultural ideas to seep across the borders of particular situations, uniting diverse political groupings or different organizational units under one cultural umbrella, adds a further layer of complexity and interest to the idea of the contextual field. Although the meanings established by such cultural movements are not always as closely entwined with specific contextual fields as many other factors are, one should never lose sight of the relationship between the two, which is almost always significant.

To repeat, the key point about this additional layer of complexity is that – in some ways but not in others – the dissemination of culture and ideas can be less anchored to, less restricted by, social structural location than most *in-situ* interactional practices. That is, within a contextual field it is useful to be aware of the relative fluidity with which cultural ideas, impressions and value-judgements can 'leak' from one institutional site to another – through direct techniques of persuasion or through routine cultural osmosis. This possibility is inherent in the configurational nature of causal processes within contextual fields. This means that the influence of single powerful actors, or a coalition or bloc of actors with similar ideologies and interests, can often permeate beyond their immediately obvious direct actions, commands, orders and so on. For if one of these mega actors or macro coalitions[11] has a particular ideology or set of goals, which is made known across configurations of networks, then other actors, many steps removed, can be influenced by this. Distant or external actors may be influenced because the ideology strikes a chord with them and they enthusiastically embrace the ideology, as can happen through the influence of a charismatic figure, the messages attached to an inspiring cause, or the eloquence of ideas that seem to articulate feelings that previously had no voice, no vocabulary.

On the other hand, people may be influenced in a more negative fashion, fearing the consequences of not being seen to support an ideology that is clearly on the ascendant or whose dominance has already been established. Something of this kind, according to academic historians, was the case with Hitler within the institutional power structures of Nazi Germany, with people further down the hierarchical chain 'working to Hitler' in the sense of second-guessing what would receive his approbation rather than following direct orders.[12] On a similarly banal level, but with less dramatic consequences, a fear of the consequences of going against the prevailing orthodoxies, against the current taken-for-granted ways of doing things, can have powerful causal effects on people in their everyday occupations. Such fear can inhibit people from engaging in critical analysis once ideas have started to find a foothold in a given institutional setting.[13] Once a tipping point is reached, moral dissatisfaction with such ideas is silenced as individuals consider their priorities, and weigh up the chances of success against the possible impact idealistic resistance might have on their candidacy for increments or promotion, on their job security and pension prospects, on the quality of their personal working conditions or on the kind of references they might receive when moving on. The advent of new ideologies or cultural movements – such as neo-liberalism and new management orientations, both aided by computer-assisted business models[14] – often, in fact, develop incrementally and organically, and without us being able to point to any one group to say that their input was decisive. In any event, both individual and collective actors, variably positioned in segments of contextual fields, will contribute to such movements of ideas, inhabiting them and helping them to emerge, and deploying the ideas, intentionally and unintentionally, in their direct and indirect influence on others.

Twenty-first century television drama and audience capacities

The minimal conceptual repertoire of the contextual field that I've listed as objective and subjective elements in this and the previous chapter (**see boxes 2 and 3**) can be used as a basic set of benchmarks against which to map out news and current affairs accounts. When television news bulletins are assessed in this manner, it is their thin, sparse, quality that stands out, as we shall see in the next chapter. By way of contrast, what is striking about such mapping when it's applied to a political drama such as *Borgen* is that so many aspects are in fact covered, and are covered in a way that is almost entirely adequate. We get to know the main characters, together with their relevant relationship to the primary collective actors, such as the Cabinet or Ministry, and we get a sense of the duties and obligations attached to their role, and so on. The drama very quickly positions these actors in networks of relevant relationships, building up a keen sense of shared and opposing ideologies, of their various principles, goals and objectives, of the intractable and possibly malleable constraints that confront them, of the variously easy and strained relations between individuals and groupings, and a key overall sense of the configurations of power and interdependence. The kind of fictional drama that *Borgen* represents does this because its *raison d'étre* of successful storytelling means that it must provide the context within which that story will make sense. It won't be good enough, as it is thought to be with television news, to be left with just a vague, desultory, sense of what is going on. Much could be gained through more reflection on the reliance of many kinds of drama, and novels even more so, on the capacity of their audiences to draw on quite complex understandings of the relevant contextual field.

It is not insignificant that *Borgen* belongs to a new generation of original television dramas that have emerged from around the turn of the century.[15] *Borgen* sits alongside other political dramas such as *West Wing* and *House of Cards*, as well as alternative or overlapping genres of drama such as *The Sopranos*, *The Wire*, and *Breaking Bad*, as well as other Danish series such as *The Killing* (*Forbrydelsen*). Each of them draws from art cinema in being able to develop storylines at varying speeds, with some unfolding very slowly over several episodes or series, in being able to present complex, reflective and conflicted characters, and to place greater trust in the audience to work out what is going on than would be the case in some more traditional film and television genres.[16] This more recent kind of drama series provides the opportunity to construct a quality of knowledge analogous to that which we would ideally want to glean from news and current affairs. It provides audiences with enough substance to be able to situate its rich, developed characters in their social and institutional contexts, including many of the elements of the contextual field I've set out as objective and subjective factors. Set within this perspective, one can see why it can be unrealistic to expect too much from television news, which doesn't have the same advantages of these television dramas. The positive message, however, is that television news bulletins are just one source for the information required to grasp what is happening within current affairs processes and events. This means that the ways in which capacities of audiences are implicated in the understanding of television drama series can be transposed to the realm of current affairs if audiences can manage to sustain their attentiveness towards particular stories and themes across items and genres of news and current affairs in a creative, systematic fashion.[17]

There is a fairly conventional, realist, dimension to the storytelling in all of the drama series mentioned, however they might otherwise depart from tried and tested formulas. In most of these series, for much of the time, there is a dynamic of equilibrium driving the story, with the disturbance of this equilibrium marking the beginning of a narrative, which then makes its way through various twists and turns, with a denouement of some kind establishing a new state of affairs, a new equilibrium.[18] This new situation is either a return to the previous status quo or marks the establishment of a new order. The story dynamic, which is known to the authors and directors in advance, or at least before the final edit, guides what is shown and what doesn't need to be shown. Much rests on the authors of the production having a clear sense of 'the point' of their story from the start. This means the writers and directors can be parsimonious and highly efficient in what they show and tell, thus allowing them to get across all, or almost all, of the background information required to make sense of what is going on.

This is clearly not the case in news and current affairs, where there usually isn't an undisputed 'point' of the story, and where much less is known about the unfolding events or their probable future trajectories, especially when the news is about a country, region or subject matter about which the news team knows relatively little. It is because of this difference that it is particularly useful to draw on *Borgen* as a benchmark. First, it allows us to see what the contours of a more or less fully fleshed-out contextual field would look like. Secondly, it reveals just how necessary it is to locate individual events and interactions within this frame in order to truly understand what is going on and why. And finally, analysing *Borgen* by means of a social-theoretical awareness of the contextual field provides a guide to how current affairs' audiences should begin to build up analogous fields by *combining* the information they receive from different sources and genres.

A One billion euro contract for wind turbines

Audiences for 'State Visit' know that they need to make sense of the action by trying to follow 'the point' of the story. I want to argue that audiences for current affairs need to find similar 'points' to their readings of current affairs events and processes. This will involve them constructing accounts that amalgamate information from a range of available texts, and doing so with a clear goal. The goal is to create the account that is most appropriate to their concerns and questions, and which is most adequate in terms of providing substantiated knowledge relevant to these. They can do this by using the four broad dimensions of a text identified by media and communications scholars as their starting point, and interrogating these on the basis of social theory. The four dimensions have a close parallel to the point of a political drama. For in the latter, too, there is: a definition of the situation and problem to be solved; a focus on the relevant causal processes; moral dilemmas and judgements to be made; and a sense of appropriate strategy aimed at a satisfactory resolution of events. Because of this close parallel, the project of bringing social theory to bear on current affairs can profit a great deal from an explication of the kinds of skills audiences of *Borgen* bring to their construction of the most appropriate and adequate versions of a story.

In searching for the point of a *Borgen* storyline, competent audiences will take it for granted that the authors and director of the episode have provided them with the scaffolding and the details they require to find and follow it. They know, however, that they have some work to do themselves to identify both scaffolding and local detail, and to bring them together. They employ the kinds of general guidelines that we've made explicit, above, in order to create the scaffolding, employing the general categories and parameters of the contextual field. The general categories are the skeleton on which producers and audiences flesh out the more detailed, substantive, content of the forces, pressures, constraints and negotiated opportunities that weigh down on the Danish Prime Minister, Birgitte Nyborg, and which provide her with her specific dilemma, whose climax is conveyed in consecutive scenes towards the end of 'State Visit'. The audience needs to understand these forces in order to understand the equivalent background knowledge possessed by Birgitte, which is the source of her disquiet and sense of impasse as the pace of the narrative slows. A tense meeting of a sub-group, the Security Council, draws to an end, people leave, doors close and the prime minister is left alone with her thoughts, with a dossier from Amnesty International and Human Rights Watch, and with a dilemma whose resolution will be all but settled in and around the press conference, live to camera, to take place in a few moments' time.

We will return to this dilemma below, but before doing so it is necessary for me to map out, explicitly, the key actors and their objective and subjective relations forming the contextual field, which, in turn, provides the basis for the relevant background knowledge possessed by both Birgitte and the audience. It is best to begin this mapping out by drawing on relevant aspects of the *objective* elements of the contextual field we outlined above. I will present this network of relevant relations in two parts, in order to show how one set of contextual relations provides the field most relevant for one of Birgitte's goals, while another set of relations, overlapping in some key areas, provides the field most relevant for another goal. The dilemma for the prime minister and her government is that these two goals end up being in conflict with each other. The first set of relevant actors and relations are illustrated in **Figure 3.1**, below, and are described in greater detail in what follows.

In mapping out these parameters one quickly understands that a key player in this contextual field is the government of the (fictional) nation state of Turgisia, founded in 1991, bordering the Ukraine and Russia, and represented in the eponymous visit by its head of state, President Alexander Grozin, who is in Denmark for the formal handing over, from Denmark to Turgisia, of the chairmanship of another key actor, the supranational body of the OSDD, the Organization for Security, Democracy and Development (represented later,

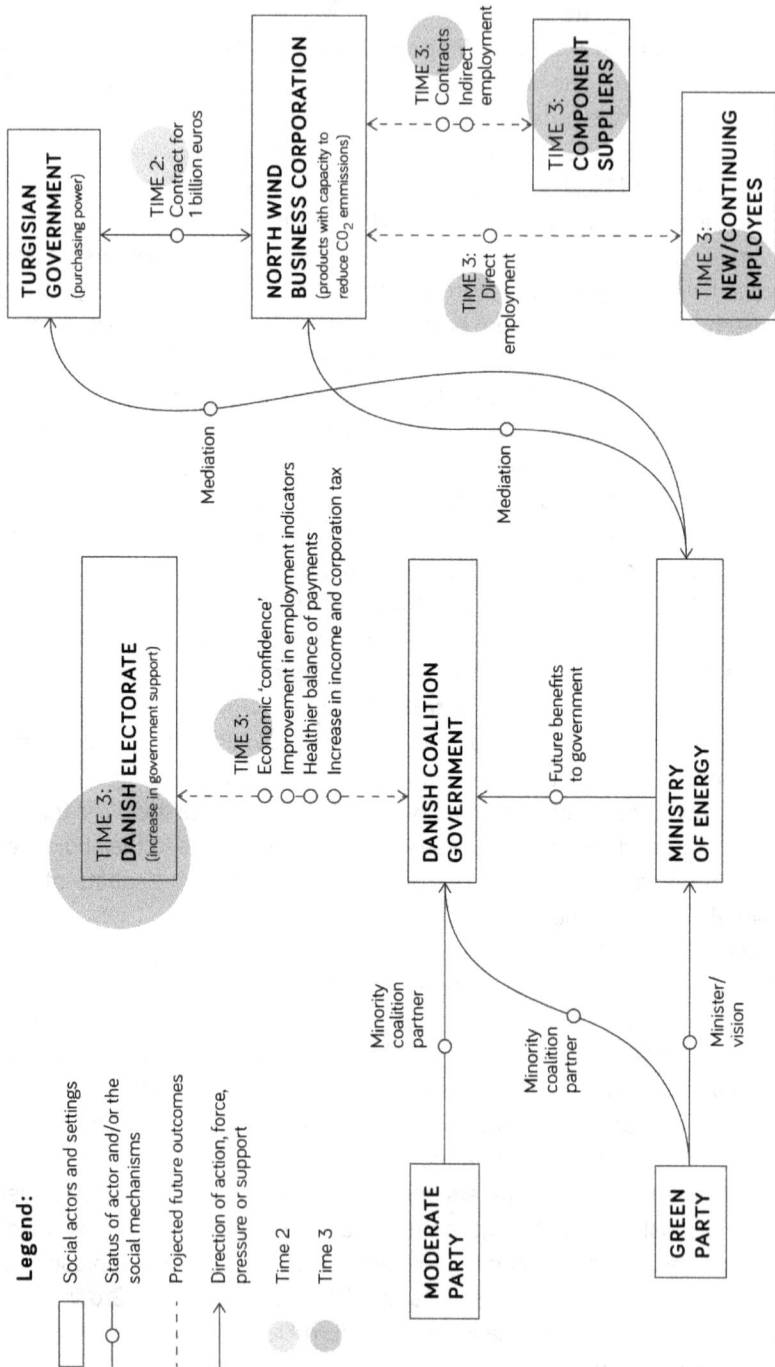

FIGURE 3.1 Borgen 1: *The wind turbine contextual field.*

in Figure 3.2). A further key individual actor within this emerging web of relationships is the Minister for Climate and Energy, Amir Diwan, a member of the coalition Government as leader of the Green Party, who announces to Birgitte and other colleagues within an inner circle that Turgisia is set to buy wind turbines worth one billion euros from the Danish company North Wind. With Russia said to also be a possible buyer in the wake of the deal with Turgisia, the combination of both sets of sales would make Denmark the largest exporter of green energy in Europe. Other actors likely to benefit if and when *the consequences* of this deal were to make their way through into the contextual field are varied and many. They include those who could find employment from the jobs that would flow from the deals, those who would benefit from the increased taxation revenue, from the improvement in the balance of payments, and from the less tangible impact on general economic confidence.

The emphasis on the pursuit of interests, political goals, and on the potential or likely future consequences of these pursuits, makes clear the requirement for audiences to quickly develop an approximate sense of the power resources and the authority actors can draw on within the contextual field. It also indicates that the mapping of the field requires a temporal, dynamic, aspect oriented to the future. This latter point is highlighted in Figure 3.1 by shading and by self-consciously dividing moments within a sequence into times 1, 2 and 3, which provides a sense of how the contextual field is adjusted, in sequence, as the action unfolds. This draws attention to objective, clock or calendar, sequential time, but also to actors' subjective orientations to the future – to consequences in the future – and the ways in which these subjective projections enter into calculations within the present. Realistically contemplating the future takes up a good deal of space in Birgitte's head as she tries to decide what practical actions to take in the present.[19] Figure 3.1 clearly also conveys an approximate sense of some of the power resources and the authority that actors will be able to draw on in pursuing their goals, together with a sense of what these goals are.

Kasper Juul, the prime minister's press secretary, immediately sees the gains in the Government's popularity that would result from signing this contract with Turgisia, and self-consciously changes his earlier tune, which had counselled caution and as little media exposure as possible given Grozin's reputation for 'being a brutal leader'. Kasper proclaims that the wind turbine contract is a 'great story': 'the cabinet creates more jobs, a greener environment, *and* embarks on an export adventure in the former Eastern Bloc'. Whereas before he'd recommended aloofness and reserve, the directive now is: 'all smiles for the press conference'. The developing story within this overall configuration of positions and interdependencies – the desire to see the potential sale of the wind turbines consummated – means that a new power dependence is set up in which something of the fortunes of the Danish

Government are now tied to the continuing desire and intent of the Turgisian Government to invest in Danish green technology. This is a dependence that, we will see, leaves Birgitte's Moderate Party, and its coalition Government, highly vulnerable to political blackmail.

The essential point made by Pierre Bourdieu about television news, which we discussed in Chapter 1, is that to truly understand an individual scene, to make it genuinely meaningful, one has to be able to place it within a network of relevant relations. So it is that to be able to truly understand what is happening when Birgitte is left alone with the reports from Amnesty International and Human Rights Watch a few minutes before the end of the 'State Visit' episode, one needs to place this scene within the relevant networks of social relations. Part of this network is the configuration represented by Figure 3.1, a configuration that Birgitte has knowledge of, and which informs her thinking and her strategic calculations. This contextual field is not, needless to say, visible on the television screen, in the frame of the camera, as Birgitte opens the dossier.

Interpretive, conceptual, skills are required to bring these currently invisible, but causally significant, dimensions into play. A key aspect of this reality that social theory insists we take very seriously is that what goes on in the heads of actors – specifically in the mind of Birgitte in this case – is closely linked to relevant configurations of actors and forces of the kind mapped out in Figure 3.1. We are now deeply in the realm of subjective factors, but these are interwoven with objective relations. For decisions are not taken in a solipsistic way, where an individual would ruminate about things that only exist in their own head, without any reference to the world-out-there. Rather, parts of the world-out-there enter in-here, into the minds of human actors. *These social configurations are internalized* in particular ways by different human beings situated in specific positions within them. These individual actors will have particular sets of cultural understandings and moral values, and will have their own goals, mediated by these cultural values but also by personal and collective principles and ambitions, and by group and institutional affiliations. In other words, parts of the world-out-there are internalized by people in particular social locations, who care in particular ways about those parts. These individuals don't function as islands unto themselves, but typically work within their institutions with colleagues who will often have internalized social configurations in very similar ways. In order to understand what happens in any news and current affairs event we need to know about relevant aspects of the cultural, interpretative, inner worlds of key actors and about the ways in which these are intimately related to the external configurations of forces.

What we have before us on the screen, visible within the camera frame, is naturally much more circumscribed than what can be represented or 'thought' as a contextual field. Let's consider in a bit more detail the scene referred to at the beginning of this section. About a minute before we see Birgitte left alone with the documents, she has just said out loud, with an air of authority, that *she* was going to have to make a decision. She had then, gently, and with an air of quiet despondency, held her head in her hands. Recovering her poise, she announced, 'let's sign the extradition agreement after the ceremony. And now I want to be alone'. This is a cue, a heavy one, for the end of the meeting. The camera pans back, allowing us to see two coffee pots of sleek, modernist design, one light, one dark, an array of white cups and saucers on ceramic trays, and croissants, mostly left untouched. Three men in ties and suits sitting opposite Birgitte, ranging in ages from late 30s to early 60s, gather up their papers from the beech coloured conference table, one of them sweeping his jacket off the back of his chair as he turns to go. They all leave the room, we hear the door close, Birgitte is left alone, phones ringing faintly in the background. She sits perfectly still, except for one finger tapping on her other hand. She moves aside her meeting papers to reveal the 'Report on Violations of Human Rights in Turgisia' that we know has been given to her earlier on in the episode by Anne Sophie Lindenkrone, the leader of the Solidarity Party, a minority coalition partner. These are documents from Amnesty International and Human Rights Watch. The camera angle is such that we view the pages through Birgitte's eyes, seeing, as she sees, bloodied corpses, scarred legs, and communal graves, with, in the latter case, uniformed soldiers standing by, leaning against an armoured vehicle, indifferent.

A viewer who had just entered the room in which the episode was showing, seeing just this scene, could quickly rustle together some interpretations. They may well intuitively conceive a sense of some of the types of general interdependencies that *might* be involved in Birgitte's palpable dilemma, and could try to look for signs that might confirm these suppositions. However, their understanding of the situation would naturally be severely impaired by having had no access to the details of the story so far. Any understanding would only be vague: the latecomer wouldn't know about the plural character of the interdependencies involved, and they wouldn't know any of the specific shapes and details. The more committed viewer, there for the duration of the episode, would have a much clearer picture of the general aspects of the configuration of forces mapped out there, and also of the details the episode has provided thus far.

Vladimir Bayanov: Poet, dissident and political activist

It's clear from the documents Birgitte is looking at that the aspects of the contextual field outlined in Figure 3.1 only provide part of the structural context relevant to her dilemma. Accordingly, the figure provides only part of the context internalized by Birgitte as she deliberates on what to do. It is only one part of the network of relations relevant to that dilemma. To more fully understand the dilemma, this part needs to be complemented by other relevant aspects of the contextual field, by a second configuration to complement the one represented in Figure 3.1. As the narrative of 'State Visit' had continued beyond the moment of elation and shared congratulation resulting from news of the potential sale of the wind turbines, another set of actors, powers and relations entered into the field of concern. Their entrance darkened the mood considerably. We've seen that the Danish Prime Minister had been advised very early on in the narrative that Grozin had a reputation as a brutal leader, and we've seen that Lindenkrone had handed documents to Birgitte from Amnesty International and Human Rights Watch. These reports, Lindenkrone insisted, described crimes 'committed by Grozin's Turgisian security services', against minorities and dissidents. We need to understand more of these aspects of the contextual field in order to genuinely understand the meaning of Birgitte's dilemma, to put ourselves in her shoes, understanding the structural context that she experiences, as she experiences it.

The first appearance of these documents in the episode cued the imminent introduction into the narrative of a key actor from the second configuration of forces. This is Vladimir Bayanov, a poet, dissident and political activist who is said to be the leader of the Sarkesian minority in their struggle for independence from Turgisia. Turgisian authorities claim that Bayanov has been responsible for a long list of crimes warranting charges of Terror and High Treason, most prominent of which is his putatively central role in the recent bombing of Turgisian Police Headquarters in which eight Turgisan policemen, including the Chief of Police, were killed. Whether or not Bayanov was involved in the planning of this act of violence is left unclear, although he doesn't overtly deny it, and even intimates it might be true, responding to a question in a TV interview on whether he feels that violence is sometimes necessary with the words, 'Yes violence is necessary because Grozin is trying to destroy my people. Should we not defend ourselves?' The testing ethical question of whether it is ever justifiable to use the techniques of terror against a regime based on terror is raised in the episode, but left hanging. Instead, the rhetoric of the text is directed towards the Turgisian regime's alleged violation of human rights, which is juxtaposed with intimations of Bayanov's basic decency through the sensitivity to language, art and human experience expressed within his poetry.

Birgitte's father, Per, a former University Professor, visiting his daughter in Copenhagen, is an admirer of Bayanov and attends a public reading of his poetry. Per Nyborg stands in, emblematically, for Birgitte's ideal principles, the ones which he, Anne Sophie Lindenkrone, and others who are positioned differently in the contextual field than Birgitte, explicitly avow and steadfastly adhere to. They can do this, however, without having to personally confront the consequences that would flow from the structured dilemma facing Per's daughter, in her role as prime minister, as the Turgisian Embassy contacts the Danish Government and asks them to arrest Bayanov. The script makes it clear that Birgitte feels that, as someone committed to democratic principles, she needs to rise above sectionalism, even when this might be in tension with her own individual principles. Although there would always be limits to how far she would compromise or adjust the latter, she is clear that she needs to be a prime minister who represents all the Danish people, including those who didn't vote for her.

Birgitte's initial response to the Turgisian demand to arrest Bayanov, is to say to her colleagues that the Turgisian Government had presented a long list of accusations but no evidence. To hand over Bayanov to a regime charged with having little regard for human rights and the due process of law conflicts with her values. She knows that Bayanov has been living in exile for the last 10 years and that Grozin and the Turgisian authorities had tried to have him extradited many times: 'And now he's trying again. We won't comply'. But this resistance is played out behind the scenes, as she is aware that a blunt refusal to hand over Bayanov would jeopardize the wind turbine deal.[20] So she plays for time, and indicates that Danish intelligence should put pressure on Bayanov to flee Denmark at the same time as she uses delaying tactics with the Turgisian Government. The structural context, however, is not always easy to control or second-guess, replete as it is with human actors. On this occasion it transpires that Birgitte's manoeuvre conflicts with Bayanov's own values, as he wishes to stay in Denmark to publically challenge the Turgisian Government and also to test the Danish Government's resolve to stand up for the principles of human rights.

The prime minister learns from her Minister of Justice, Troels Höxenhaven, that she is further constrained by new domestic 'terror' laws that give the police wide powers of arrest and extradition. The Danish Government would find it difficult to ignore, for very long, legal obligations that it has imposed on itself. The Minister of Justice is clear in his advice: 'It's a serious matter not to act.' In terms of the contextual field, this is a form of constraint inherited as a legacy, one put in place by past actors and upheld by current actors positioned within the legal system who have duties and obligations to uphold the norms of that system. While the sense of identification with individual pieces of legislation will be variable, and it is significant that the Moderate Party voted against the 'terror' laws while in opposition, the Government has a strong normative commitment to the rule of law as a principle. This means that the legal norms are more than just an externally imposed constraint on the prime minister, as the idea of the rule of law and the role it plays within the democratic framework are foundations stones of her own values and beliefs. Now that these particular laws are in place as part of the constitutional landscape they are experienced as a powerful set of injunctions that must be adhered to. They must be adhered to, that is, unless there are exceptional reasons, based on legal or moral principles of equal or superior force, for not abiding by them. In a move of some sophistication, which would probably be reflected upon by some members of the audience and not by others on a casual viewing, such an exceptional reason slowly emerges. The background dilemma concerning the law is due to the fact that impartial adherence to Danish law would aid and abet the disregard for the application of the rule of law in Turgisia. In choosing between the two, the fact that the moral claims of human rights are held to be universal, and have been translated into international law, arguably provides them with a force transcending the practices and whims of individual nation-states. This set of meanings and motives has a perpetual presence, sometimes fading into the background and at others looming large, as the plot of 'State Visit' unfolds. We will see how this plays out.

In the short term, there is no doubt that the presence of the domestic 'terror' laws, combined with the desire to secure the wind turbine contract, considerably narrows the Government's options, and greatly strengthens the hand of the Turgisians. President Grozin soon explicitly foregrounds the power balance put into play by these factors, using them as leverage as he refuses to confirm that he has yet placed the order for the wind turbines. He goes on to issue a blunt warning: 'a lack of goodwill on your part must force me to reconsider my investment in Danish wind energy'. The Justice Minister and the Minister for Foreign Affairs push towards ameliorating Grozin, with Höxenhaven angrily countering claims that Bayanov would be dead within 24 hours if returned to Turgisia, responding with the dismissive statement that 'they abolished the death penalty six years ago'. It seems to the audience at this point that Höxenhaven's declaration is at worst entirely cynical and instrumental, and at best the consequence of a narrowness of vision arising from his current institutional role and the internalized pressures and goals that are part and parcel of it. From the perspective of these narrow commitments it is in his interests to overlook the claims of Amnesty International and Human Rights Watch – already communicated to viewers – that in the last 3 years 71 political dissidents had disappeared in Turgisia. When these facts are pointed out by Amir Diwan, the Minister for Climate and Energy, during the Security Council meeting, the Foreign Minister, Bjørn Marrot, contests the veracity of the information – 'or so Amnesty International claims'.

What should be done? The contextual field and strategic judgements

A narrative tension is set up within the episode, one that is based on these two structural configurations, but which has its own inflection and inner-logic. On the one side there is the public tenor of the news coverage of channel TV1 on the events, which is one of threatening to expose the prime minister as putting economics before the principles of human rights, and even a man's life. On the other side, reinforced by the figurative role of her father, there is our sense of the private Birgitte who wants to achieve the just balance between principles. Even while she wrestles with the quandary, we never lose the sense that she is indeed personally, individually, committed to the values of human rights. More specifically, in this case, she is committed to human rights perceived as civil rights, a cornerstone of democracy, applying equally, universally, to both citizens and 'guests' such as Bayanov. However, we also see her trying to take into account the other forces pressing on her in her role as prime minister.

At a certain point in the narrative, with Birgitte positioned at the junction of such forces (see **Figure 3.2** below for the configuration of the contextual field relating to Bayanov), it becomes clear she feels she has to act to arrest Bayanov. She makes this decision in the heat of the unfolding situation – this is dramatically staged, with all present in evening gowns and tails, as the bell sounds for the end of the interval during a gala performance of Tchaikovsky's *Swan Lake* at the Royal Danish Theatre, hosted by the Queen as part of the state visit – with little time for detached reflection. The context is one in which the balance of power within and between the two sets of contextual forces is shifting as sequences of action and interaction subtly reconfigure the field. She feels she has no option but to arrest Bayanov while contemplating her next move.

The immediate context for this decision is one in which the Foreign Minister has suggested that perhaps the Government could order the arrest of Bayanov but subsequently release him before he is extradited. The idea is for the arrest to buy time without leading to any harm to Bayanov, an avenue that wouldn't permanently compromise the Government. The most immediate pressures on Birgitte's decision to arrest Bayanov seem to come from international forces as it has emerged that the Russian Foreign Minister, then the German Chancellor, and then all the OSDD countries except France, have fallen in behind the Turgisian demands for arrest and then extradition. The motivation of these international forces isn't spelt out explicitly. There is a vague sense that the OSDD must be seen to trust that all its member states genuinely

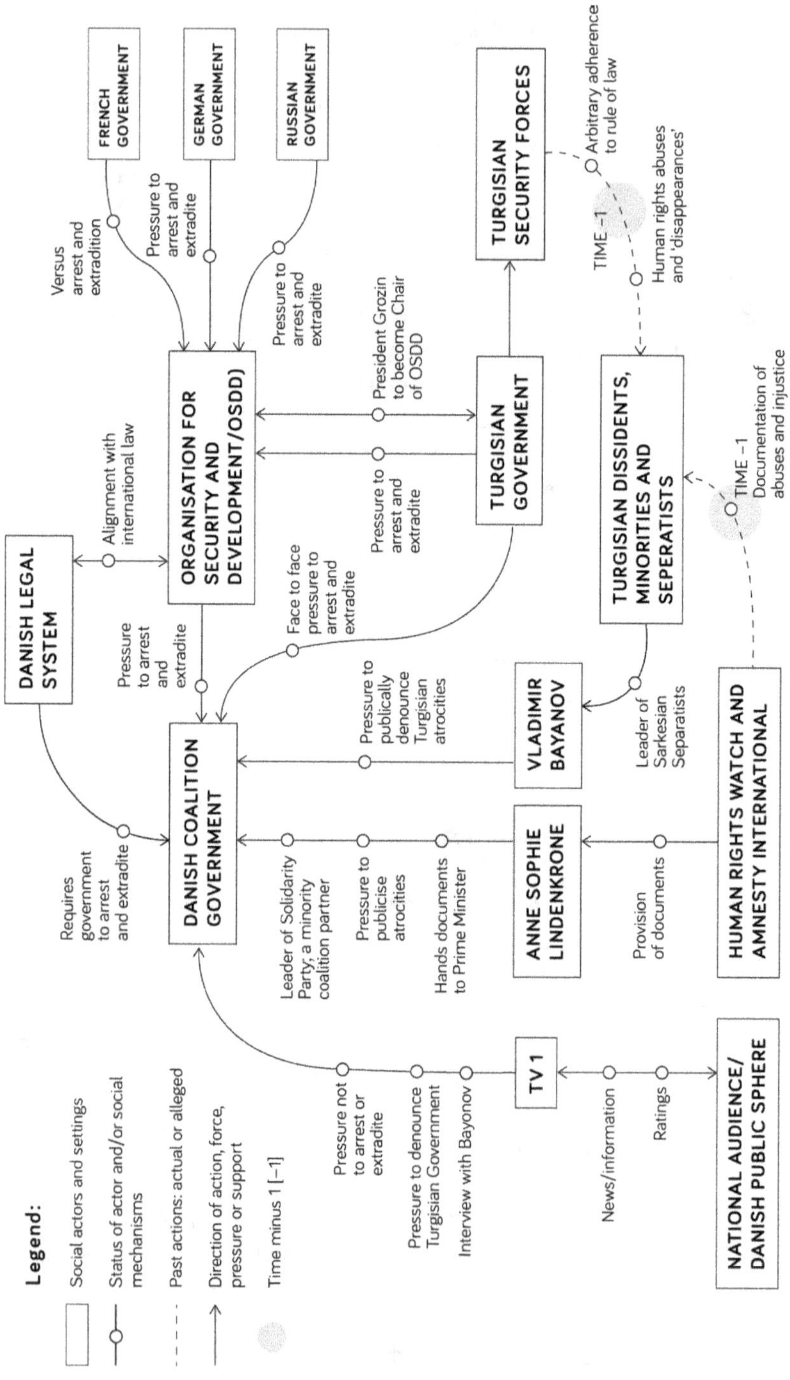

Legend:

Social actors and settings

Status of actor and/or social mechanisms

Past actions: actual or alleged

Direction of action, force, pressure or support

Time minus 1 [−1]

FIGURE 3.2 Borgen 2: *The human rights contextual field.*

adhere to its constitution, which requires an implicit trust in their commitment to democratic mores. There is a sense, also, that all the member states must play their part in a public performance conveying staunch mutual confidence in this trust. While the sense of this is vague, present only through fragments of hints and cues, the script also provides us with little to go on in considering what the other interests of the various OSDD countries might be. So, we find ourselves working hard to fathom these countries' perspectives on, and strategic calculations with respect to, the field of mutual interdependencies and potential risks, sanctions and so on, implicated in the affair.

The silences and resulting ambiguity at the international level signal those inevitable grey areas at the boundaries of a story, meaning that even a political drama with a tight narrative script cannot provide all the information one might need to truly weigh up the balance of forces and to seek out possible avenues of strategic manoeuvre. On the other hand, the role of the OSDD, and of Germany and Russia within it, in asking for arrest and extradition, is quite central to the narrative. One ultimately assumes – although one doesn't really know – that *realpolitik* is at work, that there is mutual interest with respect to the functions of international cooperation in the realms of economics and security, and therefore in the role – whose specifics we aren't privy to – that Turgisia plays in this. There is a certain public legitimacy given to the OSDD position by Denmark's apparent unwillingness to apply its own supposedly impartial laws to a particular case, a reluctance that suggests it doesn't completely trust Turgisia's commitment to due process and human rights. The fact that Turgisia is just about to take over the Chair of the OSDD will naturally inform and heighten the diplomatic positions adopted. Without knowing more about the strength of feeling within the different national diplomatic camps, or about the range and intensities of the interdependencies of the relevant parts of the contextual field, it is very difficult to know what the consequences would be for Denmark of refusing to listen to these international admonishments.

Our lack of knowledge about the international context in this case, and consequent uncertainty about the extent of international power, and of what the consequences would be of resisting external pressures, reflects a very common position of audiences when facing news concerning international diplomacy. For example, in a *Washington Post* story of 4 July 2013, about the ousting of democratically elected Egyptian President, Mohamed Morsi, head of the Muslim Brotherhood, a subsection is titled 'Complications for the US'.[21] It details President Obama's previous urgings of the Egyptian military 'to avoid any arbitrary arrests of President Morsi and his supporters', and points to how the US had refrained from criticizing the Egyptian military, and particularly from calling the ouster of Morsi 'a coup', as this would legally require the US Government to cut off financial aid to the country. The story went on to point to issues of putative control through interdependence, noting that while the

White House tacitly accepted Morsi's removal, it retained powerful leverage, 'including $1.3 billion in military aid – to help guard against a power grab or the excessive use of force'. The extent to which this amount of military aid could, in fact, on its own, guard against continued, democratically illegitimate, military involvement in politics, or against the excessive use of force, was actually much harder to say than is implied by the confident tone of this statement. Other reports at the time mentioned other powers in the Middle East sympathetic to the new regime, including Saudi Arabia's willingness to finance the Egyptian military to levels that dwarfed the US contribution.[22] And there were also the many different factors in the micro dynamics of politics within Egypt that could possibly militate against the success of any leverage the US desired to exert. We have little sense, for example, of what might follow for the military's position on the Muslim Brotherhood from, for example, the military's staggeringly vast business interests, which made up around 40 per cent of the domestic economy, employing half a million workers.[23]

One of the key lessons to take from the counsel to place issues within their relevant contextual field is that it draws attention in a more precise way to what is *not* known, and also to what would *need to be* known if a more adequate assessment was to be made of the likely consequences of particular courses of action. Taking this on board means adopting an intellectual disposition to ask how much is known or not known by significant actors situated within the field, such as by the Obama administration in the Egyptian case, and to ask questions about the ways in which their strategy is related to that knowledge. As we've noted, key actors are very often positioned in such a way that they have more 'insider' knowledge than audiences, but the knowledge they have about a strategic terrain will still be highly variable. It is important to ask probing questions about the quality and extent of *knowledge* held by both audiences and key actors.

Similar questions should also be asked regarding what we know about the *values* and *motivations* key actors bring to strategic judgements. One could wonder what was the most important determining influence on Birgitte's judgement at the point when she decides to give the order to arrest Bayanov. Was it the desire to avoid alienating international opinion and the negative consequences that would flow from this, or was her decision informed just by the desire to secure the wind turbine contract, with all its perceived benefits to the economy and the government of the day? These kinds of questions go to the heart of both drama and current affairs issues. They mark the point at which the objective factors out-there are internalized within the minds of key actors, and where decisions and strategies reflect a subjective 'ordering of concerns', or 'hierarchy of purposes'.[24] We want to know what is at stake for key actors, and to understand which balance of principles come to the fore when they take their decisions. It would be impossible to even begin to consider such questions without some conception of relevant contextual fields. The point is that the competency of both audiences and players rests on their self-awareness of how much they know about contextual fields, and so being able to reflect on such knowledge, subject it to scrutiny, and make a judgement on its adequacy to the tasks at hand.

In the field of constraints and possibilities facing the Government in 'State Visit', both major configurations of external pressures – clustered around the wind turbine contract and international pressure to respect Turgisia's wishes – were pushing in the same direction, towards the arrest and extradition of Bayanov. However, and this reinforces even further the significance of the contextual field, to genuinely understand the character of the play of forces at work it's often important to also ask what would happen if one of two (or, often, in fact, several) sets of pressures were removed.[25] In the case of 'State Visit', the dilemma would be clearer if one could know what the Danish Government would do if it could somehow assuage the international community. Would it then choose, on human rights' grounds, to protect Bayanov from arbitrary punishment, and to safeguard his right to speak openly against atrocities committed by political dictators? Or would it still go ahead with the arrest of Bayanov? Further, if the Government did go ahead with the arrest in a situation where they were unafraid of international opinion, would this be because of the desire to secure the wind turbine deal, or because domestic law was understood to brook no other outcome.

The answer to this last detail, regarding the technical nuance of the law, is one we don't learn from the script of 'State Visit', which brings it in this respect closer to a typical non-fiction account of government activity, where we often can't fully disentangle the various hierarchies and intensities of commitments. In most cases, there are all kinds of gaps in accounts with respect to what we'd need to know in order to address such questions. Moreover, the kinds of questions we want to ask of current affairs accounts are different from those we typically ask of political dramas. For in watching political drama we attempt, from the start, to decipher a narrative that has artfully guided what we have been told. In approaching a current affairs account, there can be a plurality of possible avenues we may be interested in, and this is more likely to bring to the fore many more gaps in what the text provides, and so to highlight even further its partial, limited, nature.

Novels, drama and fiction film can play the kinds of role I've been emphasizing in elucidating what happens in the presentation and audience reception of news and current affairs reports. They can also add other valuable dimensions to our grasp of current affairs.[26] Novels, for example, are particularly good at probing the complexities of internal worlds. However, there are also limits to the role these forms can play. Even if we include a very broad spectrum, embracing both popular and elite culture, each of the forms I mention shares some kind of combination of interest in aesthetics, entertainment and existential illumination in which sustained analytical focus is typically lower down in the pecking order of priorities. Too much careful unpacking of causes and reasons, and precise identification of relevant conditions, is often studiedly avoided within such forms, even at the most serious and least commercial end of the continuum. For much of the time, I readily concede, this is a blessing. There are times and places for different modes of both presentation and reception. However, there do need to be moments within the intellectual life of civil society when we are ready to invoke and harness the genres of novels, drama and fiction film to the task of strengthening our reading of current affairs. In those moments we need to break down the walls that separate different kinds of contributions to our understanding. Bringing different genres together in our interpretation of events, harnessing the forms of the arts and humanities to the social-theoretical point of view would provide a richer, more adequate, picture of the social world.

What should be done? The inner worlds and creativity of key social actors

Combinations of genres, if marshalled by social theory, can provide powerful ways of developing the capacities of current affairs audiences. From the account of the *Borgen* episode outlined here, we've been able to not only establish the basic parameters and general significance of contextual fields, but also to breathe life into quite intricate theoretical and conceptual considerations that are much more difficult to begin to broach using other means. I now want to extend this part of the exercise by looking more closely at how Birgitte's internalization of the two configurations of contextual fields we've sketched out interact with her own active agency as the plot of 'State Visit' reaches its resolution. Each moment in the explication so far has brought out further dimensions of the overall dynamic. Judgements about future consequences were important for Figure 3.1 on the wind turbine agreement. Figure 3.2, focusing on the issue of Bayanov's arrest, was presented without this temporal element, with the emphasis, rather, on mapping the various pressures, forces and potential sanctions objectively confronting Birgitte Nyborg's government at a particular point in time. In this final section, I will focus on how the prime minister responds to these pressures and forces; including in those moments when they are mediated, in unfolding interaction, by strategically powerful individuals, such as Alexander Grozin. This focus can tell us a lot about what to look for in current affairs accounts when we seek to understand, and to judge, the decisions of powerful actors in analogous positions to Birgitte Nyborg.

For actors in seemingly powerful positions are hedged in by all kinds of structural considerations, and at the same time they can be more or less skilful in getting the best out of the situation they are confronted with.[27] They can also be more or less dignified, more or less informed, rash, wise, unscrupulous or honourable. Being able to analyse what they think they are doing, and what is involved in them doing it, requires the grasp and exercise of a number of concepts dealing with action and actors. These concepts need to be defined, differentiated from one another, and then combined. We've already broached some of this, and I will start by returning to what we already know before going on to make conceptual refinements that will allow us to be more precise in our judgements when approaching current affairs texts.

The notions we've already begun to discuss in quite significant ways fall into the bracket of how social actors internalize key aspects of the contextual fields they live within. A vital element of the social-theoretical frame I'm advocating is that actors hold within them, as stocks of background knowledge, pictures of – an awareness of – the contextual fields relevant to particular actions and decisions. In this sense there is social structure inside the heads of actors. As we've noted, similarly positioned actors usually have very similar 'pictures' inside their heads. Where there are subtle differences between actors, they will characteristically spend more than a little of their energies tacitly or explicitly attempting to envisage the pictures of structural fields their colleagues currently carry around with them.

Birgitte, for one, has an acute sense of the various corners of the contextual field in which the consequences of her decisions will work their way out, including a sense of the pictures of context other players are carrying around with them. This is not least because her social position as prime minister of a coalition Government with a slender majority means there is a particular onus on her being able to combine the pursuit of her own party's values and goals with the appropriate representation of a series of competing interests. Like most people working in a complex organization in which they have the responsibility for taking key decisions, the prime minister would not be able to pass herself off as a competent and skilled actor[28] unless she had a grasp of what was going on in a whole series of different sites within the contextual field. She needs a clear enough sense of this if she is to be capable and adept. And a key aspect of this is that she also needs to have a keen sense of how the other key people within the relevant contextual field perceive their interests within it and the various ways in which they suppose they might realize those interests. At its most basic level this means that Birgitte needs to have *internalized the social context* relevant to any decision she has to make.

If she floats too far free from an appreciation of the constraints, possibilities, and room for strategic or tactical manoeuvre afforded by that context, then the decisions she takes will almost inevitably become overly idealist, utopian and irresponsible, or a combination of all three.

It's important to grasp that there are *two different aspects of the internalization of social context* that are at work here.[29] This distinction was briefly introduced at the beginning of the chapter in the process of indicating that an actor's grasp of context (*analysis of context*) is only one part of what determines how the actor then behaves. Additional subjective dimensions besides their perception of the contextual field will mediate their actions, or conduct, including one that can also be usefully characterized as a form of internalization of the social context. I noted during that discussion that we would look at these aspects in more detail later. So, let us now spell out how these two components of an actor's conduct can be seen as two different aspects of the internalization of the social.

The first is the internalization of the immediate strategic terrain, the various networks of relevant relationships we've mapped out in terms of contextual fields. We can call this *situational knowledge* of the strategic terrain, and it is the basis of an actor's analysis of context. Within the present example, this would refer to what Birgitte knows about the two sets of networked configurations we've sketched out in Figures 3.1 and 3.2. The second aspect is the internalization of society as part of a longer-term socialization process, from childhood through youth and adolescence, and into the various stages and sites of adulthood. Society here – and it may be easiest to think about this in terms of the internalization of 'taken-for-granted' ways of behaving within a culture, related to one's family, schooling, class, gender, ethnicity, religion, sexuality, trade, profession, sports and pastimes, and so on[30] – puts its stamp firmly on one's mind and one's body, and is internalized in enduring orientations and dispositions including language use, deportment, gestures, cultural understandings, values, beliefs, principles, and skills of a physical and social kind. Pierre Bourdieu gave the name of *habitus* to this kind of internalization, and the eminent Greek sociologist, Nicos Mouzelis, refers to it as the *dispositional* aspect of social actors.[31] It is important to understand that the cultural discourses that mark an age, mediated in various ways, are some of the most powerful elements entering into the understandings, values, beliefs, and principles lodged within these dispositions of an actor.[32]

These dispositions are carried around from situation to situation, job to job, contextual field to contextual field, and so they have a more transposable character than those possessed by situational knowledge, which is more restricted to particular segments of time and place. The ingrained, durable, cultural and value dimensions of a person's habitus are an important key to understanding the perspective from which that person will view a particular situation. This means that their habitus will inform the way they see and approach contextual fields, and this is where the two kinds of internalization of the external world come together. The habitus provides 'typified' ways of seeing things, situations, people, processes, which provide an initial orientation, perspective, attitude and sensibility. One can see immediately, for example, that the internalization of a particular educational, religious or political tradition would affect the way in which many of a person's typifications would be constructed. And what is true for education, religion and politics is true for cultures and sub-cultures more generally, with their many and varied assortments of inflexions of meanings and norms, of ways of seeing.

This is what I meant earlier when I noted that in order to understand what happens in any news and current affairs event we need to both know about the relevant aspects of the deeper, more enduring, cultural, interpretative, inner worlds of key actors and the ways in which these are intimately related to those same actors' perceptions of the immediate external configuration of forces. The two forms of internalization have an intimate, overlapping, relationship with each other. In the 'State Visit' episode of *Borgen*, this is symbolized by the presence of Birgitte's father in the private space of the home, evoking the deep culture and values of childhood, the inspiration for a deeply moral political life, suggesting an authenticity beyond *realpolitik*. At the same time, the narrative suggests that too much concentration on ideal values taken out of context is also naïve and overly purist, representing a wilful refusal to internalize the constraints imposed by the current strategic terrain. Developing the skills required to attempt to ascertain the inner worlds of social actors involved in news and current affairs events,[33] and so improving one's chances of understanding what is really going on, requires a grasp of both these aspects of social being.

Just how powerful these dimensions can be in terms of a person's relationship to their context can be illustrated through the example of international migration. When people move country or continent, they leave their society behind and in doing so leave behind much of what was strictly 'useful' to them in internalizing that society within their minds and bodies. The specific knowledge they have of the contextual terrains in which they operated can no longer be drawn upon, and many of the more general dispositions they had internalized in the old country, from language and physical bearing to specific social skills, will often be as much of a hindrance as a source of strength in the destination society. From now on, many of their old, intuitive and ingrained ways of doing things will fit uneasily with the culture, norms, values and demands they are confronted with.[34] Something similar is true for people who don't move, who remain in the same place, but where the society around them changes. This can be seen easily for older people as they struggle with changes in the contextual uses of technology, control, forms of communication, provision of information, and so on, so that their body and mind, moulded further back in history, no longer seem to fit, to be able to find the ease they possessed when in contact with the old social forms.

In order to have a depth of understanding of why social actors are doing what they are doing in any situation it is necessary to be able to put oneself in their shoes, not just empathetically, with pure poetic imagination – although this can help a great deal – but by reconstructing the practical detail of what it is like to live with the two forms of internalization of society that co-exist within them.[35] Such reconstructions can be built up through reference to objective, factual, information given shape by appropriate concepts. For social theory, providing the appropriate mix of conceptual shape and objective information involves two things. First, an appreciation of the two kinds of social *structures* that have been internalized within the actors, and secondly, an interpretative understanding of how individual actors *experience and respond to* aspects of these structures coming to the surface as they approach a particular task, practice, problem or issue in everyday life.[36]

Understanding this combination of internalized structures and how they are experienced and responded to in particular situations involves, however, a further element of dynamism. This element of dynamism is supplied by the social actor in the process of acting, making their actions more than just the product of the internalization of external social forces. I will refer to this here as 'creative agency', which refers to the many capacities actors have at their disposal to ward off a merely passive acceptance of the external forces pressing down on them.[37] These include the use of energy, improvisation, creativity, spontaneity, the skilful exercise of charm or persuasion, the reordering of priorities, tactical manoeuvring, vision, and the ability to respond to unfolding twists and turns in events and interaction with flexibility, reflection, ingenuity, resolve, resistance, a testing of the waters, negotiation and concession, and the use of strategic and tactical imagination. 'Creative agency' is an important notion to hang on to in order to avoid *fatalism* – the belief that social structures are so powerful and all consuming that any resistance to them is either literally unthinkable or so destined to fail that one simply succumbs to what seems the inevitable – and to protect a valuable space for positive political action and moral responsibility. Insisting upon the potential for this space, but also on *the need to place it firmly within the relevant contextual fields*, means that it is possible to accord great value to skilled, positive judgement and action, but without giving in to the wide-eyed idealism that can so easily get out of control, leading to unforeseen, unintended, unwanted, and sometimes deeply unpalatable, consequences.

These workings of creative agency can be seen in 'State Visit' in how the prime minister's orientation to the dilemma at hand is *not only* informed by the two kinds of internalization of external structures – that is, by certain cultural-moral orientations to the contextual fields (dispositional orientations/ habitus), and by an understanding of their configuration and character (situationally specific knowledge). It is also informed by a continuing openness to any potential opportunities that might be afforded by the contextual field, whether or not they have already revealed themselves. This openness can be to new possibilities that are presented as a consequence of some changes in the contextual field as events unfold and perspectives and stances are changed, subtly or radically. But the opportunity for creativity is not necessarily reliant on change in the field itself; openness also involves gathering, investigating, searching, for new information about that field, or looking for new angles on that field, even if it stays the same. For enhanced knowledge and adaptive ways of seeing can alter the sense of what the possibilities are for action within the field.

This is what happens in the final scenes of 'State Visit', when after looking at the documents recording the atrocities in Turgisia, the Danish Prime Minister suddenly requests a private conversation with Grozin. This is immediately prior to the press conference in an adjoining room in which the two leaders are due to speak and answer questions, and after which Birgitte has told her Ministers that she will sign the extradition agreement. With the international pressures to trust the democratic credentials of members of the OSDD hanging in the air, Birgitte asks Grozin for reassurances that Bayanov's case will be subject to due process in Turgisian courts: 'what will happen to Bayanov if we hand him over?' It is as if she wants to use this interaction with Grozin[38] to test out the inconsistency of the messages she is receiving from within the relevant contextual fields. That is, to test out the inconsistency between the alleged evidence provided by the documents she has just seen and the presumption of allegiance to democratic principles behind the OSDD's ruling that Turgisia's demand for extradition be honoured.[39] Much, for Birgitte, seems to rest on Grozin's response. If he had responded by providing the reassurances the Danish Prime Minister had requested then it seems quite possible that the judgement expressed at the close of the Security Council – for extradition – would have remained unchanged. In the event, however, it becomes very clear that due process and a fair trial is not what Grozin has in mind. His words express a fickle, authoritarian, approach to the rule of law, which bodes ill for Bayanov's chances of survival if he is extradited. Grozin's aggressive response triggers aspects of habitus – deep dispositions – within the Danish Prime Minister, working in tandem with her awareness of the unfolding situational context.

The cathartic power of the prime minister's equivocation and then reversal of judgement is exploited to the full in the subsequent scene of the press conference. Birgitte ignores a behind the scenes request from Grozin to veto questions from certain journalists – more evidence, if a little heavy-handed, of his anti-democratic tendencies – and arranges for a journalist to ask him whether the contract for the wind turbine deal is dependent on the Danish Government handing over Bayanov to the Turgisian authorities. The person who asks the question is Katerine Fønsmark of TV1, one of the writers on Grozin's list. Grozin is put in a situation where he is trapped by his own hierarchy of concerns – his overriding desire not to sully his democratic credentials in front of the world's press on the eve of his chairmanship of the Organisation for Security, Democracy and Development. Needing to respond immediately, his priority is not to undermine international belief in his commitment to civil rights and the rule of law. Loss of face and respect within the OSDD would be an inevitable consequence of saying the contract did depend on Bayanov's extradition. By taking such a stance he would be openly challenging his trust in Danish lawyers to establish for themselves, on the basis of a considered interpretation of the statutes of the Danish legal system, whether an extradition order was in fact appropriate. He answers with an eye firmly on maintaining the structural conditions necessary to underpin his own foremost goals. This requires his agency, including the skill of thinking on his feet, but his agency has little room for manoeuvre in the circumstances. He replies: 'I have great faith in the Danish legal system, and I can assure you that I do not link the wind energy deal with the case against Bayanov.'

As the final photos are taken by the assembled jouralists, Birgitte whispers into Grozin's ear: 'I'm glad you said that, because I'm not going to hand him over.' The episode closes with us knowing that Bayanov has been released and has flown to Paris to speak at a human rights conference. However, we are left unsure whether the North Wind deal will go through, for while it has been signed, the Turgisian government has questioned a number of the terms in the contract, leaving the outcome still uncertain. If it doesn't go through then Birgitte's moment of victory will have been short lived with respect to the wind turbine deal, with the constraints of the contextual field remaining intractable in spite of her skilful creativity, but the victory will be longer lasting with respect to the demand for extradition.

Conclusion

The purpose of this chapter has been to demonstrate the subtle appreciation of the general theoretical concepts – applying to events and their contextual field – required for audiences to be able to make sense of *Borgen*. This means that audiences who can make sense of *Borgen* are already equipped with many of the concepts necessary to make sense of news and current affairs events. This includes an intuitive sense of the ways in which key protagonists have internalized social structures, of the constraints these impose, and of the creative agency required to act meaningfully within these circumstances. It would be well nigh impossible to follow the plot of 'State Visit' without these competencies. I hope I have shown how social theory can bring the character of these conceptual and interpretive skills to the fore, making them explicit. In the process of doing this, the chapter has also, first, provided some indication as to how these skills can be transferred to the arena of current affairs, and secondly, has indicated how the concepts routinely employed by audiences can be rendered more precise, penetrating and consistent with the aid of social theory. In the chapters that follow I will apply these concepts directly to the analysis of a range of news and current affairs items, indicating what is involved, including the need to combine general categories with specific, situational details, and demonstrating more directly what audiences for news and current affairs stand to gain from a commitment to these altered ways of seeing.

4

Making the most of what we already know: Interpreting single reports on unfamiliar issues

Introduction

In this and the subsequent chapter I will directly apply the ideas introduced in the opening chapters, and illustrated in the discussion of *Borgen,* to items from news and current affairs. One key aim of this and the following chapter is to show how audiences can draw on social theory to assess the *status* or quality of knowledge provided by a given news and current affairs item as it presents a case; that is, as it transmits certain impressions, narratives, claims and arguments about what is happening in the world. However, when a current affairs item is more than just a description of what is going on, but also makes explanatory claims about causes, and strategic claims about appropriate remedies, then active, critically aware, audiences need to go beyond assessing the status of a piece to a position in which they can judge the adequacy of those causal and strategic claims. So, the second key aim of these chapters is to show how audiences can draw on social theory not just to assess the status of a piece, but also to assess the *adequacy* of the knowledge it provides when judged against the claims it makes.

In the course of the chapter, I will make a point of focusing in on discussions of quite specific social relationships, paying a good deal of attention to how these relationships are conceptualized, and to how much evidence is provided to 'fill in' the details of what the concepts suggest we are likely to find (or to meaningfully challenge those assumptions). In doing this I will draw attention to the specifics of the character of knowledge provided by each news item, and, as part of this, will indicate how items are typically made up from a patchwork of different kinds of knowledge. Awareness of this heightens the appreciation that viewers and readers have of the quality of the information they are provided with, and of the adequacy of that knowledge with respect to various purposes.

For all of the analyses in this chapter I will adopt a particular method. This is to examine single items (in one case I draw from two closely related newspaper reports) from the perspective of a reader or viewer who has no previous knowledge of the issue at hand. The assumption is that these single current affairs items refer to a time, place and social domain that readers have not previously been exposed to. This means they have no previous knowledge of the specificities of the case at hand, and so are unable to draw on such in interpreting the single item they are now confronted with. Their interpretation of this item consequently has to rely entirely on the durable background typifications of concepts, fields and so on that can be learnt about in an abstract way, or which they have transposed, on the basis of analogy, from previous current affairs situations they are familiar with. The knowledge they come away with from the latest item they are exposed to will hence be a combined product of two elements: of transposable background knowledge and of the information provided by the single current affairs item at hand.

Constructing the chapter along these lines can be justified on pragmatic grounds, because current affairs audiences often find themselves being presented with a completely new story about a part of the world they have no knowledge of, or about an unfamiliar aspect of the world they do know. However, there are also theoretical grounds for approaching things in this way, as it allows us to home in on what, precisely, can be gained from applying the transposable ideas and concepts gathered together in a social theory frame on contextual fields. Putting it the other way around, the method allows us to clarify with some precision what a single news or current affairs item provides us with, and what it doesn't provide, while allowing us to highlight the role played by transposable and durable background concepts in the making of such judgements.

Concepts within the contextual field: A focus on 'Interdependence'

I will analyse four newspaper stories in this chapter, and in three of these, as I will explain below, the concept of 'interdependence' will be the focus of attention. In examining the fourth story I will alter the emphasis, foregrounding what I've been calling the 'rhetoric of the text' or 'textuality', the ways in which the form and details of the text's presentation of events can be a powerful means of persuasion in and of itself, with the potential to deflect attention from the status and adequacy of the knowledge it provides. Critical audiences need to be aware of the relationship between concepts pertinent to a particular story – such as interdependence – and the evidence provided by that story. What does the evidence look like when judged against the relevant concepts? Audiences also need to heighten their levels of reflection on the ways in which knowledge claims are stealthily, slyly, suggested and insinuated by the text. For heightened attention to this draws attention to the need to carefully excavate and recover the shapes, textures and specificity of these claims – establishing what the claims actually are – as a prelude to the task of assessing whether the evidence to substantiate them is provided. For the sake of clarity of exposition I will keep reference to textual rhetoric to a minimum in discussing the first three reports, but will foreground these aspects in examining the fourth.

The first report is from the UK broadsheet newspaper the *Independent*, covering an Israeli high court ruling in July 2011 ordering the destruction of settlers' homes in the West Bank. The second story, whose contours are drawn from two newspaper reports appearing in the *Washington Post* on 8 and 12 June 2013, revolves around a debate in the Senate on the US Immigration Reform Bill, which would give 11 million illegal immigrants the chance to become citizens. The third, an Agence France-Press feature appearing in the *Bangkok Post* in August 2009, 2 days after an extension of the house arrest of Aung San Suu Kyi, asks how the Burmese government is able to so blithely resist international pressure in the face of this and other instances of human rights' abuse. A comparative exercise is included at this point, drawing on reports of demonstrators on the streets of the Ukranian capital of Kiev in December 2013. The interdependencies that are not far from the surface of these events are seen to have close parallels to the character of the interdependencies within the Burmese situation. Noting these similarities allows us to closely examine the extent to which a reader can benefit by carrying their background knowledge of a concept – in this case that of interdependence – from one story to another. The final story, which focuses on the need to be aware of the rhetoric of the text, is an *Independent* report dealing with renewed popular street protests across Egypt in July 2011, focusing primarily on those in Tahrir Square, Cairo, just after the fall of President Hosni Mubarak and his replacement by an interim military council.

I will marshal the analysis of the reports on these different topics around the concept of 'interdependence', which is one of the objective elements of the contextual field included in box 2 in Chapter 2. The concept of interdependence is relevant to all these pieces, albeit in varying ways that will become clear as we examine the reports in turn. A moment's thought tells us that the emphasis placed on networks of relations within the model of the contextual field means that interdependencies are never going to be far away from any current affairs story. The concept is closely linked to other generalizable aspects of contextual networks, such as the dependence of collective and individual actors on each other's power resources, the various hierarchies relating to the differential possession of such power resources, and so on. I want to convey how the nature and treatment of the subject matter in each of the reports means that it will be productive for audiences to draw on the concept of interdependence in making sense of them. Readers can begin by drawing on their background conceptual knowledge to imaginatively map out a contextual field in the way advocated in Chapter 2, using the material offered in the current affairs item as the evidential basis for this. This material is all the situational knowledge they have. In the first instance I will show how the background concept of interdependence is particularly useful in all these cases in helping to identify the status of the knowledge provided by these particular pieces.

Before moving on to the first of the pieces let me first say a little bit more about the concept of interdependence itself. The concept of interdependence can allow us to identify, with some precision, just how much and how little a report tells us about the nuance and detail of interdependent relationships. My choice of this concept as an exemplar does not, of course, indicate that it is always the most appropriate or useful one to draw on for all news items. For other pieces, other concepts could be more appropriate. The point is simply for me to focus on one concept at some length here in order to demonstrate what is involved in doing so, and to indicate how, by analogy, audiences can employ whatever concepts they decide are most pertinent in order to make sense of the current affairs item they are engaging with at any given moment.

Issues of interdependence broached in a current affairs item can initially be mapped on the basis of the kinds of objective elements mentioned above. By objective elements, it is worth reminding ourselves, we are referring to those aspects of reality that can reasonably be identified by an external observer without access to the interior worlds of the actors involved.[1] Some current affairs items are rich in such elements, allowing a very dense set of objective networks and interdependencies to be mapped, while others will only afford a very rudimentary sense of the relevant networks of relations. The same is true for the mapping of subjective features onto these objective relations, with some items providing a thick, dense, account, and others a thin, sparse, picture of how situated actors subjectively experience and mediate their objective position at the intersection of these interdependencies.

The subjective perception of actors situated within an objective relationship of interdependence lies at the very heart of the concept. One of the keys to the significance of the objective interdependence is how much value an actor places on it. If a particular relationship of interdependence is *perceived as* vital for an actor, if it is *seen as* an indispensable precondition for achieving prized goals, satisfying keen wants, sustaining valued relationships or realizing well-being of some kind, then it takes on a much greater force than it has when simply identified as an objective interdependence. In any given situation, much rests on how much the actor-in-focus will do to defend and sustain that interdependence, how much they will sacrifice for it. In attempting to grasp the meaning of a relationship of interdependence within a current affairs item, it is therefore important how much we know about the character and intensity of the relevant situated actors' attachments to that relationship. Without a sense of these subjective dimensions, of how the objective dependencies within the contextual field are internalized within the minds of key actors, it will be difficult for us to grasp what is going on. In order to understand this systematically we need to be able to combine a grasp of how to conceptualize this internalization with an ability to combine these concepts with evidence.

In discussing the various aspects of actors and agency in the chapter on *Borgen,* in Chapter 3, we laid out in some detail the concepts involved. We noted how actors internalize various forces, expectations and demands from the contextual field. These are the kinds of pressures that are often associated with a relationship of interdependence. Actors don't internalize these forces, pressures and so on in a direct, unmediated way, but from within a set of cultural, ideological dispositions (habitus). These dispositions are informed by their worldview, itself moulded by the way in which they have internalized aspects of the various discourses of the age, and by their more specific social positioning within this age. Their discourses, in turn, will have played a part in informing the development of the actors' goals and ambitions, and the development of the values underpinning these. All of this means that their immediate situational knowledge and the significance they give to it is apprehended and understood on the basis of this cluster of discourses, meanings, values and ambitions. In social-theoretical terms one would think of this as the actor's specific *phenomenological perspective* on situational knowledge.

But it is not only actors' subjective perceptions of objective relationships that are vital to the realities of interdependence within a current affairs event. We need to stay alert, also, to the objective realm itself. For the other, closely interrelated, aspect at the heart of the realities of interdependence is, as we have noted, the objective density and character of the networked interdependencies relevant to how an actor thinks about a particular event, process or decision. We've seen that in order to understand how situated actors will respond to a particular objective situation, one needs to know a good deal about how an actor's situational knowledge of dependencies and interdependencies are perceived from within *their ideological and cultural point of view*. However, as this is not a matter of free-floating perception, it matters that actors are anchored in quite specific sets of social positions situated within networks of relations. The possibilities of these actors pursuing their ideals and achieving their goals will be closely linked to the dependence of preferred outcomes on other actors, powers and processes within these networks. This means it matters, in terms of consequences, how well an actor perceives their situation (*situational knowledge),* and this places an onus on their taking into account as many relevant networks as possible. If they fail to take important networks into account then they are likely to be faced with unforeseen, unintended and unwanted consequences. Having a firm and sufficient grasp of the character and density of relevant networks matters a great deal to the actors at the heart of them.

In turn, this means that if current affairs *audiences* are to feel fully secure that a report on an event provides them with enough information to get an accurate sense of what is going on, they would, likewise, want to have been provided with an adequate picture of the character and density of relevant networks. Pulling all this together means, therefore, that in an ideal case current affairs audiences would be provided with intensive, dense, knowledge of all the objective networks of relations relevant to a story, together with an account of how these are interwoven with differently positioned actors' subjective orientations to these networks. This knowledge would include a feel for the ways in which situated actors' were likely to actively and creatively balance the various demands and pressures coming towards them from the contextual field. One salient element of this would involve an understanding of how, and to what extent, situated actors were likely to order their interests into relative priorities, into a hierarchy of greater and lesser concerns. This means that some relations of interdependence are likely, ultimately, to turn out to be more important than others.

In the discussion of the newspaper reports that follow, we'll see that active, critical, audiences need to be very conscious of the fact that: they are only provided with relatively cursory, thin, accounts of the objective networks of interdependence that are mentioned; that some significant networks are not discussed at all; and that the subjective internalization of interdependence is left more or less entirely unexplored. This latter characteristic is in marked contrast with the centrality of internalization to political drama and other arts oriented narrative forms, such as the novel, or to approaches such as oral history, biography and autobiography – including the political or professional memoir. The rarity of this dimension within news stories is a state of affairs that is to the detriment of adequate understanding. The purpose of drawing attention to the distinctive poverty of many news and current affairs stories when it comes to the interior worlds of key actors, and, of equal importance, of the thinly drawn, or entirely absent, character of the networks they inhabit, is quite simply to indicate how important it is that audiences are highly attuned to these characteristics. The idea is to foreground the silences and the presumptions of journalism with respect both to the networks of interdependencies themselves and to how these interdependencies are perceived and managed within the interior worlds of individual and collective actors.

Netanyahu and the 'Destruction of Settlers' Homes'

A story in the world news section of the *Independent* on Saturday 23 July 2011, bore the headline, 'Netanyahu may be forced to destroy settlers' homes', with the by-line, Matthew Kalman, in Jerusalem. The account is less than 200 words long, including the title, and it's almost axiomatic that the account is going to be relatively thin at that length. However, from another slant, one might well be struck by just how much information about a particular world can be conveyed in so few words, and by the skill involved in managing this. It is important to remember the achievements when looking at such reports in technically critical terms. For the most consistent underlying purpose of the critical stance I'm proposing is to enhance an understanding of what is and isn't conveyed by a text, and how this is done, rather than to always and necessarily mark out texts as falling short. Two hundred words is not a lot to play with, and, as we've noted, it's important to be realistic about what one should expect from a particular genre of news reporting.

In any event, an appreciation of both perspectives – of plenty and of dearth – can be given emphasis and precision through reference to the contextual field. In presenting the relevant field for this first example, I will continue the practice begun in the last chapter of sketching out some salient features in figurative form, something that is particularly easy to do when dealing with relatively short, simple accounts. The purpose of this, here, is to indicate how useful a visual picture can be to the intellectual exercise of thinking about what a newspaper report provides. Translating the report into the terms of a contextual field makes it easier to be clear and precise about the information being conveyed, and its relationship to relevant concepts. In turn, this provides audiences with the potential for an enhanced critical perspective.

The article's main focus has a relatively shallow time span, recounting how, the previous month, Israel's high court had 'ordered the destruction within 45 days of three permanent dwellings in Migron, near Ramallah, an outpost of 48 families mostly living in caravans', and that this period would expire tomorrow, on 24 July. The order was given because the dwellings were 'built illegally on land owned by the Palestinians.' This state of affairs is what gives rise to 'the problem' or dilemma that is said to face the prime minister, Benjamin Netanyahu, which is whether to comply with the court judgement and in doing so initiate his government's 'first major clash with Israeli settlers in the West Bank'. The fortunes of both the settlers and Palestinians with claims to this land are clearly dependent upon whether the Israeli Government complies. One can picture the site of the dwellings built on a 'hilltop outpost' near Ramallah, the three permanent dwellings, life going on around the caravans and the potential spectacle of the clash with Israeli soldiers or police. This latter image references a degree of historical depth to the story through the evocation of the last time 'Israel had destroyed permanent settler buildings', which was in 2006, 'when the bulldozing of nine houses in the Amona outpost triggered violent clashes with Israeli police'. The historical depth is suggested, but this is all the content we get, all the rest is left hanging, vague and insubstantial.

Drawing on our account of objective relations, **Figure 4.1** (below) is a very simple representation of the relevant networks of relationships between actors, conveyed in relation to that prior episode of 2006. Advocating that readers of short news stories adopt this way of thinking – a mapping or configurational way of thinking – about the events presented to them, facilitates a perspective that is different from that which could be gained by interpreting them only in terms of a linear, sequential, narrative. The linear narrative is there, but it is seen to be only part of the story, because even such a simple mapping as this furnishes a more unavoidable sense of the weight of institutional orders, of their spatial relatedness to each other and of their continuing existence beyond the story at hand. It gives a sense of situated comparative powers, of interests embedded within relatively enduring positions and roles. In doing all of this, in directing an attention to these matters that is more than fleeting, it also nurtures a greater sense of how much more there is to know that isn't covered in the account. Even more clearly, it offers a different perspective to the one called forth by a more spontaneous reading of the kind of live action available to film cameras, and made central to television news bulletins.

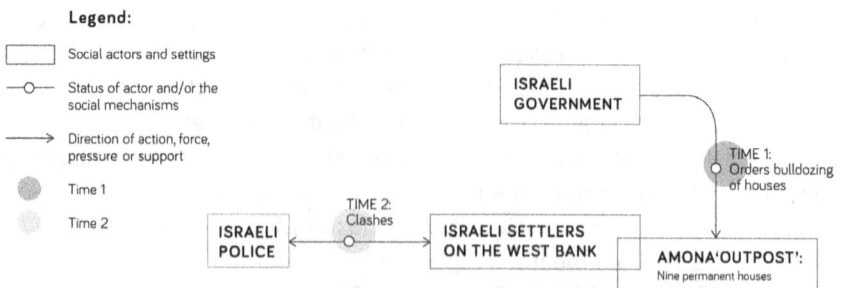

FIGURE 4.1 *The last time Israel destroyed settlements – 2006.*

As we've remarked, texts often work in surreptitious ways, whether or not their authors intend this. The parallel drawn by the author of the *Independent* article between current events and those of 2006 serves to reinforce a taken-for-granted view that the demolition of the dwellings in Migron would lead to clashes between the Israeli authorities and the settlers. This goes beyond description and is a causal claim about probable consequences within this contextual field. Interestingly, it also plays another role, inherently challenging the confidence of any overly presumptuous world weary reading presupposing the authorities would inevitably ignore the injunction of the high court; this is so even though we aren't explicitly told whether the high court played any role in the previous sequence of events, in 2006.

Figure 4.2 (below), as with the previous figure, is derived entirely from the short newspaper report, and represents a similar ambition in suggesting a reading that lingers on relevant networks rather than the spectacle of dramatic events. The most visually compelling scenes nestling in this story, which a television news team could prepare itself to record, would be the possible bulldozing, the subsequent clashes between settlers and police, and, less of a spectacle but often deemed necessary and acceptable, men in suits, protected, deliberating, walking, shaking hands and making brief statements. The reading of the newspaper report that I'm suggesting directs attention somewhere else, to the configuration of institutions, individuals, interdependent relations and events wrapped up together in an organic process of mutual influence and response.

It's instructive here to focus on the roles that time and space play in how interdependence is handled within this contextual field. Time 1 was not explicitly indicated in diagram 3.1 (page 74), as this period covered simply all the represented activity except that indicated by 'Time 2' and 'Time 3'. I do label Time 1 in the current figure (4.2), in order to draw attention to a degree of historical depth, one that stretches over months and years. It is a fairly substantial period of time, covering as it does a period in which the Israeli Government was responsible for the provision of roads, water, phone lines and electricity, as well as establishing and sustaining permanent army patrols. The relationship between this provision to the settlement at Migron and the broader provision to the other Israeli settlements on the West Bank is left unaddressed, and so these spatial aspects remain vague and imprecise. The absence of something as simple as a conventional map of the region is significant in that it means that a reader new to the subject, even if they have a rough idea of what constitutes the West Bank, will have little idea of where to situate Ramallah, let alone Migron and Amona. In terms of this kind of raw information, the advent of news' websites affords a number of very positive opportunities, in their capacity to provide links to general contextualizing features such as maps, timelines and regional and actor profiles.

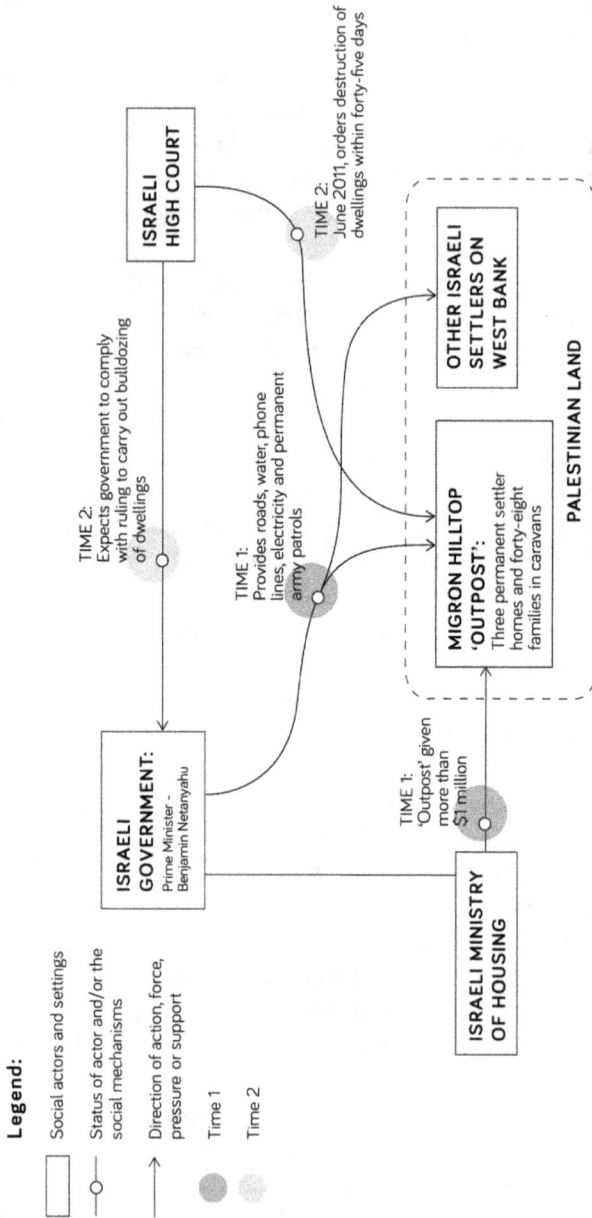

Legend:

Social actors and settings

Status of actor and/or the social mechanisms

Direction of action, force, pressure or support

Time 1

Time 2

ISRAELI HIGH COURT

TIME 2: June 2011, orders destruction of dwellings within forty-five days

TIME 2: Expects government to comply with ruling to carry out bulldozing of dwellings

TIME 1: Provides roads, water, phone lines, electricity and permanent army patrols

OTHER ISRAELI SETTLERS ON WEST BANK

PALESTINIAN LAND

MIGRON HILLTOP 'OUTPOST': Three permanent settler homes and forty-eight families in caravans

ISRAELI GOVERNMENT: Prime Minister – Benjamin Netanyahu

TIME 1: 'Outpost' given more than $1 million

ISRAELI MINISTRY OF HOUSING

FIGURE 4.2 *Netanyahu and settlers' homes – 2011.*

Time 1 also embraces the period in which the Ministry of Housing gave $1 million to the Migron hilltop outpost, although we don't know exactly when this was, or whether it was in the period in which Netanyahu's government was in office. Visualizing the network of relations between Netanyahu's government and the Ministry of Housing raises these and all kinds of other questions about the relationship between the two organizational units of the Israeli state, including the possibility of various degrees of autonomy and control, and issues about the degree to which they share ideological perspectives and values. When there is the mention of 'land owned by Palestinians', graphically represented in Figure 4.2, the emphasis on time within the contextual field would draw the attention of anyone with even a basic background knowledge of the Israeli–Palestinian situation to large gaps in what we can glean from this particular article. But a reader new to this subject would be unaware of how much they would need to know, for example, about the events of 1948 and 1967, in order to place this statement within a meaningful context. Without at least some idea of the role that history has played in the current configuration of relations readers would struggle to understand why the Ministry of Housing gave $1 million to the Migron settlement '(a)lthough illegal, even under Israeli law', or why the journalist felt it appropriate to include the qualifier 'even' in this observation.

There are two sets of social mechanisms embraced by time 2, a period whose starting point I've drawn 44 days before the newspaper report, at the point the High Court made its ruling that the three dwellings had to be destroyed within 45 days. Drawing the boundaries around the period of time 2 in this way, indicates that it is useful to think about everything in time 1 as providing the past and enduring structural context in which the various actors of the High Court, the Israeli Government and its proxies, the Migron settlers, and other Israeli settlers will soon engage, or refuse to engage, in actions. It gestures towards certain potential constraints, such as the formal obligation of the Israeli Government to abide by the rule of law, the time frame for this and the apparent powerlessness of the settlers in material terms against the might of the Israeli state. Relations of interdependence and dependence are clearly evident. The Palestinians, whose land the article unequivocally says this is, are heavily dependent on both the willingness of the Israeli High Court to rule in their favour – the officials of the High Court, in turn, may well feel their actions are dependent upon, constrained by, what the law itself requires – and on the Israeli state to implement that ruling.

I haven't yet mentioned the final few lines of the article, which are ominous but ambiguous in terms of their implications for what will happen the day after, on the 45th day. I also haven't included the import of these words in Figure 4.2, although the reader should add a sense of them to their visualization of the contextual field. This final, very brief, paragraph states that '[c]ommunity leaders and politicians, including prominent members of Mr Netanyahu's Likud Party, pledged their support for the settlers.' This might seem ominous for any hopes that the Palestinians and advocates of the rule of law might have that the Netanyahu Government would, in fact, comply with the High Court ruling. As well as ominous, however, it is also markedly and significantly indeterminate. By this I mean that it is elliptical in all sorts of ways relevant to the reader's ability to make an informed judgement as to the likely effect this pledging of support for the settlers by the group of actors mentioned (the members of the Likud Party) will have on the Government's compliance. There is so much that we don't know about the contextual terrain that we would need to know to fathom what is likely to happen.

Many of the questions one needs to ask here are generic. They are dependent upon the reader's general, transposable knowledge of social relations, networks, meanings and strategy, all of which may have been learnt elsewhere but which are sufficiently generic to be useful here. Even without knowing very much about the Israel-Palestine situation, a politically literate reader wanting to reflect further on the import of these last few lines would recognize, for example, the importance of knowing whether Netanyahu shared the views of the community leaders and members of his own party who had taken the side of the settlers. This by itself, however, wouldn't be enough to know which way Netanyahu would lean. For as we have insisted (see above, and also the discussion of *Borgen* Chapter 3), in order to understand how social actors will behave we typically need to know about their principles and values (embedded in their value *dispositions or habitus*), but not only about these. We also need to know about their *situational knowledge* of the more immediate networks of relevant relations in which they are embedded.

Hence, if we take the viewpoint of a critically competent reader with no prior knowledge of the Israeli-Palestinian situation, reflecting on Netanyahu's own *internalization of the social context,* we might also query whether the reference to 'Mr Netanyahu's ruling Likud Party' was to a party that had formed the government by itself or in coalition with other parties. It might be that Netanyahu did share the views of those who supported the settlers but that his knowledge of the balance of power within the immediate contextual terrain of a working government majority – that might be functioning on the basis of a majority within his own party with different views to his own, or on the basis of a majority opposing the settlers within a broader government coalition – told him that he needed to ignore the pro-settler views and pragmatically follow the injunction of the courts. However, given the very limited nature of our reader's knowledge both of relevant networks and of the subjective perspectives on these, any one of these variables may be other than what we have just supposed. Netanyahu may oppose the views of those supporting the settlers, and oppose them intensely, or he may be relatively indifferent to the whole issue. Alternatively, it might be that he shares the views of those supporting the settlers; that he feels he can command a majority to follow through on this; and that he will be able to avoid any sanctions from the legal context in doing this. From the point of view of a reader who knew little about this issue before reading Matthew Kalman's article, exposing the fact that any one of these various scenarios could represent the actual state of affairs, is a way of shining a light on just how little we get from the article itself. Again, it's not that we should be surprised at this. We've already noted there are limits to what a 200-word article can do. The point is that social theory provides tools that help us to be much more attentive, and precise, about what we do get and what we don't get from the piece.

Netanyahu's knowledge of the relations of dependence and interdependence within the immediate strategic terrain may tell him he has a lot of room for manoeuvre, or very little. In addition to the relevant factors already discussed that the article doesn't cover, there may also be other relevant but absent factors emanating from the interdependencies within the contextual terrain and entering into his deliberations as he considers the space he has for autonomous decision-making. These factors might lie, as with consideration of majority support within the government, within the terrain that is relatively proximate. An example of this could involve thinking about straightforward legal considerations, or about possible effects on the electoral support for his party. Or the salient factors might come from the broader contextual field, akin to the consideration of international forces that played a pivotal role in the *Borgen* episode. It's clear that considerations emanating from sites that are spatially more distant, such as general international opinion or the predicted response of major financial donors, trading partners or military allies, can still be highly relevant to local decision-making. These spatially distant forces can also be just as *immediate* in the sense that all of them enter into the decision maker's subjective thoughts and consequently into his reflections and discussions. Our conceptualizations have told us that these areas of subjectivity are a critical part of the real processes that take place within the contextual field, but they are not covered in the *Independent's* report.

Identifying the status of knowledge in current affairs stories

The two figures shown below, **Figures 4.3 and 4.4,** are a way of illustrating in graphic form key aspects of the *status* of the knowledge provided in current affairs items in general and in the reports we're looking at in this chapter in particular. The figures are designed to distinguish between varying degrees of

	Subjective Analysis	Combined Subjective and Objective Analysis	Objective Analysis
Contextualising			
High level of Contextual Detail	1a) Detailed subjectivity	2a) Detailed subjectivity situated within dense networks of relations	3a) Detailed, dense networks of relations
Floating			
Low Level of Contextual Detail	1b) Thin, partial subjectivity	2b) Thin, partial subjectivity situated within thin, partial networks of relations	3b) Thin, partial networks of relations

FIGURE 4.3 *Types of knowledge of contextual field conveyed by current affairs accounts.*

	Subjective Analysis	Combined Subjective and Objective Analysis	Objective Analysis
High Level of Contextual Detail	1a) Detailed subjectivity	2a) Detailed subjectivity situated within dense networks of relations	3a) Detailed, dense networks of relations
Low Level of Contextual Detail	1b) Thin, partial subjectivity	2b) Thin, partial subjectivity situated within thin, partial networks of relations	3b) Thin, partial networks of relations e.g. fig 4.1 see page 102

FIGURE 4.4 *Illustrative examples of variations of types of knowledge of contextual field.*

coverage of objective and subjective factors within current affairs accounts. They do this along the lines we sketched in before embarking on the analysis of the Netanyahu article, with attention paid to the density of the relevant networks of relations provided by an item, and to the depth of relevant subjectivity conveyed by the text.

There are three key differentials to pay attention to, corresponding to the three headings along the top row of **Figure 4.3**. The first, which refers to boxes 3a) and 3b) is whether a current affairs item situates the spectacle or events it focuses upon within a dense network of relevant relations, or only provides a thin or partial network of relations. We'll remember that Bourdieu believed it necessary for a news item to place the events it covered within an appropriate network of relevant relations in order for it to genuinely enhance understanding. The implication here is that when a report includes only a thin and partial network of relations then this will substantially limit the understanding that can be acquired from that report. This is graphically illustrated in **Figure 4.4**.

The kind of knowledge indicated by boxes 2a) and 2b) is that in which the knowledge provided about networks parallels that in boxes 3a) and 3b), respectively, but in which there is also a corresponding degree of knowledge provided of relevant actors' subjective perceptions of, and orientation to, those networks. As such, box 2a) represents that *ideal benchmark*, mentioned earlier, in which current affairs audiences are provided with detailed, dense, knowledge of the relevant networks of relations, but also with a full understanding of how these are interwoven with differently positioned actors' subjective orientation to these networks. This type of account allows the reader to grasp the internal worlds of actors in an intricate manner, as if able to step into their shoes as they engage in the social practices we are interested in. One could refer to this sort of knowledge of interior worlds as 'experience-heavy'.[2] Such 'ideal' accounts foster empathy and a grasp of the actor's own internal experience and deliberations, in what we have called *agents' conduct analysis* (see Chapter 2), but they also allow the reader to have a clear cognitive grasp of the external, objective, worlds that provide the contextual fields for the situated actor's perceptions and judgements. This is made possible because the heavy subjective experience of actors is placed in a context that is also 'structurally dense'.[3] This can be contrasted with accounts that fall into categories 1a) and 1b), which refer to accounts of subjectivity that are uprooted from context, in which the point of view of actors, no matter whether detailed or 'light', is presented without any useful anchoring in a defined contextual field.

The Netanyahu article, as can be seen from **Figure 4.5**, below, is a long way from the ideal of 2a), and is better represented as falling into a combination in which most of the account falls into the category represented by box 3b). This is because there is, for the most part, an exclusive, but relatively thin, emphasis on the objective structures mapped out in Figures 4.3 and 4.4. However, a fleeting, subsidiary part of the article, as we have seen, alludes to the subjectivity of community leaders and politicians 'pledging their support' for the settlers. The status of the knowledge provided here falls into box 1b)

	Subjective Analysis	Combined Subjective and Objective Analysis	Objective Analysis
High Level of Contextual Detail	1a) Detailed subjectivity	2a) Detailed subjectivity situated within dense networks of relations	3a) Detailed, dense networks of relations
Low Level of Contextual Detail	1b) Thin, partial subjectivity	2a) Thin, partial subjectivity situated within thin, partial networks of relations	3b) Thin, partial networks of relations
	┊ Aspects of ┊ Netanyahu article		┊ Aspects of ┊ Netanyahu article

FIGURE 4.5 *Positioning of different aspects of Netanyahu article within types of knowledge of contextual field.*

rather than 1a) as, in fact, we are told very little indeed about these actor's subjectivities. It is also 1b) rather than 2b) because our analysis quickly revealed that the report provides no anchoring at all of the subjectivities it does allude to in any of the relevant networks of interdependencies, which could potentially help one to consider the subjective orientation to priorities, alliances, strategy, tactical manoeuvre and negotiation. This is a problem for, as we have seen, internal worlds shouldn't be thought of as radically separate from the external world. Rather, the external social structures, cultures and practices of the external social world, while naturally having their own existence, should also be seen as entering into the consciousness of individual actors as they make judgements on courses of action and perform their roles, duties and so on.

The various features of the article all fall into the bottom half of Figures 4.3–4.5, and hence when looked at according to the categories in Figure 4.3, they are appropriately characterized as 'floating' accounts. The category of a *floating text* suggests an analysis made from a viewpoint metaphorically akin to that of traversing geographical space and historical time from the vantage point of a hot air balloon, taking a somewhat distant, bird's eye, view of what is going on below. Accounts provided from such a vantage point often have the strengths and advantages of breadth and scope, but can lack the ability to provide a more detailed fleshing out of, and contextualized embedding of, the relevant networks of relationships, events and processes in focus. It is not unusual at all to find that much of the content of short newspaper accounts, such as that within the Netanyahu–Migron article and in others we will come to below, is of this kind. To this extent, they fall squarely into Bourdieu's category of news accounts that require greater embedding within networks of relationships in order to truly make sense. Floating accounts are also typically uneven, missing out important tranches of time and space and the relevant social processes that went on within them, as if their hot air balloon has periodically sailed above the clouds, shrouding the events below from sight.[4] In terms of time one can see this in the Netanyahu-Migron article in the missing tranche of years between 2006 and 2011. At other times, the position of the balloon in relation to the clouds means that spatially some networks can be seen, but others are occluded from view, leaving a partial, incomplete appreciation of the sum of networks that are relevant to an understanding of the account. In the Netanyahu case, a number of the key relations and interdependencies sustaining the government are entirely invisible to the reader. The distinction between *contextualizing* and *floating* accounts will always be a relative judgement made when comparing one account with another, or made against a benchmark of what a reasonably exhaustive account would look like.

Border controls, the Latino vote and the US Immigration Reform Bill, 2013

Similar themes arise in the accounts provided by two *Washington Post* articles of June 2013 discussing deliberations over the 867-page US Immigration Reform Bill. Again, one can usefully begin a critical understanding of what lies behind the immanent spectacle – in this case the debate on the bill taking place on the floor of the Senate – by focusing on key actors within the relevant contextual field and then looking for key objective interdependencies. An article appearing on 8 June covered the beginning of the floor debate, and noted that the legislation would give 11 million illegal immigrants the chance to become citizens.[5] It reported that a small bi-partisan group of senators – four Democrats and four Republicans – negotiated with various key actors whose situated practices would be affected in one way or another by aspects of the bill. These actors included labour unions, the US Chamber of Commerce, technology companies and pro-immigration groups. Republican dissenters denounced what they saw as the failure to sufficiently take account of the lobby for the radical strengthening of border security measures, which they saw as a basic precondition before support for other aspects of the bill could even be considered. The article conveys tensions between Republican dissent with respect to the bill and the party's electoral dependence on the votes of those who could be alienated by such opposition. The Grand Old Party was said to be aware that this could provoke a 'backlash among immigrant groups that Republicans have sought to woo since Obama won more than 70 per cent of the Latino vote in the 2012 election'. Given that the Republicans' perceived reliance on the support of the Latino vote might have been expected to substantially temper their opposition, the report raises queries for an attentive reader as to the precise source of their continued resistance. Not least, one could wonder whether it is to be found in enduring principles relevant to the issue, or in more transient dependent relations with another set of key actors in one or other part of the contextual field that offset or neutralize their concerns about alienating the Latino vote. In not providing answers to these questions the piece also necessarily leaves the reader in ignorance as to the intensity and likely durability of the resistance in the face of potential electoral costs.

We can see from this and a second article – appearing on 12 June, focused on a speech in support of the bill from President Obama in the East Room of the White House[6] – that the Republicans would want to use the bill's dependence on their support as a means of leveraging various concessions from the Democrats. A key potential concession is identified as that of giving Congress more authority over measures the Department of Homeland Security would be required to implement along the United States–Mexico Border. However, without greater insights into the details of the interior worlds of the dissenting Republicans, and of the character of their debates with more acquiescent members of their own party, it would be impossible to know how they weighed the kinds of electoral concerns we've mentioned against other factors, or to know what the most important of these other factors consisted of. We are very low down in the territory of box 2b) in the terms of Figures 4.3 and 4.4. That is, the *Washington Post* articles provide us only with very thin, limited, knowledge about the subjectivity of the relevant actors. Moreover, they embed these actors only very vaguely and partially within the objective networks of interdependencies that would inform their subjective deliberations and judgements. From the perspective of a newcomer to this issue, there could be all kinds of unknown external structural or contextual issues vying for priority within these politicians' hierarchy of concerns. Such a reader would be hard put to know, to spell out the point, whether the agitation for additional border security measures resulted from long-standing, durable, personal principles concerning citizenship and immigration, or whether it was to do with more situational pressure from, or concerns about, lobby groups of various kinds at state or federal level.

It is worth pointing out here that a significant part of the interest commanded by these articles stems from their concern with *causation* and with *strategy*, which we'll remember were the second and fourth elements of media frames, as identified in Chapters 1 and 2. In fact, many short newspaper articles, or large portions of them, are so diffuse and fragmentary, lacking a clear focus, it is difficult to say they are anything more than *descriptive* of a general domain, lacking a discernible position on causation or strategy. However, we have noted concerns with issues of causation and future consequences in the Netanyahu article, and in this discussion of the US immigration bill there is a concern with causation – whether in the form of certain aspects of the bill producing resistance among groups of Republicans, or about what such republican resistance could do to the Latino vote – and with intimations of related strategic manoeuvrings behind the scenes. It isn't possible, however, to identify any detailed concern with precise causal mechanisms within the pieces, and here there is a grey line between what one would label as description and what should be seen as (causal) explanation. Explanation requires that an *explanandum* – an event to be explained – be raised within the text, within its *definition of the situation*, the first element of the media frame. The problem-to-be-explained (e.g. why are Republicans risking the further alienation of the Latino vote?) naturally needs to be cogently identified before it is possible to ask whether it has been adequately addressed. A text can often imply the existence of such a puzzle, and can also imply that this or that factor explains it without making these cases explicitly. In such cases audiences need to expend some energy in order to mine these claims from the text, to bring them clearly to the surface, as this is a precondition for examining the adequacy with which they have been substantiated.

The distinction between an account's status and its adequacy is important here. For the ability to ask whether the quality of information actually provided by an account (its *status* as a particular kind of knowledge) is *adequate* to establishing a specific claim made by the text, or is adequate to answering a particular question the text has set up, will naturally depend on whether such claims have been made or questions set up. This is significant because the virtue of establishing clear claims and questions is that it greatly narrows down the aspects of an account one needs to pay close attention to. Questions and claims narrow down what it is relevant to focus upon. Where an explicit or implicit question can't be found, it is still possible for critically alert, active, audiences to introduce their own questions of causation and strategy on the basis of what the text has provided. The issue in these latter cases would not be whether the status of the text is adequate to its own claims, but whether the knowledge it allows is adequate to answering the questions set by the reader or viewer. Sometimes addressing a question or substantiating a claim will require dense, contextualized, accounts that are both experience-heavy and structurally dense, but at other times, the issue at hand can be resolved with an experience-light, structurally sparse account. It depends on exactly what the issue is and how the claims about it, or the problem posed in relation to it, are characterized.

Rights abuses and Burma's powerful neighbours

An Agence France-Presse (AFP) report, 'Burma "protected by its powerful neighbours"', appearing in the *Bangkok Post* on 13 August 2009, is a story of interdependence with plural causal mechanisms at work, but with one of these said to be more powerful than the others. The article appeared 2 days after the Burmese state had extended the house arrest of the Nobel laureate and 'democracy icon', Aung San Suu Kyi, by 18 months. Suu Kyi was the focal point for opposition against the Burmese Junta. A virtue of the report for our purposes was that it clearly stated both its *problem-at-hand*, or outcome to be explained and what it believed to be the key *causal* mechanisms producing this outcome. The problem-to-be explained was how Burma seemed to be able to ignore the widespread condemnation by the international community of this and many other instances of rights abuses.

One possible approach to answering this question would be to place all the emphasis on individualistic, agency-based, or culture-based factors, putting the entire explanatory weight on a lack of moral resolution or will power on the part of either key individuals or the international community as a whole. In the latter case, the international community would typically be thought of as a homogeneous, undifferentiated, whole, thus over-simplifying matters twofold. Such answers pay little attention to the positioning of key actors within networks of contextual fields, to the balance of power and interest relations within these networks, and therefore to the constraints and potential consequences facing variously positioned actors within the international community. A significant part of a more adequate answer can already be found within the news report in the *Bangkok Post*, which identifies Burma's positioning within a network of interdependencies with its powerful neighbours, China, India and Thailand. These interdependencies provide the causal basis for a more adequate, less free-floating, explanation. That is, the existing system of mutually beneficial interdependencies was such that those parts of the broader international community who could well have been minded to place human rights and democracy at the apex of their dealings with Burma were stymied by the support for the junta provided by the powerful neighbours just mentioned. This support prevented any effective international response to Suu Kyi's arrest. Relations with China are said, in the report, to be the most decisive within this contextual field, 'keeping Burma afloat through trade ties, arms sales, and by shielding it from UN sanctions over rights abuses as a veto-wielding, permanent member of the Security Council'. This was part of a reciprocal set of arrangements whereby:

> In return, China is assured of a stable neighbour and gets access to Burma's natural resources – overall, trade between the two grew 26.4%

to US$2.6 billion last year, according to China's Ministry of Commerce. Yesterday it called for respect of Burma's judicial sovereignty in reaction to Mrs Suu Kyi's house arrest. India was once a staunch supporter of Mrs Suu Kyi but shifted its strategy in the mid 1990s as security, energy and strategic priorities emerged. It is also eyeing oil and gas imports from Burma, needs Rangoon's help in countering separatists operating along their common border and is particularly concerned about not losing strategic ground to China in the military state.

However, it would be a mistake to feel too comfortable just reading off the perspective and the intentions of a government, or other key actor, directly from knowledge of some structural relations. Thus, in this case it is important to be aware of exactly what we know from the text of the article about the perspectives of the actors involved. The AFP report tells us directly that the Chinese government 'called for respect of Burma's judicial sovereignty', and, very precisely, that it did this yesterday. However, we should be clear that the link between China's statement of support and the prior information about its interests in having a stable neighbour, access to natural resources, and in mutual trading arrangements, is imputed rather than directly stated or evidenced. No matter how plausible it seems, it is important to note that the claim is an interpretative (hermeneutic) one about the intentions of the Chinese, and that there is no subjective analysis or evidence to accompany it. We would certainly have very little to go on if we were minded to try and reconstruct the relevant interior world – the relevant phenomenological perspective – of either the Chinese Ministry of Commerce, or whichever actor it was that made the call to respect the judicial sovereignty of the Burmese. A similar picture of inference and imputation is evident in the textual presentation of India's relations with Burma, as the mention of certain objective interdependencies is likewise used as licence for the conclusion that these are causally responsible for India's withdrawal of vocal support for Aung San Suu Kyi, and for its support of Burma within the sphere of international diplomacy. We are simply told that this shift happened 'in the mid 1990s as security, energy and strategic priorities emerged'.

Taking the time to adopt the insights gained from the socio-theoretical perspective alerts us very quickly to the fact that we actually know very little about the nuanced details of the internal motivations, values and strategic calculations of the Chinese and of the Indian politicians and officials that have shown their support for the Burmese authorities. The text claims some knowledge through a coarse imputation from their actions, from the timing of shifts in their strategy, and from certain visible actions of the two states. In addition to this, however, it also makes some direct references to the internal worlds of these actors. It does this through references that rely more on the rhetorical use of third-person attribution than on any suggestion of evidence, as in the intimation of close familiarity conveyed in the reporting that the Indians are 'eyeing' oil and gas imports from Rangoon, and in the suggestion that they are 'particularly concerned' about not losing ground to China with the military state. We may, it is true, think this is quite enough for our purposes, especially if we have learnt over time to place our trust in the sources and the interpretation of AFP as opposed to, say, less esteemed new media sources lacking equivalent status and lineage. However, we need to be clear that this is the evidence we are agreeing to base our conclusions upon, and that these are the grounds for whatever convictions we form.

In terms of the contextual field as outlined in Chapter 2, there is, it seems, a less than substantiated jump within the report from the identification of some objective relations of interdependence between actors to assumptions about how this translates into a subjective sense of obligation or desire to support that actor. In this instance, as we've said, it seems a reasonably plausible jump, and one that is facilitated by thinking in terms of interdependencies within contextual fields, but, precisely because it is indeed a jump, with only the slightest of attempts to provide evidence, we need to be aware that we cannot be entirely sure of our ground. We have made a leap from knowledge claims befitting the perspective of an external, relatively distant, observer (box 3b) to claims that would need to be derived from a much more involved and intimate position. For there are claims here that presume knowledge of intricate inter and intra-organizational webs at the meso- and micro levels, and of how these webs are internalized within the subjective worlds of key actors. There is a mismatch between the claims and the basis for the claims, which means that although we have learnt a good deal about interdependencies, there are still question marks over both the status and the adequacy of what the text purports to know.

Employing the contextual field as a conceptual benchmark allows us to make something of the fact that the report does not provide us with any information on the finely textured webs of interdependent relations *within* the relevant national policy spheres (hence, with reference to box 3b, the networks that are presented in the text are not only thin but also 'partial'). And, clearly, without such an account it would be impossible to go a step further and look for the ways in which objective and subjective factors are interlaced within national policy arenas. In terms of causation and likely future developments, we would need to know much more about these *meso-level* domains in order to judge with any degree of confidence that the Chinese, Indian and Thai support for Burma is likely to be robust and enduring rather than fragile and potentially short lived. A stronger causal account, one able to provide greater confidence about the durability of the current state of affairs, would need to look not only at the macro-level objective interdependencies it outlines (see **Figure 4.6,** below), but also at

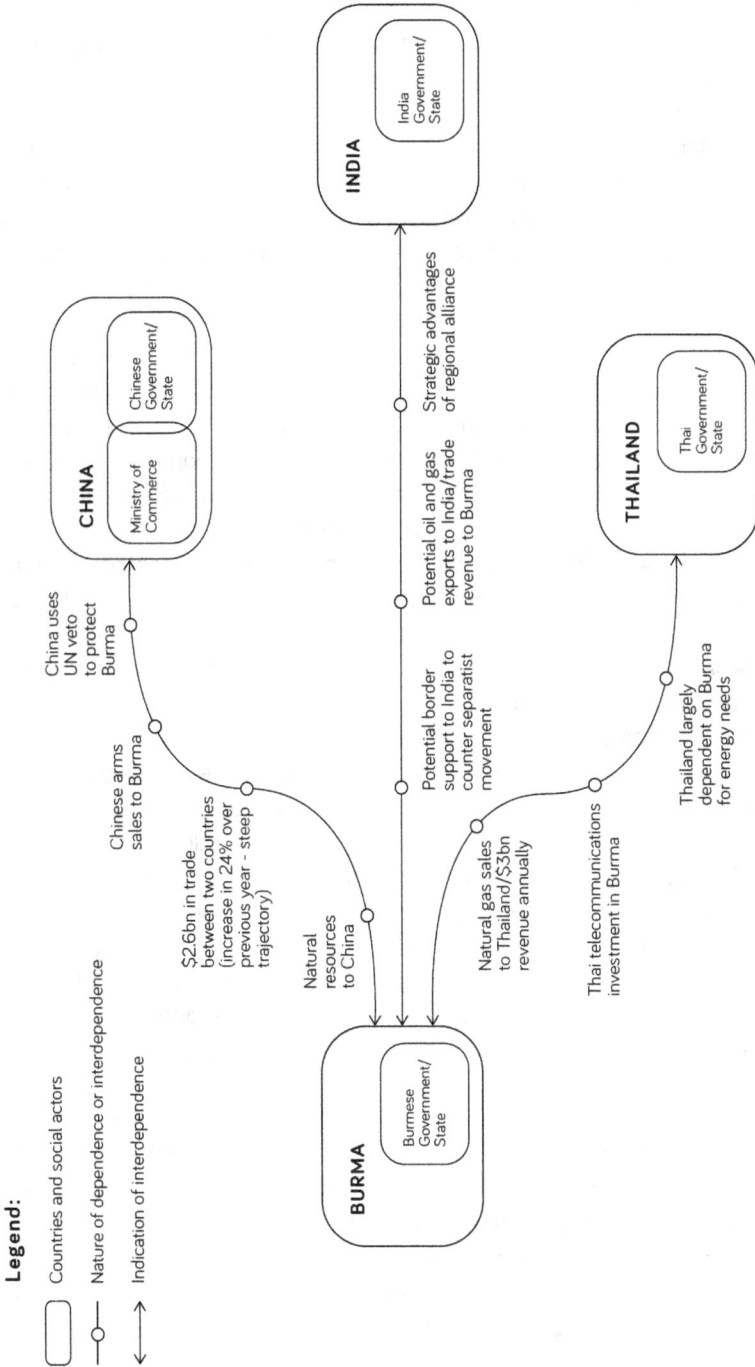

Legend:

Countries and social actors

Nature of dependence or interdependence

Indication of interdependence

INDIA

India Government/ State

CHINA

Ministry of Commerce

Chinese Government/ State

THAILAND

Thai Government/ State

BURMA

Burmese Government/ State

China uses UN veto to protect Burma

Chinese arms sales to Burma

$2.6bn in trade between two countries (increase in 24% over previous year - steep trajectory)

Natural resources to China

Potential border support to India to counter separatist movement

Potential oil and gas exports to India/trade revenue to Burma

Strategic advantages of regional alliance

Natural gas sales to Thailand/$3bn revenue annually

Thai telecommunications investment in Burma

Thailand largely dependent on Burma for energy needs

FIGURE 4.6 *Burma's macro-level interdependencies as context for diplomatic protection.*

more middle-level and micro-policy spheres, and to show how the objective and the subjective interweave within these.

One can see the same kind of presentational handling of objective elements at work in the article's subsequent observations about Thai–Burmese relations. An argument about causation is constructed by simply juxtaposing objective interdependencies. Thailand's maintenance of diplomatic relations with Burma in the face of the latter's human rights record is simply noted and then placed alongside the fact that Burma's 'biggest source of foreign exchange earnings is by far the revenue it receives from gas sales to Thailand – around $3billion annually. Thailand, meanwhile, is largely dependent on Burma for its energy needs and also has investments in telecommunications there'. The imputation about causation is clear, and again is highly plausible. At the very least we should be fairly confident, unless we are to conceive of a highly dysfunctional national policy sphere, that such major objective factors would enter into the subjective calculations of Thai policy-makers. However, a moment's reflection on general categories of policy-making – including further elements of structural interdependence we may have overlooked (but which could loom large in the internal worlds of key actors), issues of competing vested interests and their refraction through different national ministries, divergent ideological motivations and the balance of domestic forces at any one time – would alert us to the fact that the level of our detailed knowledge of many parts of the relevant contextual field is exceptionally low.[7]

Once these important caveats to any simple and straightforward acceptance of the strongest claims of the AFP report have been made and incorporated, it remains the fact that the objective interdependencies providing the basis for the article's argument, relating to trade, energy resources and finance, are significant enough to provide a major *initial*, provisional, orientation to the reader. They are key structural types that can be profitably incorporated into an audience's general 'stocks of knowledge'. Their generalizable quality means they are ready to be transposed into new situations, suitably adapted to the specifics of those situations and contextual fields, just as long as they aren't made to take on too much of the burden of explanation all by themselves.

Analogous interdependencies were at play, for example, in the structural relations underlying the spectacle of hundreds of thousands of demonstrators on the streets of the Ukranian capital city of Kiev in December 2013. The protesters were attempting to occupy government buildings to force out the government of President Viktor Yanukovich and his prime minister, Myakola Azarov, with the trigger for the protests being the failure of the government to sign an association deal with the European Union.[8] But not far behind these sights and scenes was said to be a struggle between the two trading blocs of the European Union, with its $US18 trillion market, and Russian President Vladimir Putin's ambition to bring former vassals of the Soviet Union back into a powerful Russian-led trading zone.[9] Key mechanisms within this contextual field revolved around energy and economics, including: Ukraine's almost total reliance on Russia for its gas imports; and the fact that more than 60 per cent of its exports are to the former Soviet market. Both of these dependencies were offset to a degree by the leverage afforded to Ukraine by the fact that it is the major transit route for Russian gas to the European Union.[10] It is clearly important to include a consideration of these interdependencies in looking at any Ukrainian government's actions and room for manoeuvre. In 2006 Ukraine agreed to pay almost twice the former price for Russian gas after the latter cut supplies, a move that the Russians repeated in January 2009 in the midst of a subsequent dispute over unpaid fees.[11] The structural analogies between the Ukrainian and Burmese contextual fields are clear to see, and raise interesting comparative issues about the influence of power relationships in the two cases.

We must always remember, however, that the transposable, typified, conceptual ways of seeing are always only the beginning, the initial orientation. They can't be a substitute for the more extensive and detailed knowledge of the case at hand. As a simple point of reference, it is chastening to reflect on the clear truth that in both the Burmese and the Ukranian cases, the structural dimensions alone would be an inadequate basis on which to construct the best available picture of how events would be likely to unfold over the next 2 years and more. In complex, open, systems, there are always likely to be other significant objective elements that haven't been taken into account. It is also the case that the relations between the objective and subjective elements will play a major role in any unfolding process. If we use the case study of the relatively closed world of the *Borgen* episode as a close to ideal point of reference, then we can note that the most adequate knowledge comes from a combination of objective and subjective typifications *and* the specific details of the unique situation. It is this combination that allows audiences to follow the twists and turns of that story, and to be able to begin to anticipate what might happen. This is analogous to audiences for current affairs items being able to combine a keen and fulsome sense of the relevant objective and subjective transposable concepts, an immersion in the details of the specific case, including the pertinent details of all the networks of relations relevant to the problem-at-hand, *and* the capacity to combine the two dimensions with skill and acuity. In the *Bangkok Post* story, we ultimately just have a few transposable typifications acting as the organizing basis for a thin sprinkling of evidence, and all of this is overwhelmingly focused on just objective elements.

A major difference, however, between a political drama such as *Borgen*, with its beginning, middle and end already plotted out, and real-life current affairs processes, is not only that observers of current affairs items are all too often situated in the middle of events that are still unfolding, but also that it is much more likely that there are key causal factors still lying beyond our sight. Significant, far from entirely predictable, events have taken place in Ukraine and in Burma between the time the newspaper reports were filed and the time I now write, and no doubt the situation will have changed further by the time you are now reading this. Uncertainty about the future, even with the finest, most contextualized, plausible apprehension of relevant contextual fields, places a particular set of limitations on the confidence we can have in judgements about probable consequences, and on strategic and tactical advocacy regarding the future. A certain set of political and ethical sensibilities should come along with this recognition, sensibilities not all that different to those fitting the awareness that our knowledge of current contextual fields is almost never sufficient to allow us to say with certainty that we have grasped the essence of what has gone on thus far.

Renewed protests in Cairo's Tahrir Square, July 2011

As mentioned at the beginning of the chapter, before it's possible to carefully evaluate what a current affairs account is claiming about the relationship between arguments, concepts and evidence, it's necessary to be very clear what the text is actually saying about this relationship. And there is much in the power and rhetoric of many texts that is not easily and straightforwardly translated into clarity on this issue. In this final section I'll try and demonstrate further what I mean by this, indicating how one sometimes has to work quite hard in order to recover the claims to knowledge embedded within a text. Such recovery has to be undertaken, however, if one is to construct even a rudimentary mental map of the contextual field, and the processes said to be going on within this field, contained within a news report.

The report I will use to illustrate this point is a fairly typical article in a UK quality newspaper, the *Independent*, on the unfolding Egyptian situation of 2011, just after the fall of Hosni Mubarak and his replacement by an interim military council.[12] Appearing on the 9 July 2011, the title of the piece is 'Return to Tahrir Square: Egypt Erupts in Protest', with the by-line of Alastair Beach, in Cairo. In line with the standpoint adopted throughout this chapter, I will look at this from the perspective of a reader who has little prior knowledge about the subject, and so has to rely heavily on the report-in-focus.

At first glance, as is the case with many articles positioned in the world news section of the quality press, the 'media frame' for the article seems almost entirely *descriptive* in style, simply and neutrally relating 'what is happening' with respect to events of the day deemed significant enough to merit coverage. However, one soon also sees rudimentary elements of *causal explanation*, with the narrative indicating that the reason the hundreds of thousands of protesters have come out again onto the streets of Cairo, packing themselves into Tahrir Square, is because of their simmering 'suspicions over the conduct of the ruling military council' that had replaced the ousted Hosni Mubarak in February. *Moral judgements* can also be discerned, as the article constructs a set of meanings in which the two sides are conveyed in very different ways, coming to be identified with two distinct clusters of symbolic associations.[13] The protesters gathering in Tahrir Square are presented as energetic and vivacious, and these qualities are conveyed in an easy, positive register, with Beach writing that '(T)ens of thousands of men, women and children arrived throughout the day carrying Egyptian flags and banners, and by the afternoon central Cairo was awash in a sea of street vendors, tents and ebullient slogans'. The rally is said to have been boosted by the official support of the Muslim Brotherhood, 'Egypt's largest political organisation', and this implies the consolidation of a new unity as the Brotherhood had 'until now' refused to take part in most of the protests since February. On the other side of the binary divide is the newly installed government, the ruling generals, who are the target of the demonstrators' demands for quicker reforms and for the punishment of those responsible for abuses of power and the deaths of more than 800 protesters during the uprising that led to Mubarak's ousting. Any pre-existing qualms the protesters harboured with respect to the government are said to have been further fuelled by perceptions that it is colluding with members of the establishment, allowing a judge, for example, to suspend the trial of Habib-el-Adly, who the author characterizes as 'the widely loathed former Interior Minister accused of ordering police to fire on civilians'.

Through these kinds of characterization the journalist, Alistair Beach, sets up a sense of identity between himself and the protesters, and a degree of distance between himself and the military, old and new.[14] This is probably only partly conscious and intentional, and mainly a consequence of professional training, convention and the exigencies of getting a story out quickly. The sense of identity he creates is compounded by the fact that the only speech reported in the piece belongs to the protesters, who are consequently afforded a privileged position in establishing the perspective from which events are to be seen. The mechanisms of identification between the journalist and particular groups involved in the story are overlaid by what the cultural anthropologist, Clifford Geertz, talked about as the literary transmission of a sense of 'being there' or 'I-witnessing'.[15] The article's rhetoric suggests that both journalist and protesters share an authenticity, and an authority, derived from being there, on the ground. The implication is that they can quite straightforwardly tell it like it is. The effect of the combination of these textual devices is to guide audiences to a particular point of view, and to do so through means that can easily pass by unnoticed.

These devices, establishing the credentials of credibility and guiding the audience's point of view on the authority of this, are reinforced by the *faux* solidity created by what the French semiotician and literary critic, Roland Barthes, called a 'reality effect'. This is when the impression of intellectual mastery of context is rendered through textual conventions of 'knowingness'. These can include, at an elementary level that is no less effective for being so straightforward, the confident, naming of individuals, organizations and the places where demonstrations took place – in the northern Mediterranean city of Alexandria, Sharm-el-Sheikh, and Islamia on the Suez Canal, and, of course, in Cairo's Tahrir Square.[16] A range of key collective actors is introduced through little more than the names of their organizations or groups: the ruling military council, the Muslim Brotherhood, the police and the Interior Ministry. Two high profile individuals are named: Hosni Mubarak, the toppled president, and Habib el-Adly, and also a number of demonstrators, alongside quotations expressing their views. We learn very little of any substance about this configuration of entities, or of the relations within the configuration, to provide us with raw materials as we begin to try and map a contextual field. Much of what we are able to gather has to be inferred from the reported worries and grievances of the protesters. The latter include the summarized view of 'many Egyptians' that the ruling generals are using the bad health of Mubarak as a 'ruse to scupper' his impending trial, and that of his two sons, set for 3 August. At a similar level, and as an indicator of a possible counter-trend, we learn that the Interior Ministry had just announced that 'hundreds of senior policemen would be sacked over their alleged roles in the killing of protesters'. Also, this time by way of the testimony of a protester identified as being from the Muslim Brotherhood, Khalid Dawood, we learn that in recent months the Brotherhood has been riven by internal splits, but was 'persuaded to attend because it was worried about the ruling military council's lack of transparency'. The last two examples do begin to convey fragments of potentially significant information about internal relationships and force fields between the police and the Ministry of the Interior, about relations within the Muslim Brotherhood, and about elements of the political-normative discourse of the latter with respect to issues of government transparency and accountability.

However, so much of this attribution of causal and moral responsibility is a combination of rhetorical textual certainty and weak (conceptual and evidential) substantiation. When measured against the benchmark of a socio-theoretical frame on contextual fields, it is the *absence of knowledge* of relative powers, or of positionings, pressures and forces within and between organizations, and of the interpretative processes internal to positioned individuals, that are most apparent. Rather than the text providing depth of knowledge about networks of relevant relationships, its rhetoric serves to push into the background those things of which our knowledge is vague, insubstantial or non-existent, to gloss over or efface significant gaps in what we know. The idea of contextual fields allows critical audiences to make an assessment as to the *quality* of what a text has communicated. However, it can also play a significant prior role in prompting audiences to initially interrogate the rhetoric of the text in order to recover exactly what the text *has* communicated.

Conclusion

Given the emphasis I want to place on the situated and partial quality of our knowledge, it is worth noting that I wrote most of the analysis of the final news report in this chapter immediately after the article was published, before the elections that brought Mohammed Morsi and the Muslim Brotherhood to power, and so also before the subsequent fate of that government was played out.[17] It was already clear, then, how little one could glean from one article, but it is sobering to look at it now from the vantage point of the future, where that initial sense is greatly magnified. In the next chapter I will move from an emphasis on how much knowledge we can acquire from quite short single reports covering relatively specific, demarcated, processes, to looking at current affairs accounts that attempt to interpret the bigger picture. The initial focus will be on accounts that do this within a single text, while subsequent sections will suggest ways in which audiences can combine knowledge acquired from different current affairs accounts and genres, making creative connections between them, as they build their own more complex accounts, accounts that are more adequate for the purposes they have in mind.

5

Interpreting the bigger picture

Introduction

This final substantive chapter is divided into two main parts. In the first I will examine two current affairs pieces whose coverage is much broader in scope than those we've been looking at thus far. These items are broad ranging, covering larger sets of social relations, with a greater spatial and historical span, than those covered in the last chapter. I want to explicitly thematize the *plural character* of causation within these pieces, and also – drawing on the analysis of types of knowledge introduced in the last chapter – to thematize the ways in which these pluralistic, spacious, stories with a large historical or geographical sweep are typically made up of a patchwork of different types of knowledge. It is necessary for critically adept audiences to be sensitized to these characteristics and their implications. I continue the method of approaching these items from the perspective of a reader or viewer who has no previous knowledge of the issue at hand, for the reasons outlined at the beginning of Chapter 4.

The first analysis focuses on a newspaper feature which argues that key aspects of Germany's recent economic success have been dependent on a deep, embedded, set of structural preconditions, and the second analysis examines the script of a radio broadcast situating the Rwandan genocide of 1994 in its historical and political context. The strengths of these kinds of account come, first, from their expansiveness, including their recognition that momentous outcomes – both successful and tragic – flow from a plural combinations of causes, and secondly, from their ability to see things with a wide-angled lens, with historical depth, or with both. However, because the characteristics of the knowledge they provide are uneven – as a result of sometimes zooming in on details and diligently tracking processes as they unfold, and at other times seeing things from a distance and losing sight of processes for substantial periods – there is a premium on being highly attuned to this fact. The implications for plural causation is that some of the relevant processes will be brought much more sharply into focus than others, and tracked more assiduously than others. The more attuned that audiences are to the status of the knowledge offered by any one part of a text, and to the mix of knowledges within the text as a whole, the more likely they are to be alert to both the inherent strengths and limitations of that text.

In the second half of the chapter I will continue the theme of plurality, approaching two sets of news and current affairs accounts on very different issues with a view to foregrounding the complexity of relevant causal forces at work within their respective fields. I will also, however, introduce a new theme of making creative connections *between different items*, either from within the same genre or from different genres. We will have prepared the ground for this with the emphasis on the patchwork of different types of knowledge *within* the single items on German manufacturing and ethnic genocide in Rwanda. This theme of making connections between items is a natural corollary of recognizing the patchwork quality of the knowledge provided in a single item. We can remind ourselves that, in single items, the detail and quality of some parts of a piece are usually more richly textured and contextualized than others. One needs to notice the thinner, sparser parts of accounts, as these tend to be the places where these single items fail to live up to the lofty rhetorical pretensions of their own claims and arguments. Instead of the consistently solid weight of evidence required to substantiate a strong and vigorous line of argument, one so often finds, instead, patches of relatively convincing and compelling empirical reference nestling among a diffuse and motley array of vaguer, more threadbare, fragments. These swatches of variegated status and quality are typically all stitched together into a less than satisfactory whole by the tropes of imprecise and hazy summary. The recourse to creative connections between items is a way of supplementing, filling out, the uneven knowledge provided within these single pieces – filling them out with complementary, enriching and completing, kinds of knowledge gathered from other items and genres. Connections can be made to sources that provide more detail and coverage within areas already encompassed, or they can be to sources that extend the analysis into new domains, domains that have been ignored but which have a bearing on the issues and claims at hand.

The audience is at the heart of this approach, as the implication is that audience reception and interpretation of single texts about an issue needs to be integrated into a slowly evolving stock of knowledge about this issue, and about the same complex of questions with respect to this issue. From this perspective, a television news bulletin is potentially just one source from a kaleidoscope of sources that a viewer can access and draw from in making sense of a particular event or outcome, and of the things that have brought it about. This places a significant onus on the creative capacity of viewers to combine information from different sources in a manner that is conceptually coherent and empirically adequate.

The two news and current affairs issues focused on in the second part of the chapter are the violent clashes on Bangkok's streets in May 2010, and the revelations about the chronic ill-treatment of patients in a UK National Health Service hospital run by the Mid-Staffordshire Trust between 2005 and 2009. Both involve a good deal of complexity, and it is no straightforward matter to be able to combine the information provided by different sources in a way that adequately addresses the four dimensions of stories identified by media frames. To remind ourselves again, these are: (i) ascertaining the appropriate definition of the situation or problem-to-be-explained; (ii) identifying the relevant causes of that situation; (iii) identifying moral judgements made with respect to this causation (and we should want to seriously probe and evaluate these judgements); and (iv) formulating strategies to improve or remedy the situation.

We've seen that social theory allows us to approach these preoccupations of media frames with a greater level of sophistication, and a greater degree of conceptual refinement. It allows us to identify the status of the knowledge provided within a current affairs account, and therefore to judge how adequate such knowledge is for the questions we want to address, or for the claims that have been made for it. Having this capacity to identify the status of the knowledge we already have, incorporating a sense of how such knowledge has been conceptualized, makes it easier to think about what knowledge we still lack. These are powerful capabilities, and all the more so if they can be combined with a sensibility alert to the full range of avenues through which to extend the conversation so as to deepen the interpretation. Such a combination allows us to be open to the possibility that the further knowledge we are looking for might be provided by, for example, one or other of a specific news report; a documentary film; a specialized essay; an academic text; official documents or reviews; or a memoir, literary novel or photograph; or such serendipitous sources as, say, the unexpected surfacing of hitherto hidden items of personal correspondence. In extending the range of the sources we look out for, and are ready to examine, we hope to find, on those occasions when we are lucky, that a new source provides us with some of those pieces of information that were missing and which we were looking for. At other times we will discover illuminating, and highly relevant, pieces of information that it would never have occurred to us to look for. The key, in both cases, is to be able to identify, with some precision, exactly which bits of missing knowledge have been provided, and what their implications are.

In analysing how to combine texts in order to make better sense of the political conflict in Bangkok, and of the mistreatment of patients within Stafford

Hospital, I will draw attention to the accompanying process, introduced at the end of the previous chapter, of recovering the status of knowledge in any one piece from the rhetoric of the text. For, as we have seen, the textual tropes and rhetoric that have their own intrinsic power to rouse, direct and persuade audiences, quite apart from any question of their truth or accuracy, should be taken seriously. The insights and tools of social theory, with the idea of the contextual field at the heart of these, can be invaluable in facilitating and guiding this process of recovery, as well as in the subsequent assessment of the knowledge that has been excavated from the text. The *media frames* literature is a useful bridge here as it directs us to typical aspects of media texts, training us to look for how a media text defines the situation it is covering and how it then, in one way or another, avers certain causal claims, makes moral judgements and advocates particular remedies with respect to that situation. The *social-theoretical frame* adopts these guidelines but provides greater focus and rigour; it also asks us to think carefully about the links between the different aspects of the media frame. What, for example, are the links between a documentary film's definition of the situation and its causal claims? Is it saying that a particular cause has been solely responsible for a particular aspect of the defined situation, or has it combined with other causes to produce this outcome? In either case, the combination of media frame analysis and social-theoretical frame analysis guides one to look for, and to recover, specific kinds of knowledge and knowledge claims contained within the text.

It is only once one has a grasp of the recovered or excavated status of the knowledge provided that one can start to consider what further knowledge is required. As noted, the identification of the problem or outcome to be explained – the *explanandum* – is key to being able to ascertain which different sets of causal forces might provide the key to the explanation. The outcome to be explained (as in Bourdieu's outbreak of violence in a high school) helps to guide one towards the networks of social relations that are 'relevant', relevant to a causal explanation of how that outcome came about. Care must be taken to show how processes within certain networks, within certain clusters of institutional practices, interact with other networks in producing the outcome. The process of thinking things through must be conceptually astute if it is to be able to identify this interaction in a coherent and plausible manner. The performance, within this, of creatively, but systematically, combining information and understandings from different items is of particular significance now, in the age of information technology and communication, an age in which one internet link can lead seamlessly to another, but which all too typically results in a simple overload of random, inadequately integrated, fragments of information. The alternative to drawing on the guidelines of social theory, even in a pragmatically 'light' way, is for audiences to settle for information being received in an *ad hoc* and fragmentary manner, and for us to be content that interpretations and arguments are based on nothing more than this.

If this is something we don't want to settle for then we need to develop ways of being able to combine seemingly endless quantities of information with disciplined, systematic and adequate ways of conceptualizing and making sense of them. In order to combine knowledge from different sources on a particular news issue in a systematic and coherent way, audiences need to know how to excavate, conceptualize and contextualize the information they receive. Once they can do this effectively, and they begin to stick with particular stories, seeing them through from one day to the next, the background knowledge they will have on hand to bring to the interpretation of each new item *within* this issue at hand will, soon, consist both of generalized typifications drawn from other places, times and social domains and of a developing body of conceptualized knowledge on this particular issue. At each stage of this process, each new item will be subjected to scrutiny in ways analogous to those discussed in the previous chapter, but now on the basis of a slowly accumulating stock of situational knowledge.

Large sweeps of the social world: Patchworks of knowledge from single texts

The broader, more pluralistic accounts, we shall look at in the first part of the chapter, texts that cover larger sweeps of history, geography, or both, tend to share the shortcomings of the more narrowly directed reports examined in the previous chapter, but to also have other limitations that are more specific to type. One might say that these limitations are the flip side of their strengths, as concern with detail is sacrificed for the sake of breadth of vision. It is a particularly fruitful exercise, when confronted with such texts, to pay close attention to the patchwork-like quality of types of knowledge they rely on. In these accounts, for example, one is more likely to encounter the pithy and sententious summary that condenses into a few words the narration of what are, in fact, complex, enduring and deeply networked processes. Such processes may have persisted for years and have taken many years before they produced certain outcomes, and they could have involved the co-ordination of many different kinds of differently situated practices over large tracts of space and have involved the combination of several key causal mechanisms. But they are often dealt with in a sentence, where they are mentioned at all.

It is certainly the case that it is just not possible to do full justice to all the elements involved in large-scale processes. One must necessarily engage in a complex scheme of selection and judgement about what to focus on at all, and about which of these elements to treat with greater or lesser degrees of reflection and awareness. The summaries within texts thus necessarily highlight only some processes, and only some salient parts of these processes, pushing into the background key dimensions of their entanglements with other aspects of their context. They therefore typically compress or efface many of the details of the sum total of all relevant entanglements and the processes and mechanisms they are a part of. They routinely conceal significant gaps in the analysis. More than this, their scale means that the details and aspects of processes they do focus on are typically, inevitably, wrenched away, uprooted from, the contexts in which they were embedded, in which they made sense. The scale also means that many aspects of the things that are perceived are perceived from afar, from a bird's eye view rather than through the eyes and ears of an actor at the heart of the action. The credibility and integrity of the accounts should begin with the extent to which their authors are able to successfully believe in, and convey, the value of their narratives. However, in order to be appropriately robust intellectually, and not just simply persuasive, an author's own conviction about the value of the narrative must also be able to withstand and incorporate any valid charges that, for example, their narrative is uprooted and decontextualized in one way or another; that their point of view is a distant one; or that there are many significant gaps in their coverage of key processes.

Plural conditions for Germany's manufacturing success

The lead article in the *Guardian Weekly* 7–13 June 2013 announced a causal argument in its headline: 'How Germany Rode the Storm: Progressive Business and Labour Principles Underpin Europe's Economic Giant'. In reflecting upon and assessing any causal argument it is first necessary to establish what the state of affairs is that has been brought about. What is the end state of affairs, the definition of the current situation, we are focusing on? If a current affairs item does not tell us what this outcome is, then it will naturally be more difficult for us to look seriously at what has caused it. While this is all very clear at a logical level, it's not something we would necessarily notice as readers or viewers, and this makes it necessary to place a premium on ways of making ourselves alert to it. It is necessary to find ways of heightening the awareness of audiences on this issue as it is on so many others.

To begin with, in defining the situation to be explored, one needs to rule out one clear possibility raised by the first part of the headline. The focus of the article was not, as might be assumed, about Germany's direct management of all the elements that are usually raised when discussing the global financial crisis. It doesn't cover the exposure of banks and savings institutions, home loans, the ratio of national debt to GDP or balance of payments positions and their composition.[1] Neither does it target the performance of the financial and service sectors more broadly. Instead, the focus is, rather unfashionably and possibly unexpectedly, on manufacturing. The state of affairs the article draws to the reader's attention as a prelude to explaining how it has come about is the health of Germany's manufacturing sector. This is the *explanandum* – the outcome to be causally explained by the article: that is, the success of these German companies, despite intense global competition from low wage economies, and the attendant contribution of the manufacturing sector to continued economic growth in 'a recession haunted eurozone'. The performance of Volkswagen is cited as an illustration and indicator of this success, with a 'reported $15bn profit for 2012, making it the most profitable car manufacturer in the world, ahead of Toyota and General Motors. The new VW Golf also won "world car of the year" at the New York motor show in March – not a bad way to celebrate the company's 75th anniversary'. Another illustration is provided by Tital, a leading manufacturer of precision parts for aircraft and racing cars, which has increased its exports around the world 'by 50% over the last decade, as the market for high-class titanium products booms. Revenue is up. Apprentices are being taken on. A new plant for small aluminium castings has just been opened in the Chinese town of Nantong, near Shanghai'.

The article presents these indicators of success as a narrative puzzle that it sets itself to solve. The core of its answer, its explanation, is that German manufacturers have concentrated on the high-quality niche product end of the market, the upper part of a trading triangle which is said by Tital's managing director, Philip Schack, to be protected from the global competition. It is, he says, only if you are producing in the much wider base of the triangle that globalization is a threat. It is this that explains why Germany has been able to buck the global trends. This is clear enough, but it is only really the beginning of the explanation rather than its end state. This is because the reasons that Germany came to concentrate its ambitions on the high-quality market and then was able to pull this off are things that themselves need explaining. And in a modern, complex society with a finely tuned division of labour one would expect such an explanation to involve the coming together of several facilitating factors. In other words, in looking for an explanation the reader should be on the lookout for a contextual field that contains several causal factors, and to look at how these combine to help bring about Germany's success.

The author of the article, *Observer* journalist Julian Coman, approvingly quotes an academic, Wolfgang Streek, the director of Cologne's Max Planck Institute, in framing an overall argument that Germany was in a position to seize current opportunities because, for many years, it had been pursuing a different kind of economic agenda to that of the many other advanced economies, based on a different set of structural arrangements. In the 1980s and 1990s when all the talk was of Silicon Valley, the dotcom boom, financial deregulation in both the United States and the United Kingdom, and the Conservatives' erosion of Trade Union power under the leadership of Mrs Thatcher, Germany continued to embrace an alternative model. Streek is quoted as saying that it

> remained a manufacturing economy, true to its artisanal roots. That was strongly criticised at the time. . . . Worse, Germany's economy was highly regulated. Power was locally held. Employers had obligations to their workforce and the local community. Wages were high and workers had the right to influence decisions and sit on boards. In countries like Britain and America, that way of organising things was seen as a kind of death sentence for the economy.

The twist in the unfolding of events was that German management and labour are said to have been able to convert these conditions, which from the Anglo-American perspective of the time were seen as severe constraints, into a set of potentials to be realized. The challenge this posed was met by innovating in relation to the global market-place, focusing on quality rather than price, and tying customers into various forms of dependence as a result of this quality. This was another way. In taking up this idea of an alternative model, Coman's argument has two overlapping strands, which are readily apparent. One of the strands deals with corporate giants, where the emphasis is on the importance of skilled and progressive management and consensual labour relations. In articles of this kind it is standard for general claims to be enlivened and given weight by one or two illustrative examples that show the general trends at work in particular instances, with local detail and colour. The literary trope at work is that of metonymy, where a part stands in as an illustration of the whole. This is duly the case here. In 2001, Volkswagen, in a context in which its plant at Wolfsburg had been relatively low-tech for years, threatened to transfer production of new cars to cheaper locations such as Portugal. Making a strong causal claim the author of the article tells us that this future was avoided because the Wolfsburg workforce, through the mediation of the IG Metall union, agreed to new flexible hours and pay, along with performance targets and training schemes which combined with strong leadership from management to make the Wolfsburg plant, by 2013, 'one of the most sophisticated in the world'.

Indeed, the Volkswagen case turns out not only to be an illustrative example of a wider phenomenon, but we are also told, through the use of the direct speech of Streek, that it was instrumental in the consolidation of such a strategy nationwide: 'The then Chancellor, Gerhard Schröder, urged other industries to follow the example of VW and IG Metall to create new jobs in Germany'. Coman then indicates that Schröder's admonishment had a powerful causal impact. This claim is not, of course, conveyed by an explicit statement about causation, but through the simple and routine textual technique of simply following Streek's comment with the observation that 'Labour market reforms, negotiated between employers and unions, followed across German industries and have been embraced by today's chancellor, Angela Merkel.' This combination of sequence and authoritative summary gives the impression of solid and unproblematic knowledge about the order of events and what caused them to happen. The Volkswagen Wolfsburg case and the chancellor's championing of this model, it is strongly implied, played key causal roles in creating a kind of cultural revolution among management and unions throughout the nation. These key players within industry internalized this world view, and it directly affected the subsequent nature, direction and strategic complexion of employer–labour relations. One knows there was much more to this process, but the constraints of the genre require that the narrative is selective and pithy.

The creative thought of Yale Sociology Professor, Jeffrey Alexander, which has provided the inspiration for the setting up of Yale's Centre for Cultural Sociology, has devised an approach that characterizes this kind of process as primarily a 'cultural' revolution or 'cultural' process.[2] It encourages the acknowledgement that a significant causal factor in the relevant developments is a cultural change of mind. In the current case, this change of mind was brought about by a change in the guiding ideas about how key actors should work together to meet the challenge of cheap labour, low-quality economies. The article's message at this point is that this cultural message was diffused throughout Germany, in particular within its industrial 'supergroups'. Coman may or may not have possessed this degree of knowledge about the nature of this cultural diffusion and the chancellor's direct impact upon it, but for good or ill he leaves the unguarded reader with the overwhelming sense that he does. The presentation of his argument, relying as it does on summary and implication, means that if we are to believe him, then we need to do so on the basis of trust, because we are not actually told anything about the unfolding processes that connected the chancellor's admonishment to subsequent developments. The textual form of the causal argument here is, again, *summary*, and the degree of detail we get is akin to that we would get if looking down from up on high and from a great distance, so that the details and mechanisms within the relevant processes, within the relevant networks, cannot be seen. Because these networks can't be seen, it follows logically that we know nothing about the interweaving of objective and subjective factors within them.

In the terms of **Figure 4.3** (on page 108 of Chapter 4), the status of the knowledge in this part of the analysis should be placed at the very bottom of box 2b), that is, at the lowest possible level of contextual detail from a perspective that purports to say a great deal about the combined subjective and objective elements of a causal process, but does so with hardly any evidence of either of these elements. When confronted with this kind of sweeping account of processes putatively taking place in plural sites across a nation, it is worth pausing for a moment to remember our point that the distinction between *contextualizing* and *floating* accounts is always a relative judgement. For when, earlier, we positioned most of the account of the contextual field recounted by the report on the West Bank as having a 'floating', objective status (box 3b), we didn't really need to say where in that box it should be placed. But now, as we compare that account, with its thin but discernible networks of relations – allowing a degree of mapping to take place – with the part of 'How Germany Rode the Storm' we are now focusing on, we can see that the network of relevant relations it provides is significantly greater. Both are floating accounts, but the account of the cultural revolution within Germany's manufacturing companies sails much higher, making it even harder to make things out in the fields down below than it is from the narrative of the potential bulldozing of settlers' homes on Palestinian land.

The second strand within the explanation put forward by the article to account for Germany's miracle recovery from the low point of being talked about as the 'new sick man of Europe' in the late 1990s to being 'the last economy left standing, following the hurricane of the debt crisis', focuses on small to medium-sized (*Mittelstand*) businesses. This strand has a similar structure to the first to the extent that it starts with a generalized picture, and then picks out – zooms into – a particular company to illustrate a thesis about the broader whole. Adhering to this logic, it begins by noting that Germany's *Mittelstand* businesses, of which Tital is to be the primary exemplar, are often family owned, typically have up to 500 employees and specialize in high-quality niche products. They are said to own an astonishing 499,525 patents for specialized technological innovations that are developed, typically, for niche markets. The concept of interdependence comes into play again here, and we are told that Tital itself developed a patented casting process that uses a unique cooling liquid, which has 'made it indispensable to its clients'. *Mittelstand* enterprises as a whole employ more than 70 per cent of the country's workforce and provide 83 per cent of apprenticeships. Tital, Sennheiser, the audio equipment manufacturer, and Lunor, a six-person manufacturer of high-end spectacles, are used to indicate the variety within the general phenomenon. It is implied that these companies shared in the general cultural process outlined above in relation to the industrial supergroups, but their success is also said to owe a great deal to another set of more specific, localized conditions.

To highlight this, the article again uses the trope of metonymy, using the example of one particular part to illustrate the whole. The main illustrative focus of attention is, as noted, Tital, and the *status* of the knowledge in this part of this strand of the argument now comes much closer to the ground, as if the hot air balloon has lost height, and its occupants are taking a close interest in a particular stretch of land, able to make out in more detail a series of social actors and institutions within a relatively dense networks of relations. We learn that Tital employs 520 people in Bestwig, a town of 11,000 near Dortmund in North-West Germany (North Rhine-Westphalia). The journalist, Coman, is crystal clear about the generalization he wants to make: 'What goes for Tital goes for Germany'. Geography is important, as Tital's embedded-ness within localized socio-structural relations is offered as the causal explanation for its success, illustrating what is also said to be the case on a general level for such companies. These socio-structural relations are mapped out in the contextual field of **Figure 5.1**, below, and involve links to communities, and the banks, businesses, schools and other institutions, that go back generations. The continuity and stability of these links are said to be key to giving *Mittelstand* companies a competitive edge. This embeddedness over time, indicating the continuity in actor's lives and consciousness of enduring institutions, together with the interdependencies that sustain them, is represented in Figure 5.1 by the explicit inclusion of a historical dimension. This is accompanied by a representation of the density of the spatial configuration of objective relations between key actors at any point within this stretch of time. In addition to what we already know of these relations, we learn that Tital is financed by the investment arm of the local co-operative bank, that the company takes 18 apprentices each year from local schools in Bestwig and the surrounding area, that it pays a grant to allow the more academic to go to university on the condition that they return to work for Tital after graduation, and that it provides in-house supplementary education for the others. The enterprise also has a works council 'with power and influence over company strategy', including one full-time paid member.

Phillip Schack has a clear vision, from the position of managing director, about how this structural nexus facilitates, and is reinforced by, an ethos of mutual trust and autonomy, which is said to be a critical factor: 'We need continuous improvement and collective ideas: employees who think as they work. The system functions because we need to be up there at the quality end of the market. So we pay top dollar because we need to compete at that level, and that gives us the luxury of having this consensual way of acting.' As with the national 'cultural revolution' mentioned above, the argument is that the ethos encompassing the structural nexus in which Tital is embedded is also in some ways cultural. The implication is that Tital works because the objective nexus is matched by the cultural diffusion of a shared set of dispositional meanings,

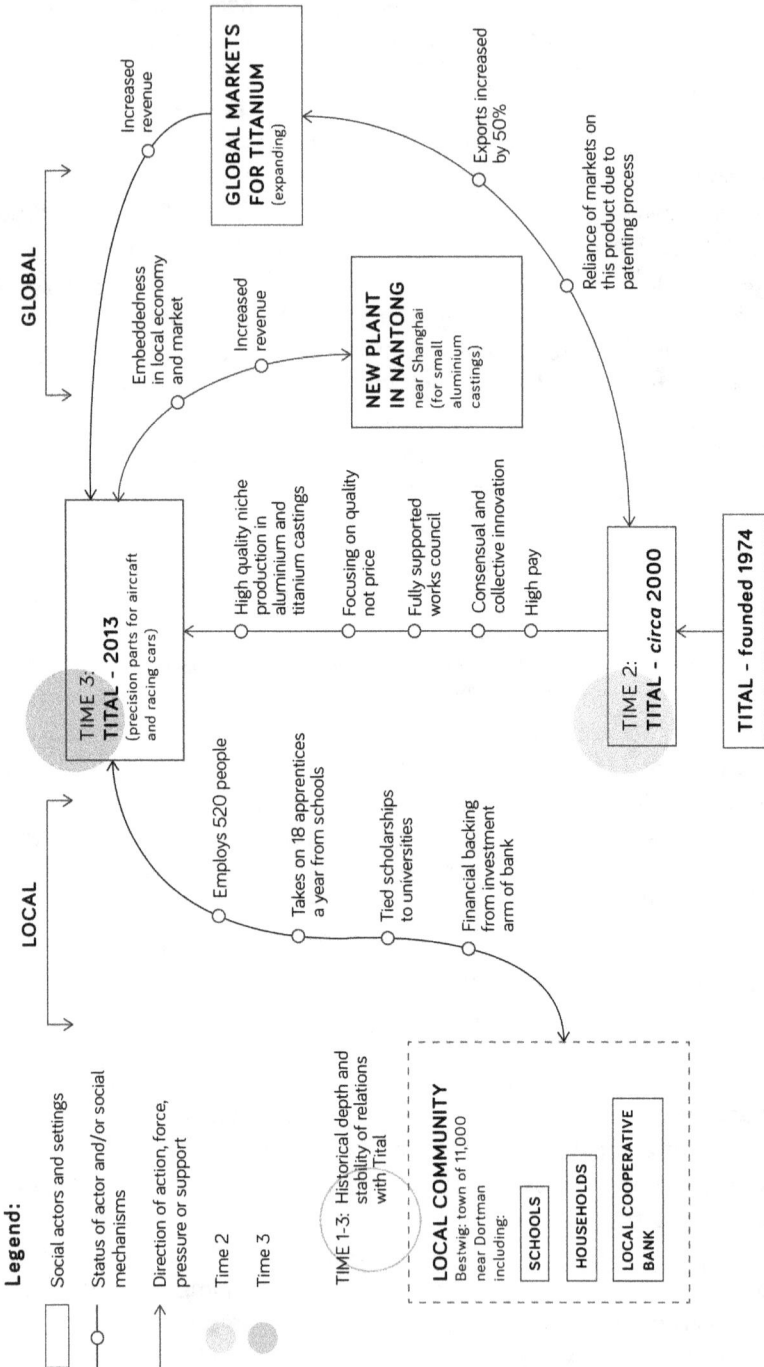

FIGURE 5.1 *Conditions for German manufacturer's global success.*

values and norms. The difference between the two parts of the account is that, in the Tital case, these more specific cultural or ideological factors are now embedded in a concretely identifiable configuration of institutional practices and relations. A virtuous circle is implicit within this vision, with the people involved subjectively responding to a working environment reliant on (causally sustained by) the various sets of relations sketched out in Figure 5.1 and overlaid by the broader cultural-political climate.

Despite the emphasis on the cultural and the consensual ethos that is a part of it, however, *this aspect of the report* doesn't include the perspective of any of Tital's employees besides that of Phillip Schack. To this extent it remains as overwhelmingly objective account, more 3b) than 2b), but with a status much higher within its box than that of the more generalized parts of the report. Nevertheless, the cumulative picture presented by the various objective factors, along both spatial and temporal axes, provides a rich initial context for anyone wanting to think more deeply about the issues involved. For example, we have a solid basis on which to consider how these objective factors became interwoven with the subjective elements we see much less of, and of the implications of such interweaving for the causal claims of the *Guardian Weekly's* report. On its own terms, the account leaves us with a powerful, if provisional, sense that the personal fates of each of the apprentices taken on each year, the fate of Philip Schack, and of all the other people employed by Tital are closely bound up with a set of social relations which has developed over time, and which has been sedimented in a series of complex interdependencies within which the parts are dependent upon the whole.

The Rwandan genocide of 1994

In 1996 the BBC reporter, Fergal Keane, highly respected for a trademark blend of combative politics, personal compassion and compelling prose, put together a compilation of his own favourite pieces of journalism from the past 6 years of his work, *Letter to Daniel: Dispatches from the Heart*. He concluded the book with two extracts from radio talks exploring the issues of identity, ethnicity and nationalism. I had recently heard the second of these, 'A Letter from Africa', on its original broadcast earlier that year, and it had stopped me in my tracks. I couldn't ever remember a report so moving me and educating me in the same breath. There was Keane's consummate ability to conjure empathy with a few well-chosen sentences, but there was also his ability to place the people whose suffering he invoked in a social context which explained how that torment had come to be. The talk was about a subject I was interested in knowing about, felt I should know about – the Rwandan genocide of 1994 – but which, amidst the busy flow and demands of day-to-day living, I had not managed to get any decent grasp of. In a matter of minutes I felt that this had changed. It wasn't that I now knew all that I wanted to, but I now knew enough to feel I could easily learn more, and that I had an idea of how to make sense of further information.

'Letter from Africa' had done exactly what the sociologist C. Wright Mills, mentioned earlier, had advocated and fostered in promoting the idea of the 'sociological imagination'.[3] It had combined an acute sensitivity to individual lives, with a very broad mapping out of some of the macro-level social and historical forces that had positioned those lives, and that had also infiltrated and inhabited them. Moving between the larger picture and the human experiences that took place within it, Keane's account provided a way in to those horrific events, a way in that somehow managed to combine the intellectual with the emotional, hard analysis with the sensitivity of human concern, which has always been the enduring appeal of Mills' vision to generations of scholars in the social sciences.

Keane's earlier pieces from Rwanda, some of them included in *Letter to Daniel*, had been powerful and numbing evocations of what it had been like to be there during the riot of cruelty and killing, among the machetes, the rotting corpses and the haunted survivors. There was little, however, at this point in the life of Keane's relationship to the events that was able to position the horrific, emotional texture of being there within a set of social relations that would help one to understand how they came about. Two years later, in 'A Letter from Africa', Keane writes candidly that when he had been dispatched to Rwanda, he wasn't able to adequately situate the events he was to witness in any meaningful social and historical context. As such, he wasn't able to properly question the received and simplistic Western stereotype of Africa, which was that if there was slaughter, if there was genocide, then it was simply 'a matter of tribalism. A crazy African thing. A horror somehow mitigated by the knowledge that Africans have always been prone to this kind of behaviour. Genocide prompted by implacable and ancient tribal antagonisms'.[4]

There are some hints in the 1994 pieces that Keane was searching for more adequate explanations, and beginning to find his way towards his later account. In writing about the 'hundred-day orgy of killing' in 'Seasons of Blood', dispatched from Nyarubuye in 1994, elements of the wider context responsible in great part for these events begin to emerge. In a room at the very back of the abandoned building housing the Office of the Bourgmestre of Rusomo, Sylvestre Gacumbitsi, one of the most influential perpetrators of the carnage, Keane and his colleagues come across a library of index cards. Each of these is an identity card for every local resident:

> [T]here are thousands of these thin paper cards on to which are fixed the photographs of the bearers. Each card is marked with the name, address

and ethnic identity of the resident, Hutu, Tutsi, Twa, or other. Dust has gathered on the cards, and when I flick through it rises up and stings my eyes and nose. The colonial government introduced this system of population registration and their Rwandan Hutu successors entrenched it as a means of political control.[5]

In 'A Letter from Africa' these remarks have been consolidated into a more developed conception of the socio-historical forces signified by this incident. In the terms we've been using, Keane now places the genocide more squarely within a historically informed contextual field, and advances the broad features of a causal argument on the basis of this. He believes that such an account can mount ' a profound challenge' to the kind of analysis that reduces all to unfathomable tribal antagonisms: '[S]cratch below the surface of this genocide and you will not find a simple issue of tribal hatreds but a complex web of politics, economics, history, psychology and a struggle for identity'.[6] Beginning the process of translating this complexity into a more focused causal account, *three key categories of explanation* emerge from within Keane's later, more reflective, account. He doesn't use these terms, but the *first category* of explanation is clearly bound up with the large forces of history and social structure. This category can be broken down further, and using social-theoretical language, we can say that these involve elucidating three temporal moments in the following ways: identifying the social positionings and relations within the broad contextual field of Rwandan politics at the beginning of 1994; identifying the role that history had played in creating and consolidating these forces (historical depth); and specifying how this configuration of forces, of power and culture, were necessary, causative, conditions of the genocide that was to unfold.

The *second category* has to do less with broad contextual conditions in themselves, and more to do with the biographical history of particular men and women growing up within these conditions. That is, with the ways in which forms of socialization prevalent in Rwandan society moulded and forged the deeper dispositions and potential orientations of its citizens. This is explanation by way of societal influences on the lifetime development of what we have called a person's *habitus*, profoundly affecting not only their own sense of identity, but also the way they perceive others and can behave towards them. The workings of these first two sets of explanatory forces were intertwined with each other, as they always are, blending to create the profound effects that societal forces have on the way people behave. But a *third category* is also required. This is to think about how, for example, an individual Rwandan Hutu, socialized over years and finding themselves positioned in a certain place within society, sees an immediate situation, and responds to it in a particular way. The genocidal response is both personal and collective, and its potential is present within the habitus of its perpetrators and in the configurations of forces and culture that have slowly moulded that habitus. It is also something brought forth within and made possible by the current web of social relations. Finally, it is something that requires the agency of people who actively, purposively, translate their habitus and their immediate social context into a multiple series of unfolding – never entirely inevitable – scenes of unimaginably harrowing human interaction. When Keane gave the title 'No Man is an Island' to his concluding chapter, some or all of these categories would have been lurking somewhere, somehow, in his mind.

The social relations of the early 1990s in which – and in large part because of which – the Rwandan genocide took place had deep roots in colonial times. In what I've called a 'floating' mode (see Figure 4.3), Keane relates how in colonial Rwanda and Burundi the German and then later the Belgian rulers 'cultivated the notion that the Tutsis were somehow less African, more European and, by extension, superior to their Hutu fellow countrymen. They ruled through and with the assistance of a Tutsi elite built around a king and a group of land-owning clans'.[7] All kinds of what Keane calls 'racial nonsense' was invoked to justify this form of rule, including the Belgians citing the tallness of the Tutsis, their aquiline facial features, and their preference for cattle rearing over tilling the land as evidence of a superior civilization. Keane is clear that the purpose of this raising of the Tutus was to 'create and preserve an inherently unjust power structure'. In reflecting on the subsequent consequences of this he moves from a concern with these objective cultural, ideological and positional aspects of the colonial period to claims about their effects on the subjectivities of those who were subordinated and oppressed within this process:

> The effect of this injustice and of the stereotyping of Hutus as lesser beings was to create murderous feelings of inferiority and resentment among the majority. When, at the end of the fifties, the Belgians relinquished power, the Hutus rose up and began the first of many campaigns of massacre against their former Tutsi rulers. . . . The eruption of violence which seemed to the world like a matter of tribal hatred had its roots in the politics of power and privilege.[8]

In thinking about the 1990s it is again important not to slip into the lazy and distorting supposition that the genocide is simply another variation on the crazy tribal hatred thesis of African history. All major social events are anchored in one way or another in socio-structural relations, and history works through these, both being shaped by them and, in turn, affecting them. If we look to the 1950s for clues about the 1990s, it is not because we will find in the latter an identical manifestation of deep and timeless tribal hatreds. Rather, it will be because we have a sense that specific, time-bound, forces emanating from the configuration of the 1950s could have played a part in the configurations and actions of the later period. Keane has suggested how the social structure bequeathed by the colonial regimes created resentment and backlash, and he goes on to relate how the historical legacy of this hatred manifested in the immediate post-colonial period was to play a direct part in the genocide of 1994. It did so, however, in specific historical conditions which, as with understanding Bourdieu's more local outbreak of violence in a high school, need to be grasped in order for the role of that legacy to be understood.

Rwandan society remade itself in the years that followed the withdrawal of the Belgians, and Keane maps out how he sees the new configuration in a way that embeds the events of 1994 within it, at the same time as emphasizing its deep links to the past. The panoramic picture Keane paints in a few broad, carefully applied, brush strokes is one of a society that is unjust and divided, but one that is also relatively stable. A corrupt aristocracy from within the Hutu was led by former army chief Juvenal Habyarimana and a clique of his supporters from northern Rwanda. While the dictatorship flourished, with wealth and power concentrated among its elites, most Hutus eked out an existence at subsistence level, so the objective social hierarchies cut across ethnic lines. The Tutsis, for their part, 'were a cowed minority, discriminated against in every sphere of life but left largely unmolested because they no longer represented a political threat'.[9] This equilibrium of forces was not disrupted arbitrarily and ahistorically but by the reappearance of a group initially formed by the colonial regime and forced into exile by the post-colonial regime – again, traces from the past emerging powerfully within the present. This was the Rwandan Patriotic Front (RWP), made up of those children of Tutsis who had escaped death, unlike thousands of their family members and friends, and been driven into exile in Uganda in 1959 when the Tutsi aristocracy had been overthrown. The RWP swept into Rwanda, ready:

> to claim a share of power. The reaction among Habyarimana and his supporters was one of barely concealed panic. They called in French military support and without this would have been defeated by the RWP in 1990. Worse still, Habyarimana now faces growing calls for democratization from moderate Hutu groups, tired of his corrupt and authoritarian rule. There is strong evidence to suggest that Habyarimana feared losing power to the moderates. Threatened from within and outside, Habyarimana and his northern Hutu clique seized on the one element guaranteed to mobilize public support behind the government: hatred of the Tutsis.[10]

Keane thus sketches in the situation on the eve of the genocide, taking a wide-angled view on the current contextual field and its colonial and post-colonial history. As a 'floating' account, surveying the landscape in a panoramic mode, much of the fine grain of actual events is inevitably sacrificed. This means that claims made within it are open to further scrutiny on the basis of greater detail and contextualization, and as audiences we should be keenly aware of this. Such scrutiny, however, is made easier by the fact that the picture provided is historically and socially anchored, with the main actors identified and some of the dispositions, power hierarchies, vested interests and stored resentments briefly indicated. These are all said to be components of the causal nexus that provides the conditions necessary for the genocide to happen. However, it is apparent that the most proximate cause, according to Keane's account, involves the utterly cynical and self-interested creation by the ruling clique of *a cultural process* designed to demonize the RWP and the Tutsis. At the same time, the creation of militias, the Interhamwe, among the Hutu meant that the means were in place to translate the cultural demonization into violence. The cultural process was one of the diffusion of crude typifications of the character and intentions of the Tutsis. Its effective production relied on a range of positioned social actors with investments in the current regime, and a related infrastructure of performance and dissemination.[11] Newspapers and radio stations began to exhort the Hutu 'to drive the Tutsis out and show them no mercy.'[12] The impoverished Hutu peasantry were told that the Tutsis were about to take their land, the rhetoric summoned up cultural memories of the not so distant past when the Tutsis and the colonial overlords had combined to subjugate the Hutus. Keane's textual presentation draws on indirect and free indirect speech, reporting and mimicking the voice of the exhorters, and melds this with more sober commentary in order to both evoke and condemn the atmosphere of hysterical fear the discourse was intended to bring about:

> Remember your shame. Remember how they humiliated us. Be proud of your Hutu blood, they told the peasants. Intellectuals were recruited into the cause of creating a pan-Hutu consciousness. University professors, churchmen, journalists – all travelled the country disseminating the propaganda of hate. The Tutsis were characterized as vermin. *Inyenzi in Kinyarwanda* – cockroaches who should be stamped on without mercy. Mercy was a sign of weakness. Show them any mercy and they will make slaves of you again (italics in original).[13]

Specific, embedded, details of local memory were involved in the production and power of this discourse, and the argument is that its efficacy couldn't be understood without these. Little Tutsis, the message went, will grow into adult Tutsis, and sparing them in 1959, when the aristocracy had been overthrown, meant that they had now returned to make 'eternal slaves' of the Hutu. The only way to avoid this mistake again was to 'kill the children'. The peasantry, it is implied, were primed to be receptive to these messages by the selective resurrection of deep cultural memory combined with the invocation of a current socio-structural terrain in which one of the only things they had left, their land and livelihood, was in imminent danger. Keane's overriding moral message, grounded in his mapping of causes within this historically stretched contextual field, is that it is not humanity, or preordained ethnic hatreds, that are to blame. Rather, one needs to look at what the wrong kind of society can do to humanity, and to ethnic differences. Moral culpability lies first and foremost, for him, with the powerful men who knew how to connect their own current interests to the fears and the socialized, latent, prejudices of the vulnerably positioned peasantry.

Creative connections between different sources

From Keane's powerful evocation of the structured presence of the past within current affairs, we will now, in a long final section, focus on two cases – political conflict in Thailand and the ill-treatment of patients within Stafford Hospital – in which the scope and vision remains that of the wide canvas, involving many actors, relations, and interdependencies within the processes relevant to the outcome-in-focus. But we are now adding the issue of how audiences can combine their knowledge from one source with knowledge from other sources. The emphasis is on making connections between different sources, amalgamating what they each tell us into a richer, more developed, understanding of specific processes.

In the course of the book I hope that it has become very clear just how important the 'outcome to be explained' (the *explanandum*) is to the whole process of grasping which knowledge is *relevant* and which is not. In terms of the four key elements within media frames, this is something that links the 'definition of the situation' – which, among other things, identifies the outcome to be explained – with the second element of 'causation': the actions and processes that do the explaining, that indicate how and why the outcome has come to be as it is. We have seen that these aspects of media frames are indispensable guides to help one home in on the essential claims within a text, and that social theory provides additional tools that can refine this focus, allowing greater conceptual refinement and empirical precision. I now want to make some additional, generic, points about media frames and their relation to social-theory frames as they help to further sharpen the focus. These points are about the *close internal relationships* between the first two aspects of media frames, which we've just indicated, and between these and the third and fourth aspects, namely, moral judgements and remedies, once these are considered from within a social-theoretical frame.

Let's start with moral judgements. Moral judgements made within a media text are closely entwined with how the surface situation is defined and with causal questions of what brought this situation about. This is because moral judgements, by their nature, point towards the process that produced the outcomes that are judged, morally evaluating certain aspects of that process and the actors involved in them. Put another way around, the aspects of situations or outcomes that are thought to be problematic, and therefore to demand a causal explanation as to how they came to be as they are, are typically those that attract moral judgement of one kind or another. It is clearly essential that care is taken to properly characterize the moral judgements that are being made, and to match these assiduously with an investigation of the corresponding networks of relevant relations within the contextual field. And if a current affairs text makes moral judgements about specific aspects of a state of affairs but does not focus on the actors, networks, forces, situated judgements and processes that brought about these outcomes, then there will almost always be something remiss about the text. I say this on the reasonable assumption, already noted, that moral judgements should usually be made not only with an eye on moral principles, but also with an eye on the context in which such principles are applied.[14]

Looking at this from within a social-theory frame, one can see the need to have a defensible grasp of the relevant contextual field before making all but the most fundamental moral judgements. One can say without compunction, for example, that genocide is simply wrong whatever the circumstances, but most moral questions are not as clear cut as this. And in these other cases, in order to subject the practices of particular actors to moral judgement, one needs first to position those actors within the relevant contextual field. Part of this will involve trying to grasp the contours of that field from the perspective of an external observer, but another part of it will involve attempting to understand how the context looked from the perspective of the key actors whose decisions and actions are being morally questioned (their *agents' context analysis* – see Chapter 3, pp. 60–2 and pp. 64–6). In looking at the contextual field through their eyes one would hope to grasp something of their perception of the constraints and possibilities, risks and potential costs and gains afforded by the situation, and of the motivational grounds behind them taking the actions they took. These two points are themselves closely connected as the actor's perception of the risks and potential consequences of alternatives, including those implied by moral critique, will usually have played some role in their following the course of action they decided upon. This needs to be taken into account in casting moral judgement. It might well be that the judgement of the actors-*in-situ* was that pursuing the alternative strategy advocated in the moral assessment of the media frame would have led to unpalatable, unintended, consequences. Without a situated sense of constraints, possibilities and likely consequences, moral judgements can very easily be blindly utopian, and sometimes disastrous in their outcomes.

We've already journeyed right into the heart of the fourth element of the media frame, which directs attention to the 'remedies' advocated by a current affairs account. The strategic question about *what future-oriented remedies actors should pursue in the present,* and how to pursue them, is structurally very similar to the question we have just been discussing with respect to morally evaluating past actions.[15] There, we were discussing the considerations that should have come into the picture *when situated actors, acting in the past, decided on a particular course of action.* The only difference is that now we are explicitly focused on remedies, on fixing things, or improving things, rather than on why someone did something in the past. This considers actors' orientations to the future from a perspective in which this orientation is benchmarked against some conception of a future that would be an improvement on the present. This conception will be more or less well defined, and, in fact, will often be very ill-defined, notwithstanding the moral intensity with which any departure from it is condemned.

Moral judgements should enter into this picture about the future in a similar way in which they entered into the picture about the past. There should be an eye on whether someone's actions are motivated by self-interested or narrowly instrumental values, or are underpinned by more expansive, ethical considerations. In either case, as we've previously noted, in order to genuinely grapple with issues of moral responsibility it is important to not only look at *pure moral principles* (what moral philosophy discusses under the heading of 'deontology'),[16] but also at *the probable consequences* of advocating the pursuit of a particular set of remedies. For exactly the same structural considerations apply with respect to the constraints and possibilities, risks and potential costs afforded by the situation. We've seen that the future is not as open and pliable as we too often fancy it to be.[17] Not only are many avenues already entirely closed off, but the power dynamics, trajectories and action orientations already in play within a contextual field can provide heavy intimations of the consequences that will follow from attempting to mould the future according to an alternative plan. In order to negotiate the best way through the openings that are still possible, and to avoid unintentionally calling down the wrath of the gods in the shape of social forces, it is necessary to have a keen grasp of the relevant contextual field. Again, without this, the consequences can be unintended and, at times, catastrophic.

We will explore these close internal relationships between the four aspects of media frames – their characteristics deepened by social theory – as we look at both of the case studies in this section. How a media text *defines a situation* is always the place to begin, moving out from there to linkages with one or more of the three other elements of causation, moral judgement and proposed remedies. Sometimes it will be one of these three themes that have primarily determined the definition of the situation, and sometimes the definition of the situation will have a different rationale – often, in news and current affairs items, dictated by issues of drama and spectacle – and the connection with the other three elements can be tangential, dispersed and fragmented. In addition, it is noticeable how frequently the presentation of current affairs issues, and the subsequent discussion of these, is dominated by moral judgement unencumbered by any genuine concern with the relationship of such judgements to the other three perspectives on the contextual field.

The precise focus of a current affairs account, and its linkages with other elements, will vary from case to case, which means reflection has to be both disciplined and flexible, creatively adapting general categories to the specifics of the case. Whatever the specifics, however, systematic thought is required, and will always be illuminating. In looking at the two cases, I will draw attention to how close reflection on the relationships between the four different elements of media frames can help audiences to decide on the extent to which they have been offered appropriate and sufficient knowledge by an account. Such awareness provides the grounds on which it is then possible to search for the relevant additional knowledge from complementary sources and genres.

Democracy and conflict in Thailand 2001–10

For the Thai case I will begin by organizing my comments around the striking similarity of the narrative form shared by four news and current affairs accounts of the political conflict leading up to the street protests of May 2010, in which more than 90 people died.[18] In the process I will indicate aspects of the distinctive contributions made by the different genres of current affairs within the four accounts, and how they complement each other. I will also use social theory to reveal the limitations of these accounts, pointing to the precise *status* of the knowledge conveyed by their preoccupations and arguments. In the process I will bring to the fore the close internal relationships between the definition of the situation, moral judgements, implications regarding causation and strategic advocacy regarding remedies. In the texts that I will discuss the most prominent moral theme is that of democracy, which *guides the definition of the situation* in a similar way in every one of the items, directing the analysis to look at certain aspects of the contextual field and not at others.

This common thread is very striking. We shall see that the characterization of the moral theme of democracy is skewed and partial, as the accounts emphasize only one out of four key aspects of democracy, to the detriment of the others. This has a knock-on effect in guiding the analysis of the contextual field to just the domains and networks that are *relevant* to this one aspect of democracy while neglecting or downplaying the others. We shall see that this has clear implications for reflecting on moral and causal responsibility and strategic remedies, as only part of the truly relevant field is in vision.

Finally, I will indicate how audiences could begin to address the limitations of the four current affairs accounts by turning to other sources to complement the knowledge they already have. The other sources in this instance are readily accessible items of academic literature in both empirical and normative domains, which, likewise, can be judiciously sifted and guided by social theory towards the appropriate actors, dispositions, forces, interdependencies and so on within relevant networks of relations. The academic literature on these events and processes, as needs to be the case with any source or genre, is itself subjected to a reading and interpretation that is informed and organized by the guidelines of media and social-theoretical frames. An advantage of approaching academic literature in this way is that straightforward connections are made to the concerns of the public sphere, providing points of mutual engagement. It also serves to demystify academic accounts of the social world, refusing to ring-fence them as a separate domain of 'expert' knowledge, immune to meaningful critique. Instead, they are subject to the same theoretically informed criteria of status and adequacy as other media sources.

The four initial accounts on the Thai case cut across genres and include two accounts that formed part of double page reports in the UK broadsheets, the *Independent* and the *Guardian,* on, respectively, 14 and 15 May 2010; a substantial article in the *London Review of Books* (LRB) by Joshua Kurlantzick, fellow for South-East Asia at the Council on Foreign Relations (Kurlantzick, 2010); and an hour-long BBC2 documentary, *Thailand – Justice Under Fire*, directed by Jonathan Jones and presented by Fergal Keane, broadcast on 7 August 2011. The newspaper reports were written in the midst of the tense street stand-offs and eventual bloodshed of May 2010, the documentary was produced during the year after these events, and the LRB piece was published in the month before they took place. The report in the *Independent* was combined with an informative table of the timeline of events leading up to May 2010; the *LRB* article made close reference to academic studies and the writer is clearly knowledgeable about the history of the events; and while the documentary doesn't eschew the moments of spectacle, it embeds them in exposition, interactional dialogue with academic experts and with a range of differently situated actors relevant to the events in question, including those within powerful organizations at the apex of the state.[19]

Rich as they are in many respects, the definition of the situation provided by all of the accounts is oversimplified in a way that leads them to neglect key dimensions of the relevant contextual field when making moral judgements, discussing causation and suggesting remedies and political strategies to secure those remedies. All of this raises serious questions about the ethical judgement of the pieces, and reinforces the argument for more intellectual engagement with social theory. Keane's piece is interesting in that many of the strengths we met in the Rwandan case are also here, including the sense of eye-level visual and emotional involvement with people at the heart of the events, and the framing of this in a broader historical and political context. However, the virtues of switching between individual experience and the broad sweep that is so effective in the Rwandan case, where the moral judgement is beyond doubt, lead to misapprehension in the Thai case. This is because the moral issues are more complex and because the additional focus on future strategy in relation to those issues demands a more fine-grained grasp of the contextual field and the forces and dynamics that populate it.

Each of the accounts highlights the following elements, in more or less detail: the electoral victory of Thaksin Shinawatra and the *Thai Rak Thai* (Thais Love Thailand) party in 2001; the ensuing success of populist schemes in health care, village credit and other forms of financial support directed by this government towards the rural poor; the success of Thaksin in presiding over the first elected Thai Government in history to see out a full term of office, followed by a stunning increase in its mandate in the 2005 election, gaining 377 out of 500 seats, and raising its number of votes from 11.6 million in 2001 to 19 million in 2005 (FTN – Pasuk and Baker 2009: 237)[20]; the overwhelming concentration of Thaksin's electoral support in the poorer, agricultural, regions of the north-east and the north of Thailand; the subsequent formation of the anti-Thaksin People's Alliance for Democracy (PAD – the 'yellow shirts') in February 2006; the military coup that ousted *Thai Rak Thai* later that year, with strong intimations that this was backed by the monarchy; dubious legal interventions that forced two successor governments (led first by Samak Sundaravej and then by Somchai Wongsawat) loyal to Thaksin from office in 2008 after electoral democracy had ostensibly been restored; the civil disobedience protests by the PAD – including the occupation of Suvarnabhumi airport that left 350,000 travellers stranded – designed to force the resignation of the Somchai government; the military-brokered collation agreement that saw the installation of Old Etonian, Abhisit Vejajiva, as the Prime Minister; and the reaction of the rural poor to all of this, with the revival of the United Front of Democracy against Dictatorship (UDD) in May 2008, and their identification with the wearing of red shirts; and the ensuing violent confrontations on the streets of Bangkok in May 2010.

It is a relatively simple affair to recover a shared master narrative of causal explanation from these accounts, a narrative that is organized in terms of a simple binary antagonism between two sides, one bad and one good. The clearly implied argument of the accounts is that it was one of these sides, the Bangkok elites, which repeatedly drove Thaksin and the rural poor he represented away from the power they had legitimately achieved through the ballot box. The moral and expressive tone of the pieces is that it was patently wrong, because undemocratic, for Thaksin and the subsequent governments allied to him to be ousted from power by the military, the monarchy and others in what is presented as an unflinching and unchanging alliance. The strong, ethically informed, strategic message is that this situation must be reversed immediately; the bad must be ousted by the good.

The definition of the situation is one in which democracy has been defeated by anti-democratic forces, represented most visibly by the yellow shirts, but including the most prominent and powerful institutions of the Thai establishment. This is the outcome that the four pieces set about explaining and judging. The problem, however, with this presentation is that the situation has been defined from the outset in an overly narrow, and therefore misleading, manner. The perspective offered by this master narrative is inadequate because while the moral principle invoked by its definition of the situation is that of democracy, it focuses attention on only one aspect of this – the electoral dimension of democracy, which I will label Democracy 1. It neglects three other defining aspects of democracy widely accepted within the normative literature, and hence it also neglects the correlative networks of *relevant* relationships and sequences of action these further aspects of democracy would draw attention to. The three are: open and accountable government with respect to the rule of law, and responsiveness to public opinion (Democracy 2); issues of civil, political and human rights (Democracy 3); and a democratic, participatory, civil society (Democracy 4).[21] If these other aspects of democracy had been included in the defined field of investigation of the *explanandum*, then it would have made it very difficult for the four pieces to concentrate their dominant moral and emotional tone, and their attendant ethical-strategic advocacy, so exclusively on Thaksin's electoral mandate. The other dimensions of democracy, demonstrably held in contempt by Thaksin, would have had to be considered.

It is possible to explore what the consequences would be of defining the situation more appropriately, which would mean introducing the other three aspects of democracy into the analysis. This can be done by combining these generalized theoretical points with evidence that can be gleaned from a series of additional academic sources covering these other dimensions of Thai politics. A concern with Democracy 2 would highlight the moral and causal significance of Thaksin's involvement in major asset concealment and myriad abuses of position to further his multi-billion baht business interests, and his government's illegitimate interference with institutional actors such as the National Counter Corruption Commission and the Constitutional and Administrative Courts designed by the progressive 1997 Constitution to strengthen democratic accountability. Likewise, such guidance would draw attention to the appalling record on civil and human rights of Thaksin's governments (Democracy 3) and the increasingly autocratic and unresponsive nature of his rule when it came to social movements and active expressions of local, grassroots opinion (Democracy 4). If the pieces had identified these practices, and the four different configurations of socio-structural relationships that provided them with their context, they would have needed to construct a much more complex narrative.

As it is, the neglect of those areas of the contextual field pertaining to these key areas of democracy means that much of the structural background informing resistance to Thaksin and his government is missing. The narratives of the four pieces are consequently informed by an analysis in which prominent actors are largely uprooted from their relevant contexts. Order is imposed on events by means of a de-contextualized analysis that subsumes the many differentiated organizations, groups and individual actors from the four configurations, as well as their varied specific concerns and activities, into a simple binary opposition, summed up in the title of Kurlantzick's article, 'Red v. Yellow'. In reality, it is highly misleading to treat all the forces relevant to the downfall of Thaksin as one collective grouping, the 'Bangkok elites', and to represent all of the forces involved in bringing about the coup as motivated primarily by the wish to deny the rural poor their rightful voice in politics. There is little doubt that this was the motivation of some, but a more adequate understanding would really have to consider the plural sequencing and configuring of events. Academic literature on the anti-Thaksin movement of 2006, for example, suggests that the PAD was in fact a broad coalition of differentiated forces set up in direct response to various anti-democratic actions of Thaksin in his first 5 years in office. The yellow shirts' movement thus combined within itself a variety of more sectional interests, each of them bruised, in a significantly varied range of ways, by Thaksin's governments.[22] The provisional and unstable degree of unity and cohesion consolidated within the yellow shirts' protests against the *Thai Rak Thai* and successor governments thus emerged over a period of time as a response to their policies and behaviour.

The resistance was produced by co-evolving processes in a range of different socio-structural domains related, primarily, to Democracies 2, 3 and 4.[23] The unity was a provisional outcome produced by this plural combination of processes. It was, in turn, reinforced through 'sacred' rituals and celebrations around the King's Diamond Jubilee, which produced a heightened emotional intensity within the political culture.[24] This emergent cultural, ritual, process,[25] in its turn, produced a mood that facilitated subsequent responses from the Monarchy, the Privy Council, the opposition parties, and sections of the military. It should be pointed out that these responses were themselves dubiously justified by their own very selective appeal to democratic principles, often singling out activities in Democracy 2, in highlighting Thaksin's putative corruption with respect to activities of the executive branch of government, and to his interference with the impartial rule of law. Not only was this opportunistically selective, but it also quite brazenly neglected to consider the long-term culpability of many prominent members of many of these groups in similar practices, practices which seriously, and persistently, undermined the impartial functioning of the institutions of democracy. Any genuinely adequate telling of this story would have to move well beyond a simple, exculpatory, reversal of good and bad.

Against this backdrop, one can see clearly the importance of the guidelines we've constructed for dealing with complex narratives – ones that can integrate differentially situated and relationally configured actors into a conception of plural and co-evolving sequences of events. The need for these can be highlighted by the quandary, or *aporia*, encountered by all four current affairs pieces under consideration. For each of the accounts does mention or allude to, at one time or another, negative, anti-democratic, aspects of the Thaksin governments, and this honest acknowledgement threatens to subvert their binary opposition between good and bad. However, and this is a key point, it is conspicuous that none of the pieces finds a satisfactory way of thinking about these anti-democratic practices in the same breath as their master narrative on the putatively homogeneous Bangkok elites and their supposed antagonism to democracy. The master and minor narratives are kept separate rather than brought into dialogue with each other, with propositions in the minor key systematically relegated in each text's hierarchy of significance.

Once discerned, these interdependent intellectual and narrative deficiencies can be seen to run right through the form and surface rhetoric of each of the texts. Let us focus on just one characteristic example taken from *Thailand – Justice Under Fire*. At nearly 8 minutes into the film, against a visual backdrop of farmers working in the rice fields intercut with images of exuberant, flag waving, supporters at a rally for Thaksin in the capital, Fergal Keane's commentary declares that 'here in the rural heartland, a charismatic politician started a social revolution'. After switching to a farmer, Manot Triprawat, speaking side-on to camera – his words translated in simultaneous voice-over – extolling the virtues of life under Thaksin, Keane resumes in the same vein, with visually illustrated remarks on Thaksin's notable biographical accomplishments culminating in an emphasis on the two popular electoral victories that made him 'Thailand's longest serving Prime Minister'. The reporter is then shown on a train journey in the countryside, in and among rural people, metonymically juxtaposed with shots of shanty-style dwellings flashing by along the side of the tracks. His next words mention, only to subordinate, Thaksin's dark side: 'Despite widespread allegations of corruption and of major human rights abuse, he remained hugely popular with the poor'. Not only are Thaksin's anti-democratic, and sometimes abhorrent, practices confined to a subordinate clause within the sentence, the sentence itself is also positioned between the positive traces of what we had just seen and heard and the immediately ensuing return to images of Manot, walking by the fields, continuing his exaltation of Thaksin: 'Every household had a better life, better living. They had money that belonged to them, and which they could spend. The economy in the village improved'. The minor narrative is thus not ignored or entirely effaced, but the *aporia* is evident in its positioning as the subordinate clause, and in the tone and sequencing of the commentary and the visual editing, and also in the sympathetic identity relations set up between Keane and the rural poor within the text. The negative comments on Thaksin and his record thus remain marginalized, awkward and irrelevant supplements to the argument.

A critical reading of these texts on Thailand, all focused on a curtailed notion of democracy, reveals an *aporia* – an inability to resolve a significant quandary – resulting from the failure to create a narrative complex enough to acknowledge the full configuration of forces and processes relevant to the outcome of the dramatic and deadly conflict of May 2010. The consequence is a stark contrast between the certainty of the rhetoric of the texts and the inadequacy of support – morally, conceptually and empirically – for those certainties. By way of contrast, reference to a contextual field truly appropriate to a 'definition of the situation' focused on a more appropriate and satisfactory conception of democracy, makes it clear that the character of Thaksin's and *Thai Rak Thai's* practices in each of the four democratic domains during the years they were in power was directly relevant to the emergence of oppositional forces and to their subsequent sense of the dangers inherent in his return to power. Moral judgements and strategy for the future need to be thought about in this context. These aspects can't be marginalized without distorting the causal explanation of events or the genuine moral choices to be made.

Power and hierarchy within the UK National Health Service: The case of Stafford Hospital

I will end this final, substantive chapter by returning to where we began, with television news. Through an analysis of a BBC news report, 'Scandal Hit Mid Staffs "Faces Being Dissolved"', entered on to the BBC News Website on 28 February 2013,[26] I will continue the theme of combining sources and genres. This time, however, I will do this through indicating the junctions in the narrative where other sources are required in order to address issues that are raised but not adequately addressed within the news bulletin. I will draw on the conceptual device of contextual fields to indicate how audiences can gain from what is available from television news, but can combat its limitations by knowing how to identify the points at which its claims exceed its substance, and how to think about finding and drawing from complementary sources in a conceptually consistent manner.

Between January 2005 and March 2009, an estimated 400–1,200 patients are believed to have died at Stafford Hospital, in the English Midlands, as a consequence of inadequate care. The scandal that ensued was one of the most severe and damaging the National Health Service (NHS) has ever endured. In February 2013, the 31-month public inquiry chaired by Robert Francis QC, set up to look into what happened at Stafford, published its report. The report was widely interpreted as providing a 'damning indictment of NHS attitudes, practices and organisations.'

The BBC news report came in the wake of the publication of the Francis Report, and this was a significant part of a background context in which the BBC bulletin makes links between its definition of the situation, including the outcome it focuses upon, and what it indicates has brought about that outcome (its causes). Notwithstanding this, the link between the actual 'outcome to be explained' and what is supposed to do the explaining turns out to be remarkably weak within the bulletin. The report is driven by a combination of aesthetic and dramatic spectacle and moral judgement, and works more through impressionistic intimation and connotation than through sequential, logical reasoning about the contextual field. It begins with the off-screen voice of the reporter informing us that, 'Stafford Hospital failed badly on care resulting in the unnecessary deaths of hundreds of patients. Now, the trust that runs it is failing financially, heading towards administration, its board likely to be dismissed and services cut back'. The words are spoken against a visual backdrop that begins with an external view of the front of Stafford Hospital, and which then pans away to the interior of the hospital through a series of stylized soft lens images. The images fade into view from different points in the centre of the screen and then drift slowly away towards its bottom left hand side, the movement set against the stable background of a gleaming corridor rendered in the same shades of light green and blue. The images include a glimpse of a human figure – a nurse or a doctor – engaged in activity by a wall of shelves above a desk, medical equipment, documents, filing labels and so on, evoking the many kinds of activity that go on in this or any NHS hospital.

The invocation of the deaths of hundreds of patients at the beginning of the bulletin is entirely appropriate given the public interest that followed the revelations of events at Stafford Hospital. Defining the situation in the way it does, combining the deaths with the issue of financial failure, is a reasonable enough means of engaging the interest of viewers by moving to the main focus of financial failure through the already familiar, and emotionally compelling, theme of the failure of care. The introduction has made it clear, however, that the focus of today's report is finance – '(n)ow, the trust that runs it is failing financially'. Some kind of causal link is intimated, through association, between financial failure and the failure of care but this is not spelt out. There is also intimation that the financial failure is the result of mismanagement as we are told that the board of the trust that runs the hospital is likely to be dismissed. We are left with an indistinct impression of incompetence on two fronts, and with the sense that there is some connection between the two, the most straightforward inference being that financial incompetence played a notable part in the unnecessary patient deaths. The argument of the bulletin continues in this melodramatic, vein. It is built up in successive steps as the piece develops, constructed almost entirely through connotation and rhetorical suggestion. The sequence following the introduction takes up a third of the entire bulletin and, given this, is worth describing in some detail. The scene immediately following the opening shots I've described shows protesters from Cure the NHS who, according to their own website, are 'a small group of relatives, patients and community members who successfully campaigned for a public inquiry into the failings at Mid Staffs Hospital' under the Inquiries Act of 2005. The camera shows members of this group holding placards, grouped together on the pavement outside a meeting of the NHS Commissioning Board in Manchester. They are, the commentary tells us, 'calling for the chief executive to resign'. This off-screen narration is accompanied by a visual close-up of one of the placards showing a photograph of the bespectacled head and suited shoulders of the chief executive, Sir David Nicholson, with the word 'RESIGN' in large bold red upper case letters above the photograph and, below, the phrase "The Man with No Shame" written in black and wrapped in quotation marks. This was a phrase used about him in an orchestrated campaign for his resignation conducted by the English newspaper, the *Daily Mail*. The other type of placard held by protesters showed a gravestone indented with a row of skulls and the letters RIP, with 'Too Many Deaths, No Accountability' written above it and 'RESIGN' in the same font as the first placard.

The piece then segues into a shot inside the meeting of the Commissioning Board, capturing Sir David mid-sentence, addressing his colleagues, appearing comfortable, without his jacket and with hand gestures of measured involvement, declaring '. . . when actually what you need to do is to absorb the criticism, understand it in a deep way, and . . .'. His voice is muted as the reporter's off-screen commentary explains the intercut of images: 'inside, that man, Sir David Nicholson received a vote of confidence. These pictures were provided by the NHS Commissioning Board. What they don't show is the moment when some members of Cure the NHS walked out in protest'. There is a concerted combination of both irony and conspiracy in the narrative here, irony in the decision to select the business-as-usual message for the commentary that the chief executive received a vote of confidence, and in the knowing, sardonic tone in which the reporter delivers this line. There is drama in the focus on the moment when the NHS members walked out, and conspiracy in the attention given to the point that this is 'what the film doesn't show'. The reporter's spoken reference to the source of the pictures, just before he tells us about the walk-out, reinforces and underlines exactly the same information conveyed in a caption on the screen reading, 'Pictures from NHS Commissioning Board'. This belts and braces emphasis is presumably there just in case we are in danger of missing the point. The next shot in the edited sequence takes us back out onto the street to a close-up of the spokesperson for the Cure the NHS protesters, speaking to an out-of-shot reporter, saying they were not asking for the resignation of an innocent party as 'this man failed as the leader of the NHS'.

Almost a minute into a 2-minute bulletin on a story whose ostensible topic is the financial failure of an NHS trust, all of the coverage has been on the much more emotive subject matter of the poor and inadequate care given to patients. All that has been achieved by a few strokes from an impressionistic and ill-defined narrative so far is a vague and free-floating binary opposition[27] between the forces of light and the forces of shade, both positioned around the issue of care, but not embedded in any meaningful way in the networks of relevant relationships. Lined up on one side, there are: Cure the NHS; the patients they represent; Julie Bailey, the spokesperson for Cure the NHS, whose mother died in the hospital in 2007; and wider populist sentiment appalled at the poor care, the suffering, and the perceived irresponsibility and insensitivity that led to it. One could also make a strong argument that the report itself is lined up on this side of the divide. The primary framing of the story focuses squarely on this perspective, and a value perspective takes shape in the respectful and sympathetic way in which relations are set up between the reporter, Dominic Hughes, and the identities and concerns of key actors on one side in the unfolding drama. On the other side of the divide there is the NHS Commissioning Board, and its chief executive, Sir David Nicholson.

These binary oppositions prepare the ground for the issue of finance that does, eventually, follow. Key actors introduced in such a way as to be associated with financial rectitude are added to the first side of the binary divide, to the side of light. The report indicates that misguided choices about financial arrangements made by the Foundation Trust were ultimately responsible for the failures in patient care. In the scene that makes the transition to the financial segment of the bulletin, following the scene of the Cure the NHS spokesperson calling for the resignation of Sir David Nicholson, Dominic Hughes speaks directly to camera. He speaks precisely and authoritatively: 'This is the first time a Foundation Trust Hospital has failed in this way, but in Stafford's case that's significant, because many believe that it was the push for foundation trust status that led to the terrible collapse in the quality of care.' Great emphasis is given to the words 'Foundation Trust', 'significant' and 'quality', as if a revelatory answer to a grand conundrum is being revealed. In reality this is an extreme form of textual 'summary' of elements directly relevant to the bulletin's argument. Summary is no doubt always necessary, and particularly necessary within a 2-minute news bulletin, but critical audiences need to be aware of what it does. For summary typically serves to subsume and efface the details of the relations, processes and social mechanisms it purports to relate. Reflection on the reporter's words from the perspective of a contextual field, using this as a benchmark, would indicate just how much there is to unpack in terms of the various trails of causation within configurations of relevant relations.

The subsequent scenes are very simple in content, straightforwardly providing some headlines of a situation of financial failure, establishing in sound and pictures that Monitor, the relevant financial regulator, has decided that the trust is 'not financially or clinically viable'. The chief executive of Monitor, Dr David Bennett, speaking to an out-of-shot interlocutor to the left of camera, notes that 'at the moment' the trust 'is losing money. It's losing around £15 million a year, so we have to address that, but they have also said that while they are providing safe care today, the current arrangements aren't sustainable in the longer term.' On the face of it, this comment indicates that there is good patient care at Stafford Hospital in 2013, but that it is costing more money than is affordable under current financial arrangements and accounting systems. This clearly suggests a tension between prevailing conceptions of financial rectitude, on the one hand, and adequate patient care, on the other. Although this tension seems to be a key aspect of causation, the moral judgements to be made, and the optimum remedies, it isn't explored at all in the bulletin. Such issues are subordinated to spectacle and melodrama. If the financial issues around the push for NHS trust status are significant regarding the quality of care, and invite the suggestion of moral condemnation, then, one might expect a greater exploration of how this came about. Also, logically, one might expect that the same kind of moral rebuke should be aimed at the current financial forces militating against adequate care. There is a striking absence of any attempt to place action within networks of relevant relations in which one could genuinely understand causation. There is no attempt, for example, to look closely at the external forces, pressures and constraints being internalized by key situated actors, such as Sir David Nicholson and the trust's board members, as they assess the *in situ* alternatives available to them. As it is, the simple, us versus them, melodrama we are provided with – reflecting the dominant popular simplification of news, uprooted from all meaningful context – manages to place Monitor, which has financial rectitude at the apex of its value priorities, and Cure the NHS, which has care at the apex of its value priorities, on the same side. This provides a bogeyman but simplifies the configuration of forces to the point of distortion.

It's worth spelling out explicitly what kind of contextual field the BBC news report does allow us to construct. Starting with identifying the key actors, the institutional actors included in the report are the Commissioning Board, Stafford Hospital, Cure the NHS and Monitor. We have also seen that a number of individuals belonging to these institutional actors have also been identified, with an indication that at least two of these individuals are in positions of authority within these organizations. However, this is virtually all we have, and perhaps all that television news bulletins can be expected to provide. There is no account of the hierarchies, relations and processes that connect the institutional actors to each other, or of the nature of the roles inhabited by particular individuals, with the duties and obligations these roles carry with them. To make even rudimentary sense of the bulletin viewers would need to already know that Sir David Nicholson was chief executive of the West Midlands Strategic Health Authority, the strategic health authority overseeing the Mid Staffordshire NHS Foundation Trust during the period when the poor care and resultant deaths occurred. Without a sense of this basic positioning there cannot be any appreciation of those various forces and pressures to act in particular ways, mentioned above, that the incumbents of relevant positions experience and respond to. All this means that we need to be aware that we have no account at all of social mechanisms. The link between the outcomes to be explained by the bulletin and what is supposed to do the explaining can be seen to be extraordinarily weak.

These points raise serious questions, not about whether news bulletins should take a particular point of view, as this is inevitable, nor about their ability to be objective from within a point of view, as this is indeed possible, but about how much they should claim for a point of view on the basis of so little evidence. They should almost certainly claim less, and should also attach more appropriate levels of uncertainty and confidence to what they do propose or imply. The implicit suggestion of this bulletin, which is really quite complex at the same time as it is left entirely unsubstantiated, seems to be the following. It is that Sir David Nicholson is guilty as charged by Cure the NHS because of a process involving two stages. The first is that, due to his position within the organizational hierarchy of the National Health Service, he would have had a connection of causal, and therefore moral, responsibility with the Mid-Staffordshire Trust. The second is that the pursuit of foundation trust status was bound to lead both to financial failure and to a 'terrible collapse in the quality of care', and that he should have predicted this and, accordingly, should take responsibility for it. This implied argument may ultimately be right or it may be wrong, but in either case the presentation of the news in this form makes it very difficult to formulate any kind of independent critical response to it.

The contextual field in this bulletin is virtually empty, with the focus on the character of individual people rather than on people embedded within organizations that are in turn embedded within networks of relations. The consequence is the same as that identified by Djerf-Pierre and co-authors in their account of the mistreatment of the elderly in Swedish care homes, discussed in Chapter 2. That is, both mistreatment and financial failure are construed as moral scandals rather than policy failures that need to be unravelled. In the Swedish case as in this case the question of the marketization of social and health services remains mainly in the background, while it should be recognized as a key factor in the kinds of pressures experienced by situated actors within such organizations. This does not settle any moral or political argument, but it is indisputably a significant part of the structural context in which individuals are positioned, and in which they have to act. If a government has endorsed and legitimized such a context then they need to be able to defend and justify it, and this means, in turn, that citizen-audiences need to know how its processes work.

Highly relevant additional information about how such processes worked within the NHS were already available in the public sphere at the time of the BBC bulletin. They were most readily accessible in the Francis Report, the result of a public inquiry into the scandal at Stafford Hospital that had lasted nearly 3 years, chaired by Robert Francis QC. A brief, even gestural, acknowledgement of some of the evidence given to this inquiry, and to the conclusions of the report, would have given viewers a more adequate sense of the real, *in situ*, causal mechanisms, policy choices and operational dilemmas. For this report contained a good deal of evidence on the character of the organizational context of the NHS, its relations with Whitehall and various other organizations, and on the perspectives of many of the situated actors within this terrain. The report would certainly have played a significant role as background knowledge for the specialist journalists preparing the BBC bulletin. Whatever the constraints on television news, making it difficult for bulletins to go into much depth on issues, audiences should be made aware that evidence available in the public sphere militates against an overly simplistic account of causality, attribution of responsibility, and strategic solution. Audiences with typified knowledge of contextual fields, and of the ways in which organizational hierarchies work within these, would be in a strong position, if they were so minded, to make meaningful links with such sources. They could do so by challenging more simplistic accounts precisely by bringing to mind the themes the media frames' perspective directs one to. Routinely working with such a perspective would immediately make one conscious of the kind of thing that is happening when a television news bulletin, such as this one, focuses on a particular outcome and makes causal and moral judgements in relation to it. Social theory can then provide the general concepts and protocols to guide more nuanced reflection. This, in turn, would provide the basis for a search for additional sources to complement the surface, rhetorical account of the television bulletin.

Audiences, without the time or inclination to directly consult the Francis Report, could find information in newspaper accounts, such as the *Guardian*'s item, 'Mid Staffs report calls for sweeping changes to improve patient safety', written by Denis Campbell and James Meikle, appearing 3 weeks before the BBC bulletin.[28] The *Guardian* piece, understanding its assignment to be one of conveying the key points of the Francis Report, is much less ambiguous than the BBC account in clearly identifying an undesirable 'outcome' that needs to be explained.[29] This was simply the shockingly poor care provided to patients at Stafford Hospital, resulting in the 400–1,200 deaths between January 2005 and March 2009.

The *Guardian* article identifies a strong primary causal argument in the Francis Report, which is that one key actor, the hospital trust, 'bore most of the responsibility for allowing the "appalling suffering of many patients" to go unchecked between 2005 and 2009':

> In a scathing assessment of the trust's board of directors, Francis accused it of a 'serious failure' of its duties. 'It did not listen sufficiently to its patients and staff or ensure the correction of deficiencies brought to the trust's attention. [It also] failed to tackle an insidious negative culture involving a tolerance of poor standards and a disengagement from management and leadership responsibilities', he said.[30]

In terms of a contextual field the picture painted here focuses on one key actor, the Mid-Staffordshire Hospital Trust, indicates that the trust had 'duties' and responsibilities attached to its position within a network of relations, and that it failed in specific ways. These failings, which would seem to be related to each other and to reinforce each other, were that (i) it did not listen to either patients or staff when they raised issues about deficiencies; (ii) it did not attempt to correct any of the deficiencies; and (iii) it tolerated negative poor standards of care among relevant staff, and, it seems, allowed a disengagement from management and leadership responsibilities, both on their own part and by unspecified others lower down in the organizational hierarchy, many of whom were presumably situated in a variety of roles within Stafford Hospital itself.

The degree of autonomy possessed by the trust in its culture and operations would depend not only on the interdependencies it had with actors further down the hierarchy, but also, of course, with the forces and pressures emanating from the interdependencies it had with actors whose authority it was subordinate to. The *Guardian* account incorporates some of these connections as it notes that Francis doesn't attribute the causal process culminating in poor patient care only to the hospital trust. Rather, according to Francis, the failure of the trust was combined with 'multiple failures by a wide array of organisations and individuals across "the NHS system"', which allowed poor care to persist and meant 'opportunities to intervene were not taken'. More specifically, Francis is said to cite:

> . . . the hospital's A & E [Accident and Emergency] unit's need to treat 98% of patients arriving there within four hours to meet the government's key NHS targets, the trust's attempts to balance its books and its 'seeking foundation trust status . . . at the cost of delivering acceptable standards of care' as contributory factors.[31]

Thus, on the one hand, the *Guardian* account conveys the message that there is a clearly stated *primary* casual argument in the Francis Report, in that it identifies a series of activities clustered around one key actor, the Mid-Staffordshire NHS Trust, that should bear 'most of the responsibility' for the failures around patient care. On the other hand, however, this is combined with the acknowledgement of an additional series of secondary causes, interweaving with the primary set of causes. Included in these secondary causes are sub-actors such as the hospital's A & E unit, which has a subordinate hierarchical position with respect to the trust, although it will have had a degree of operational autonomy and hence independence from the trust. Also included, though, are indications of the presence and force of institutional actors in a superior position within the organizational hierarchy. This is readily apparent in the mention of, and in the negative assessment of, the government's key NHS targets, but is also there, albeit more vaguely, in the references to 'the trust's attempts to balance its books' and its 'seeking foundations trust status . . . at the cost of delivering acceptable standards of care'.

Embedded in networks of relations, duties and reciprocal obligations, the trust would have been more autonomous, more able to be master in its own house, in relation to some of these activities than it was in others. With certain activities, such as the 'trust's attempts to balance its books', there were strong external forces pushing it in this direction, with the threat of sanctions hanging over it in the event of failure to do so. In a different but overlapping way, the trust's project to seek foundation status was also palpably not an entirely internal affair, for the move to foundation hospitals was a nationwide, government-sponsored enterprise promoted by a set of ideological justifications, and encouraged, structurally, by a series of institutional inducements.

These external forces are part of the relevant contextual field in which the flash bulb events inside Stafford Hospital were also strongly influenced by causal forces spatially distant from it. These are forces that would have been internalized by more and less powerful individual actors within the configuration of organizations that together constituted chains of command, influence and causation ultimately affecting the local setting of Stafford Hospital and what went on within it. This is the kind of process Francis is reported as pointing towards when he is quoted as referring to the 'wide array of organisations and individuals across "the NHS system"'.

Ultimately, there is something more than a little arbitrary about the Francis Report concluding that the hospital trust, 'bore most of the responsibility', while also acknowledging that blame also lay with a wide array of actors across the NHS system. For the attribution of primary causal weight is a complex issue, requiring *counter-factual judgements* about what would change if one factor or another were removed or altered in a non-trivial way. And it is at least a plausible hypothesis to suggest that the creeping emphasis on financial criteria to the detriment of other factors was the overriding causal influence, permeating the external structures and interior worlds of actors throughout the NHS. A key counter-factual question here, challenging the conclusions of the Francis Report, would be whether the poor care could have been avoided by more responsible policy-making within the centres of power. Genuinely, rigorously, thinking in this way is a difficult exercise. It would include thinking seriously about the spatial distance of relevant centres of power in Government and Whitehall from the poor care in the hospital wards. One would want to ask whether the incumbents of such institutions might have a deficit of intellectual and moral imagination regarding the consequences of their actions. This is a sensible question because they are indeed very likely to lack much of the knowledge and moral empathy possessed by actors working more locally. Such a deficit will, in large part, be simply because significant spatial distances between decisions and their consequences make it harder for decision-makers to genuinely understand the contextual field in which their decisions will unfold. In turn, this makes it more difficult for them to grasp the moral implications of what they are doing.[32] The counter-factual test – very difficult to construct, but essential to attempt – would involve ascertaining if negative standards of care within the hospital would ever have occurred if the financial pressures exerted by the Government and Whitehall on the West Midlands Strategic Health Authority had been less intense, or had been managed with more skill and judgement.

This counter-factual test about causation would require an analysis of the relevant networks of relations keenly focused on the conditions required for this alternate outcome (adequate care). The nature of the task would require the kind of conceptual and evidential detail suggested by box 2a) in Figure 4.3, and so is not something we can pursue in any depth here. However, just a few excerpts taken from the *evidence* contained within the Francis Report, once combined with our social-theory perspective, quickly unsettle and challenge too easy an acceptance of its own causal thesis.

The report contains a good deal about the external pressures exerted by Central Government on chief executives of NHS trusts, with the centre admonishing the chief executives to balance their books. The report quotes from a letter written by Sir Nigel Crisp, then Chief Executive of the NHS as well as Permanent Secretary, which was sent to all NHS trust chief executives but was 'addressed principally to those whose organisations had been in deficit in 2004/5. He cracked the whip in no uncertain terms . . .', pointing out that:

poor financial performance in a few organisations can erode public confidence in the management of the NHS as a whole . . .

If planned recovery is not delivered, this represents a failure by their Boards to meet their duties . . .

. . . An aggressive pursuit of efficiencies, in the way we deliver our business and maximising productivity from the resources we consume, are essential parts of the contract we have with Ministers and the public we serve.[33]

These generalizing, anonymous and distant, pressures from Whitehall to cut deficits through an 'aggressive pursuit of efficiencies', conveyed together with a conviction that there was a 'well-evidenced' case that it was possible to deliver 'better care for patients while reducing costs',[34] are a significant part of the contextual field within which the poor care of patients at Stafford took place. The NHS's West Midlands Strategic Health Authority (SHA), which was a key mediating institution further down the social hierarchy, was acutely aware of this context, as were other mediating actors. They were also aware that the Mid Staffordshire Trust had a deficit of £509,000 in 2003/4 and that this had grown to £2,158,000 in 2004/5. Sir David Nicholson's role as chief executive of the West Midlands SHA needs to be placed at the intersection between these forces and pre-existing duties, responsibilities and orientations. He described the atmosphere at the time to the Francis Inquiry as 'fevered', and while denying that the proposed measures were about compromising clinical services, he admitted that '[T]he criticism of our stewardship of the financial affairs of the NHS was under great scrutiny and great comment, and there is no doubt that the response of NHS management to all of that was to redouble their efforts to balance their financial position.'[35] Mr Peter Bell, a non-executive director at the trust, noted close parallels between the pressures on the trust, and the warnings issued to them, with the 'departure of the board of a nearby trust over financial issues'[36]:

> This is particularly pertinent; it sets the scene that as a board it was unacceptable not to balance the books. If we, as Non-Executive Directors, were overlooking an organisation where things were going wrong financially, we would probably have been expected to go if we couldn't demonstrate that we were in control.[37]

One can see very clearly here the power of external pressures on the board of the trust, pressures that would have been experienced as *independent causal forces* in the sense that the actors sitting on the board – the actors-in-focus – had no power over them.[38]

Evidence provided to the Inquiry by both Karen Morrey, director of operations at Mid Staffordshire from 2006 until 2009, and Toni Brisby, non-executive chair of the trust, indicated concerted pressure from the West Midlands SHA for the trust to 'break-even and by implication to cut staff'.[39] It is clear that both women believe that 'hitting the financial target' was at the apex of the ordering of concerns or hierarchy of purposes[40] conveyed to the trust by key actors further up the organizational hierarchy, and that little more than lip service was paid to safeguarding the standards of clinical practice and care in the process of achieving those cuts.[41] Whitehall and the SHA were careful to say that balancing the books did not have to mean staff cuts, as it could entail cuts elsewhere and 'efficiency gains'. However, it's difficult to avoid the conclusion that, in the context pertaining at the time, the external financial pressures conveyed from Whitehall through the West Midlands SHA and the Mid Staffordshire Trust were encouraging the creation of a precarious situation. The tension between financial pressures and obligatory duties seems to have expressly incited the performance of a precarious balancing act in which one slip one way or the other would have led to charges of incompetence or worse. The question arises as to whether health managers and administrators at various levels, and doctors, nurses and patients, should ever be positioned within structural complexes requiring judgements and calculations with such fine margins for error. Should such risks ever be taken? And, also, should those involved in the implementation of such unstable regimes be exposed to the intense demands and acute stress that are their inevitable accompaniment. Faced with this degree of structural strain, there is only so much that can be done with even the tightest system of regulatory control. The Mid-Staffordshire Trust was expected to make cost reductions of 8 per cent in 2006–7, which was 'the highest level of savings planned for any trust in the West Midlands, where the average was 5%'.[42] The finance director and deputy CEO of the trust at the time, John Newsham, noted that the staff establishment was in reality to be reduced by 370 posts.

Much is gained from situating other aspects of the Francis Report within the networks and power relations of the broader contextual field. For example, Francis takes members of the trust to task for failing to make clear statements about the risks entailed by proposed staff reductions. Jan Harry, the director of nursing up to July 2006 is particularly criticized, both in the Francis Report and in subsequent fitness-to-practise hearings,[43] for not raising the issue of risk assessments. One would indeed want to look closely at the absence of response at this level, and at other failings at hospital level reported by the *Guardian* article as having been listed by Francis in a letter to the health secretary, Jeremy Hunt, accompanying his report. These were such things as: 'Too great a degree of tolerance of poor standards and of risk to patients', and 'an institutional culture which ascribed more weight to positive information about the service than to information capable of implying cause for concern'. The situations these failings describe are clearly unsatisfactory, and imply the need for profound reflection on causal and moral responsibility at all levels. But it ultimately seems unjust to treat such moments of role inadequacy as discrete moments of personal failure, as if they are somehow unaffected by the powerful financial forces and pressures that have left roles without the resources they require. Rather, it would be much more appropriate to acknowledge that these forces may well have exposed the people who inhabit the roles to unconscionable demands. Reality is distorted when each separate site is treated too atomistically, where each one site within the system is insufficiently connected to relevant others, is treated as overly free-floating and autonomous, with the responsibility for too much of what goes on in each setting laid at the feet of the actors who are most immediately involved.

A further contributory causal factor to include in this mix involves the drive to large-scale reorganization that affected the efficient functioning of the NHS at every level during this period. Macro decisions within organizations such as the NHS, where the decisions of a powerfully positioned few filter out to many different middle-level sites and micro sites, can upset equilibriums and drastically reduce capacity at the local level.[44] A *Guardian* article reports Sir David Nicholson as saying that at the time of the Mid-Staffs scandal he was responsible for delivering a large-scale change within the NHS. This involved 'delivering three SHAs into one [and] for moving 70 primary care trusts into about 40'.[45] Change on this scale almost inevitably disrupts positive, well-functioning social systems, which derive much of their effectiveness from habituated, organically embedded, skills and capacities. It disrupts such systems by uprooting material, technological and informational infrastructures, and through disrupting embedded human practices and the routine skills, norms, knowledge and interactions that underpin these. For these reasons, there is something careless, desultory and morally questionable about the way in which contemporary culture has embraced constant change as a good in itself.

Conclusion

In this final section we have come a long way from the crude simplicities of the BBC news bulletin. We've done this by positioning the definition of the situation, and the implicit argument contained within it, in the midst of its relevant contextual field. This theoretical framing facilitated the further move in which we identified those places where there were gaps, with no coverage at all, or where we were given insufficient evidence. It also allowed us to reflect upon relevant issues of hierarchy, power, resources, and the internalization of external injunctions alongside other conceptions of duties and responsibilities. All this, in turn, encouraged recourse to further sources and genres as a means of complementing our knowledge, of bringing it closer to the levels of adequacy required to genuinely address the issues at hand and to assess the claims being made about them. A similar movement through stages was at work in the Thai case. Here, the resort to additional sources and genres was guided by an initial questioning of the definition of the situation and the normative framing of claims made by the various current affairs reports. The re-structuring of the 'problem-to-be-explained' in terms of a broader conception of democracy brought into view a more adequate contextual landscape, and this, in turn, allowed us to identify a broader array of relevant causal features. Both cases built incrementally upon the skills, tools and perspectives introduced in the interpretation of accounts of German manufacturing success and the Rwandan genocide, and in the case studies of Chapter 4. All of these earlier cases, in their different ways and across a range of historical and geographical scales, were focused around the knowledge to be acquired from single texts.

Conclusion

Brought into dialogue with news and current affairs, social theory has the potential to greatly improve the quality of public understanding of social and political issues. The opening chapters of *Why Current Affairs Needs Social Theory* indicated the deracinated, uprooted, character of television news and routine newspaper reports, revealing the absence of the contextualization that would facilitate genuine understanding. This was combined with a brief discussion of the audience reception of such reports. Through reference to academic studies of audience response to news and current affairs accounts on different issues, from the United States, the United Kingdom and Scandinavia, a picture emerged of audiences whose grasp of events tended to mirror key aspects of the ways in which news had been presented to them.

The absence of an illuminating provision of social context in the reports themselves – one that embedded events within their relevant socio-structural context – was thus reflected in a lack of appreciation of the significance of context on the part of audiences. It was seen that audiences have a tendency to think about events and processes in naïve, overly free-floating, individualistic, ways. It was argued that this inadequacy, and the accompanying vulnerability to, the rhetoric of news and current affairs, needs to be countered by a substantial change in the character of audience reception. That is, there is a need for audiences to become more keenly aware of how different forms and contents of news affects and influences them, and to cultivate a set of intellectual resources allowing them to interpret what they receive in a more critical manner. These are intellectual resources creating the capacity to see how much a current affairs account has provided of the context required to genuinely understand a particular story. Is it possible, for example, on the basis of what has been provided, to think adequately about causation, or about strategic approaches to improving the situation reported on? Have allusions to such aspects been included in the report's 'definition of the situation'? How adequately have these aspects then been treated? Has enough of context been provided to merit the moral position taken by the news account?

The book has aimed to provide audiences with the intellectual tools and resources required to develop critical capacities to the point they routinely incorporate such questions into their reception of news and current affairs. Chapter 2 saw the introduction of the key social-theoretical idea of a contextual field, whose purpose is to facilitate the ability of readers and viewers to situate the spectacle or drama of current affairs events within relevant networks of social relations. The *objective elements* of the contextual field were introduced here, and it was suggested these could be used to map out the historical and geographical context provided by any news or current affairs story, providing a provisional set of orienting co-ordinates from which much else could follow. The case study of Sandy, a single mother of two young children searching for somewhere to live in a contemporary American city, was drawn on to indicate what these objective circumstances looked like from the perspective of someone caught up in their web. It was shown that the objective matrix of constraints and limited opportunities facing Sandy (her *strategic context*), or any situated social actor, can also be looked at from a researcher's point of view, and that this often allows the exploration of a broader set of forces creating and sustaining the social forces bearing down on an individual, limiting their own power and possibilities. Audiences were encouraged to take the perspectives of such objectively situated actors, and to explore their actions from this standpoint, but also to explore the objective circumstances affecting situated actors from an external observer's perspective. Attention was also drawn to the need for audiences to develop an awareness of how much and how little a current affairs account has told them about such situations, and about the matrices of forces that bear on them.

The objective characteristics of contextual fields were complemented, in Chapter 3, by the introduction of the *subjective elements* populating these fields. The narration and analysis of a single episode, 'State Visit', from the Danish political drama, *Borgen*, was used to demonstrate how both sets of elements are interwoven within the events and processes of social life, and that a mapping of both sets of elements is required in order to grasp the stories emerging from them. The use of *Borgen* allowed us to see that audiences already deploy procedures of mapping in the way they interpret political drama, and that they intuitively deploy sophisticated conceptual tools in doing so. It was suggested this should make us optimistic and ambitious about the possibility of such skills being transposed to the analysis of news and current affairs. The sophistication already in place provides a solid base on which to encourage audiences to become more explicitly aware of the skills they possess, and to further refine both their background concepts and the ways in which they routinely apply them to the particulars of specific accounts.

Chapters 4 and 5 saw the intellectual resources provided by social theory applied, step by step, to a range of news and current affairs items from across the world, and from different genres. These case studies illustrated key aspects of putting social theory to use in the interpretation of current affairs texts. Particular attention was paid to the ability of audiences to identify the *status* of knowledge provided by a current affairs item; the patchwork nature of the kinds of knowledge provided within a single piece; the connections that can be made between different pieces, including from a range of genres; and to how audiences can assess the *adequacy* of the knowledge they are provided with in a current affairs item in relation to the claims that the item makes for that knowledge, or in relation to the knowledge required by audiences for their various purposes.

An aspect emphasized in these case studies was the significant critical purchase to be gained from focusing on individual concepts. The general, transposable, concept of 'interdependence' was used as an illustration of this in Chapter 4, with the emphasis placed on the relation between this abstract concept and the specific shape it takes in particular circumstances. The abstract concept can prompt and guide readers to think in terms of interdependent relationships, and as such can direct them to look for both objective and subjective manifestations of this as they attempt to map out the specifics of a particular current affairs story. In being guided to the relevant objective and subjective dimensions of interdependency within an account, theoretically informed audiences will also naturally bring other germane concepts into the picture. It is a small, and easy, step from here to taking a close interest in the 'fit' between these concepts and the empirical evidence made available by the current affairs account in focus. This concern with the relation between general concepts, social processes in particular times and places, and relevant empirical evidence, provides a firm, routine basis for systematic rigour about the quality of the claims made within current affairs pieces. These are ways of ascertaining the degree to which current affairs pieces embed the events they cover in the 'networks of relevant relations' within which they can become genuinely understandable.

This conceptual focus is consolidated, in turn, by the devices introduced to facilitate comparison between stories with respect to the geographical and historical scales they are pitched at, the kind of focus they entail, and the level of corresponding detail they provide. I refer here to the idea of 'floating' and 'contextualized' accounts, to the distinction between accounts that focus on just one causal factor embedded within a network of relations and those that focus on a plurality of such factors, and to the differentiation between accounts that get 'inside the heads' of actors and those that don't. The account of the *Borgen* episode in Chapter 3 serves as an invaluable benchmark, or point of reference, in all these respects, given its high degree of contextualization, the plural character of the causal forces involved, and the intricate combination of objective and subjective factors implicated in the unfolding of events. One only needs to think of the stark contrast between the account of the *Borgen* episode and the analysis of the *Independent*'s sparse report on Netanyahu and settler homes in Chapter 4 to grasp the critical value of these stratagems for comparison. The contrasts between the varying accounts addressing the poor treatment of patients in the UK National Health Service in Chapter 5 provide similar lessons. All of these theoretical and methodological devices serve to heighten awareness as to the status and adequacy of the knowledge provided by any particular account.

The examples presented in Chapters 4 and 5, however, only begin to scratch the surface of the variety of uses and insights to be gained from a heightened awareness of social theory focused around the notion of contextual fields. Each new case study will reveal fresh insights and will provide audiences with new angles of seeing and interpreting. Also, as mentioned at the outset, the aspects of social theory that I've drawn on here are not the only ones that can be drawn on. This poses a challenge to other traditions of social theory. It can only be to the good if theorists working within these other traditions can also find ways of directly engaging with the language and the concerns of news and current affairs, providing insights that can help audiences to make greater sense of social events and processes. If these can be articulated with the insights from the traditions in this book, thus enriching the stocks of knowledge available to audiences in a readily coherent manner, then that would be doubly positive. If we find there are tensions between theoretical approaches as they engage directly with current affairs in this way, then that, too, can be fruitful, deepening our sense of the challenges that exist and further resisting a retreat back into overly simple readings of overly simple texts.

Why Current Affairs Needs Social Theory has self-consciously directed its arguments primarily towards audiences, to developing the intellectual resources and tools through which audiences can alter the routine ways in which they approach current affairs. At heart it is boldly idealistic. It pictures a drawn-out process in which audiences begin to apply the theoretical guidelines and tools when they listen to the radio, read the newspaper in hard copy or online, watch the television news or a current affairs documentary and, mixing genres further, when they go to the cinema, read a novel or look at a Pulitzer Prize-winning photograph. At first, they may apply this knowledge, and these sensibilities, intermittently, and progress will be slow. But before too long, the ways of seeing will start to seem second nature, becoming embodied and natural (in what we have called their *habitus*). As this happens, the pace of progress should quicken, with the application less occasional, more customary, simply becoming part of the culture of how things are done around here.

Audiences are in many ways the easiest targets. Each individual reader or viewer has a good deal of autonomy to take on the challenge of developing their capacity to interpret current affairs texts at a qualitatively higher level. One should remember, also, that individual members of audiences are also members of larger institutions of many kinds, and will take their sensibilities and their ways of seeing into those institutions. Some of these individuals within institutions will be what Nicos Mouzelis has called mega-actors, in that, because of the social power and influence given to them by their position within an institution, and within the broader contextual field, their example and their actions will have effects on far more people, and often in many more spatial sites, than the actions of an individual with little social power. In a cultural contest between different ways of seeing, the battle for the hearts and minds of audiences can be truly consequential.

Journalists have been mentioned from time to time through the book, partly because journalists are also members of audiences, but also partly because one naturally shouldn't ignore their key institutional role as mediators between events and processes in-the-world and events and processes as they appear in-the-news. They are not an easy target for a book like this, because there are all kinds of institutional pressures and constraints pushing them to tell stories in certain kinds of ways, and which would discourage their telling them in ways more in tune with the message of this book. Nevertheless, it must be a hope that some of the lessons of social theory could rub off on some journalists some of the time, and that it is therefore not only the audience reception of current affairs that will develop, but also the ways in which current affairs are presented. For the positioning of journalists within society means that they certainly, often, have the capacity to be mega-actors.

Finally, to extend the sense of the work that the current argument has left still to be done, but also to indicate that it has provided the necessary groundwork for such work, I want to introduce a further sense of *objectivity* to the three spelt out in Chapter 2 (see pages 30–1). This, fourth, sense of objectivity is, in some ways curiously, the one most usually discussed in public discussion of news and current affairs, even though it is probably the most difficult to consider seriously, and even though logically it should depend on a thoughtful engagement with the first three. This, fourth sense of objectivity, is the idea of objectivity as fairness achieved through the absence of bias, where an absence of bias is understood as a somehow 'neutral' view of what is going on in the world. Such a position cannot logically be underpinned by the untenable, impossible, idea of 'a view from nowhere': a view that somehow transcends the narrowing of all situated perspectives, all value-commitments, and somehow tells it like it is. This seems to be understood, at least intuitively, as most typically the quest for neutrality is pursued by the attempt to let both sides of an argument have their say, or, where there are more than two sides, to let several voices be heard. So far, so good. But then we are left with the very real, pragmatic, question of how current affairs forums, or cultures as a whole, are to judge between accounts told from different perspectives, and so achieve a certain level of objectivity in the sum of what is presented.

The arguments in this book can't solve such a problem by themselves, but they do provide the grounds to begin thinking about this question in a more adequate way. We have insisted that all current affairs accounts are told from a certain situated perspective, and that values will inevitably enter into such a perspective, consciously or pre-consciously. We have also insisted, however, that we can judge the rigour and adequacy of each of these stories on the grounds of the three kinds of objectivity outlined in Chapter 2 (ontological, methodological and epistemological), and which have been developed in more prosaic language throughout the book. That is, we have learnt to hold statements about the world to account in terms of (i) how they have *conceptualized* the objective and subjective aspects of the world they are making claims about; (ii) the extent to which they have gathered *evidence* about those conceptualized aspects they have included in their claims; and (iii) whether the knowledge claims included in the statements about the world drawn from stages (i) and (ii) are adequate or inadequate – or *adequate enough* when judged by reasonable standards – including the 'fit' between concepts and evidence claims.

Stories, or accounts, told from different perspectives on the same set of events must consequently first be judged on whether their own claims to objectivity stand up to scrutiny. This is to impose strict, but surely reasonable, criteria of adequacy on any account told from any value perspective. Accounts that don't meet these standards should naturally be seen as suspect in terms of their contribution to 'balance'. The concern to give voice to a variety of perspectives should always be tied, as far as possible, to a concern with their objectivity in terms of the three basic criteria we have discussed. That is, it can't be a positive thing to want to give oxygen to accounts of the world and its people that can be shown to misrepresent those worlds. One should, rather, try to include a range of perspectives, but hold them to high standards of objectivity. Any conception of 'balance' – of allowing all relevant voices to be heard – needs to be built upon these foundations. It should go without saying, by now, that each one of the stories told by these voices will need to be considered in terms of their networks of relevant relations – their contextual field – if they are to truly further comprehension and understanding. We have repeatedly seen that providing such context presents all kinds of challenges to both audiences and producers of current affairs.

Audiences and media outlets shouldn't stop here, however. They should ultimately take the further step of using the apparatus of social theory and contextual fields to begin a genuine dialogue *between* adequate-enough accounts from different perspectives. This is particularly so when such accounts involve some kind of head-on clash. It is useful to employ here the famous method of dialectics, central to the work of the great German thinkers Friedrich Hegel and Karl Marx and long incorporated into the more thoughtful realms of popular culture. In the terms of dialectics, the account offered from one current affairs point of view, replete with views of causation, moral judgements and suggestions for future strategy, can be thought of as offering an initial *thesis*. Another current affairs account on the same topic from a conflicting point of view, containing a different set of moral judgements and a different set of proposed remedies, can be thought of as the *antithesis*. Serious dialogue and debate between the two accounts would naturally keep looking at how adequate these two accounts are when looked at in terms of the first three forms of objectivity. For it is important that the proponents of each recognize the extent to which the other's account is objective, and continue to be aware of this. This should include an evaluation of what each account says about the situated experiences of the people at the heart of the stories, and of how they convey those subjective experiences as intertwined with a picture of their objective conditions of existence. Objectivity should also mean interpreting both sets of accounts in such a way that neither is distorted nor impoverished.

If both accounts could be seen as adequate enough on these grounds, then it should be a requirement of responsible dialogue to search for points of agreement or *synthesis* between the two accounts. If these cannot be found, then the points of continued disagreement and contestation would be likely to have become clear in the process of attempting agreement. In such cases, one would then need to carefully explore the normative or other as yet unexplored underpinnings of the continued clash of views. One wonders, for example, what a dialogue between accounts provided by a variety of different groups within Israel and Palestine would look like if held to these disciplined standards.

This briefly sketched idea clearly needs a great deal of further unpacking, and even to mention it takes us beyond the specific arguments of this book. I have mentioned it, nevertheless, because it is suggestive of the long view, of the kind of further progress that could be made once the first steps, of the kind that *are* dwelt on in the book, have been taken and the accompanying skills consolidated. It is suggestive of the fertile possibilities that are opened up by taking our readings and viewings of news and current affairs as seriously as they should be taken.

Notes

Preface

1 Alain de Botton, *The News: A User's Manual*. London: Hamish Hamilton, 2014, pp. 99–100.

2 George Elliot, cited in de Botton, *The News*, p. 86.

3 For rewarding social-theoretical reflections on the things that people care about, and how the social sciences, to their detriment, have neglected these, see Andrew Sayer, *Why Things Matter to People: Social Science, Values and Ethical Life*. Cambridge: Cambridge University Press, 2011.

4 An argument that audiences not only might understand more, but also would be more interested, more engaged, if current affairs were to be conceived in a contextualized manner, receives support from recent empirical research. Work undertaken by Martin Scott, a Lecturer in Media and International Development at the University of East Anglia, found that audiences developed greater involvement and emotional identification with 'distant others' than was found in relation to news bulletins when they were exposed to longer documentaries and other non-news programming which embedded their subjects in socio-structural situations of greater depth and complexity. See Martin Scott, 'The Mediation of Distant Suffering: An Empirical Contribution beyond Television News Texts', *Media, Culture and Society* 36(1), January 2014, 3–19. Scott's research draws on innovative conceptual work on 'mediated encounters'. Prominent among these are Luc Boltanski, *Distant Suffering: Morality, Media and Politics*. Cambridge: Cambridge University Press, 1999; and Lilie Chouliaraki, *The Spectatorship of Suffering*. London: Sage, 2006. This work focuses more on issues around engagement, and normative questions related to this, than on any sustained in-depth exploration of the character of the socio-structural fields in which the subjects of media texts are embedded. It is not difficult, however, to envisage a fruitful synthesis of these approaches with the one offered here.

5 Rob Stones (ed.), *Key Sociological Thinkers*, 2nd edn. London: Palgrave Macmillan, 2008. An expanded third edition will be published in 2015.

Chapter 1

1 For accounts of the 'hermeneutic' tradition in social theory see Anthony Giddens, *New Rules of Sociological Method: A Positive Critique of*

Interpretative Sociologies. London: Hutchinson, 1976; and William Outhwaite, *Understanding Social Life: The Method Called Verstehen*, 2nd edn. Lewes: Jean Stroud, 1986.

2 On the pitfalls of leaving out of the picture what people care about, see Andrew Sayer, *Why Things Matter to People*.

3 See Rob Stones, *Structuration Theory*. London: Palgrave Macmillan, 2005, pp. 3–5.

4 Also see Postman's later book, co-authored with Steve Powers, *How to Watch TV News*, rev. edn. London: Penguin Books, 2007.

5 Neil Postman, *Amusing Ourselves to Death: Public Discourse in the Age of Showbusiness*. London: Methuen, 1987 (first published 1985).

6 Ibid., pp. 149–52.

7 Ibid., p. 152.

8 Ibid.

9 G. Philo and M. Berry, *More Bad News from Israel*. London: Pluto Press, 2011, p. 187.

10 Ibid., p. 394.

11 Ibid.; also see pp. 315–18.

12 Shanto Iyengar, *Is Anyone Responsible? How Television Frames Political Issues*. Chicago: Chicago University Press, 1991. Pages 17–25 provide details of Iyengar's methodology.

13 Ibid., pp. 46–67.

14 Ibid., pp. 53–4; and Gadi Wolfsfeld, *Making Sense of Media and Politics: Five Principles in Political Communication*. New York: Routledge, 2011, p. 102.

15 See Chapter 3, 'The Phenomenological Input', of John Heritage's *Garfinkel and Ethnomethodology*. Cambridge, MA: Polity Press, 1984, pp. 37–74; and also see Peter Berger and Thomas Luckmann's, *The Social Construction of Reality: A Treatise in the Sociology of Knowledge*. London: Penguin Books, 1967[1966], pp. 45–8, 53–4; and John Heritage, 'Harold Garfinkel', in Rob Stones (ed.), *Key Sociological Thinkers*, 2nd edn. London: Palgrave Macmillan, 2008, pp. 209–23.

16 See Pierre Bourdieu, *Distinction: A Social Critique of the Judgement of Taste*. London: Routledge, 1984/79.

17 John Street, *Mass Media, Politics and Democracy*. London: Palgrave Macmillan, 2001, p. 30.

18 Ibid., p. 37, original emphasis.

19 Robert M. Entman, 'Framing: Towards Clarification of a Fractured Paradigm', *Journal of Communication* 43(4), 1993, 51–8. See also, John Street, *Mass Media, Politics and Democracy*, p. 37; and Jim Kuypers, 'Framing Analysis from a Rhetorical Perspective', in P. D'Angelo and J. Kuypers (eds), *Doing News Framing Analysis: Empirical and Theoretical Perspectives*. London: Routledge, 2010, p. 301.

20 Kuypers, ibid., p. 301; also see Street, ibid., p. 37; and Robert M. Entman, 'Reporting Environmental Policy Debate: The Real Media Biases', *Harvard International Journal of Press/Politics* 1, 1996, 77–8.

21 In some parts of the world of social theory there has been a move away from any concern with judgements about the adequacy of knowledge. This is in large part due to an ever-increasing recognition of the complex and entangled nature of social life, and hence of the obstacles involved in accurately representing aspects of it in authoritative statements. I regard this retreat as unfortunate, for notwithstanding the many difficulties of making judgements about the adequacy of knowledge, the ability to take on these difficulties with rigour and sophistication is one of the greatest strengths of social theory. This ability is at the root of the most important contributions that social theory can make to public life.

22 Thought about what *exists in* the social world falls into the category of ontology and the ontic in philosophy and social theory, whereas thinking about questions of *knowledge claims* about what exists falls into the category of epistemology and methodology.

23 Pierre Bourdieu, *On Television and Journalism*. London: Pluto Press, 1998 [1996], p. 2.

24 Bourdieu 1998[1996], pp. 6–7.

25 Bourdieu 1998[1996], pp. 6–7; also see David Morley, 'Finding Out about the World from Television News: Some Problems', in J. Gripsrud (ed.), *Television and Common Knowledge*. London: Routledge, 1999.

Chapter 2

1 I have in mind here the ideas developed by the critical realist philosopher Roy Bhaskar, around the term 'existential intransitivity', which denotes the objective reality of an entity, relation or state of affairs at a particular point in time. Roy Bhaskar, *The Possibility of Naturalism: A Philosophical Critique of the Contemporary Human Sciences*. Brighton: Harvester Wheatsheaf, 1979, p. 60; also see Andrew Sayer, *Realism and Social Science*. London: Sage, 2000, pp. 10–11.

2 See Alain de Botton, *The News: A User's Manual*, pp. 99–101, for the link between this supposed neutrality and the 'stifling boredom' produced by too many news accounts. There are, by now, many traditions in social theory, from the theoretical writings of the classical German sociologist, Max Weber – who believed it was inevitable that observers bring their values to the selection and interpretation of social phenomena (he called this *value-relevance*. See Max Weber, 'Science as a Vocation', in P. Lassman and I. Velody with H. Martins (eds), *Max Weber's 'Science as a Vocation'*. London: Unwin Hyman, 1989/19, p. 22.) – to feminist standpoint theory, and various strands of postmodernism that have persuasively challenged the idea of objectivity as a view that somehow manages to divest itself of a situated, value perspective. The challenge is, rather, how to be objective from within a perspective, and then to ensure that objective accounts from disparate perspectives receive fair exposure. We shall see below that Djerf-Pierre and colleagues are, in effect, saying that the anti-marketization perspective on care homes for the elderly didn't receive fair and justifiable exposure in the Swedish press. Accepting these points does not place in jeopardy the ontological, methodological or epistemological notions of objectivity set out in **Box 1**, pp. 30–1.

3 See pages 5–6 in Chapter 1.

4 See Erving Goffman, *Interaction Ritual: Essays on Face-to-Face Behavior*. New York: Anchor, 1967; and Erving Goffman, *Relations in Public: Microstudies of the Public Order*. New York: Basic Books, 1971. Also see Philip Manning, *Erving Goffman and Modern Sociology*. Cambridge, MA: Polity Press, 1992; and Robin Williams, 'Erving Goffman', in Stones (ed.), *Key Sociological Thinkers*.

5 This is a paraphrase of the famous quotation from Karl Marx, who wrote 'Men make their own history, but they do not do so under self-selected circumstances, but under circumstances already existing, given and transmitted from the past', 'Eighteenth Brumaire of Louis Bonaparte', in David McLellan (ed.), *The Thought of Karl Marx: An Introduction*. London: Macmillan, 1971, p. 61. Also see Karl Marx and Friedrich Engels, *Marx and Engels Selected Works*, vol. 1. Moscow, 1962, p. 247. See also, Bob Jessop, 'Karl Marx', in Stones (ed.), *Key Sociological Thinkers*.

6 See Barbara Adam and Chris Groves, *Future Matters: Action, Knowledge, Ethics*. Leiden: Brill Books, 2007; and Barbara Adam, 'Future Matters: Challenges for Social Theory and Social Inquiry', *Cultura e Comunicaizione* 1: 47–55, online: www.pic-ais.it/upload/rte/Rivista_online_PicAis_aprile2010_ N1.pdf.

7 C. Wright Mills, *The Sociological Imagination (Fortieth Anniversary Edition)*. Oxford: Oxford University Press, 2000 (original publication 1959, Oxford University Press).

8 Ibid., ch. 1, 'The Promise', pp. 3–24.

9 On Filipina migration to Hong Kong, see Chapter 6, 'Domestic Labour Migration', in Karen O'Reilly, *International Migration and Social Theory*. London: Palgrave Macmillan, 2012.

10 Iris Marion Young, *Responsibility for Justice*. Oxford: Oxford University Press, 2011.

11 On the implications of taking the viewpoint of situated actors see Dorothy Smith, *The Everyday World as Problematic: A Feminist Sociology*. Boston: Northeastern University Press, 1987; and see Karin Widerberg's chapter, 'Dorothy Smith', in Stones (ed.), *Key Sociological Thinkers*.

12 For a clear introductory account, see Ken Morrison, *Marx, Durkheim, Weber: Formations of Modern Social Thought*. London: Sage, 1995, pp. 273–6. For explanations aimed at a more specialist readership, see Stephen Kalberg, *Max Weber's Comparative Historical Sociology*. Cambridge, MA: Polity Press, 1994, pp. 24–6, 48–9; Giddens, *New Rules of Sociological Method*, 1976; Outhwaite, *Understanding Social Life*, 1986; and n. 1, ch. 1.

13 See Anthony Giddens, *The Constitution of Society*. Cambridge, MA: Polity Press, 1984, pp. 1–40; and see Rob Stones, *Sociological Reasoning*. London: Palgrave Macmillan, 1996, pp. 52–8, which includes accounts of scenes taken from Peter Carey's 1989 novel, *Oscar and Lucinda*. London: Faber & Faber, and Kazue Ishiguro's novel of the same year *Remains of the Day*. London: Faber & Faber, in order to clarify some of the various ways in which internal and external worlds are intimately inter-linked. Also see the same concepts applied to documentary film in Rob Stones, 'Social Theory, Documentary Film and Distant Others: Simplicity and Subversion in "The Good Woman of Bangkok"', *European Journal of Cultural Studies* 5(2), 2002, 217–37.

14 Young, *Responsibility for Justice*, p. 43.

15 See Robert K. Merton, 'Manifest and Latent Functions', in R. Merton, *Social Theory and Social Structure*, enlarged edn. New York: Free Press, 1968, pp. 73–138; on unintended consequences of action, and Anthony Giddens, 'Functionalism: Après La Lutte', in A. Giddens, *In Defence of Sociology: Essays, Interpretations and Rejoinders*. Cambridge, MA: Polity Press, 1996, on connections to structure and agency, and on the link between unacknowledged conditions of action and unintended consequences of action. Also see Giddens, *The Constitution of Society*.

16 The detached, intellectual perspective is what the French theorist and sociologist, Pierre Bourdieu, labels the 'scholastic point of view', which he distinguished from the practical point of view of those immersed in the interactions and logics of the social world. See Pierre Bourdieu, *Pascalian Meditations*. Cambridge, MA: Polity Press, 2000/1997; also see Loic Wacquant, 'Pierre Bourdieu', in Stones (ed.), *Key Sociological Thinkers*, p. 273.

17 Young, *Responsibility for Justice*, p. 44.

18 Ibid., p. 50.

19 Ibid.

20 Ibid., p. 56.

21 Ibid., p. 44.

22 Ibid., p. 57.

23 Kim Christian Schrøder and Louise Phillips, 'Complexifying Media Power: A Study of the Interplay between Media and Audience Discourses on Politics', *Media Culture & Society* 29(6), 2007, 890–915; Monika Djerf-Pierre, Mats Ekström and Bengt Johansson, 'Policy Failure or Moral Scandal? Political Accountability, Journalism and New Public Management', *Media Culture & Society* 35(8), 2013, 960–76.

24 Schrøder and Phillips, 'Complexifying Media Power'.

25 Schrøder and Phillips, 'Complexifying Media Power', p. 900. The authors write that their understanding of discourse is based on that of the radical French philosopher, Michel Foucault, who saw it as 'a limited set of possible utterances which set the limits for what we can say, and, therefore, do,' p. 894. For a brief overview of Foucault's social theory, see Lawrence Barth, 'Michel Foucault', in Stones (ed.), *Key Sociological Thinkers*. Schroeder and Phillips also draw on the critical discourse analysis developed by Norman Fairclough, referencing, among others, his 2003 book *Analysing Discourse; Textual Analysis for Social Research*. New York: Routledge.

26 Schrøder and Phillips, 'Complexifying Media Power', p. 913.

27 In referring to the ways in which orders of discourse are drawn upon as 'interpretive repertoires' (pp. 894, 900–1) the authors follow Jonathan Potter and Margaret Wetherell, *Discourse Analysis and Social Psychology*. London: Sage, 1987.

28 The remaining category, not particularly emphasized by either party, is 'grassroots movements: growth versus the environment'.

29 Schrøder and Phillips, 'Complexifying Media Power', p. 896.

30 Ibid., p. 897.

31 Ibid., p. 898.

32 The insistence that attention is paid by social analysts to the 'skilled and knowledgeable' characteristics of human actors is closely associated with the ethnomethodological tradition in social theory. See John Heritage, *Garfinkel and Ethnomethodology*. Cambridge, MA: Polity Press, 1984; and John Heritage, 'Harold Garfinkel', in Stones (ed.), *Key Sociological Thinkers*.

33 Schrøder and Phillips note that when reference is made to the workings of *the system* within the text, the references employ distanced, dehumanizing terms and nominalizations, pp. 903–4.

34 Schrøder and Phillips, p. 909.

35 Ibid., p. 905.

36 Ibid., p. 906.

37 Djerf-Pierre et al., 'Policy Failure or Moral scandal?', pp. 961–2.

38 Ibid., p. 966.

39 Ibid., p. 965.

40 Ibid., p. 964.

41 Ibid., p. 969.

42 Ibid., p. 973.

43 Ibid., p. 962.

44 Ibid., p. 965.

45 Ibid., p. 968.

46 Ibid., p. 973.

47 Ibid.

48 Ibid., p. 971.

49 Ibid., pp. 960, 973.

Chapter 3

1 For more detail on a situated actor's *context analysis* see Rob Stones, *Sociological Reasoning*, pp. 98–102; and Stones, *Structuration Theory*, pp. 121–6. Also see R. Stones, 'Strategic Context Analysis: A New Research

Strategy for Structuration Theory', *Sociology* 25(3), 1991, 673–95. Over the years I've switched backwards and forwards between referring to this idea as 'agent's conduct analysis', when it's focusing on any kind of analysis by a situated actor of her or his context of action, and referring to it as 'strategic context analysis' when the actor-in-focus is surveying their context with a distinct strategic purpose in mind. Both are clearly useful, depending on the case in hand.

2 Some key references to the notion of habitus are Pierre Bourdieu, *Outline of a Theory of Practice*. Cambridge: Cambridge University Press, 1977[1972], pp. 87–95; and *The Logic of Practice*. Cambridge, MA: Polity Press, 1990[1980], pp. 66–79. Also see Andrew Sayer's systematic integration of emotional and ethical concerns into Bourdieu's earlier conception of habitus in A. Sayer, *The Moral Significance of Class*. Cambridge: Cambridge University Press, 2005; and A. Sayer, *Why Things Matter to People: Social Science, Values and Ethical Life*. Cambridge: Cambridge University Press, 2011. For secondary literature on habitus see Derek Robbins, *Bourdieu & Culture*. London: Sage, 2000, pp. 26–9; Karl Maton, 'Habitus', in Michael Grenfall (ed.), *Pierre Bourdieu: Key Concepts*. Stocksfield: Acumen, 2008, pp. 49–66; Löic Wacquant, 'Pierre Bourdieu', in Stones (ed.), *Key Sociological Thinkers*, pp. 266–70; and R. Stones, 'Habitus', in John Scott (ed.), *Sociology: The Key Concepts*. Abingdon: Routledge, 2006, pp. 79–82.

3 The idea of the 'hermeneutic circle' indicates a movement between, on the one hand, what one already knows or assumes to be the case, as with a typification, and, on the other hand, exposure to some details of a particular case that may either confirm or confound one's pre-judgement (or initial 'prejudice'). For an advanced discussion of this see Georgia Warnke, *Gadamer: Hermeneutics, Tradition and Reason*. Cambridge, MA: Polity Press, 1987, pp. 75–6.

4 See Stones, *Structuration Theory*, on the difference between situational (or conjunctural) knowledge and more general dispositions and capacities of the kind that Bourdieu includes in his notion of habitus. Building a layered account of social actors, Stones differentiates both of these from the further, dynamic and creative, aspects (active agency) that actors bring to moments of action as they draw on and combine both kinds of capacity within their actions.

5 See endnote 2, above.

6 On actors' 'hierarchy of purposes' see Anthony Giddens, *New Rules of Sociological Method*. Cambridge, MA: Polity Press, 1993[1976], pp. 84, 90–1. And on the parallel notion of the 'ordering of concerns' see Margaret Archer, *Being Human: The Problem of Agency*. Cambridge: Cambridge University Press, 2000, pp. 230–41; and *The internal Conversation: Mediating Between Structure and Agency*. Cambridge: Cambridge University Press, 2004.

7 See the references in endnote 19 in chapter 1 regarding the four key components of media frames.

8 Max Weber, 'The Profession and Vocation of Politics', in P. Lassman and R. Speirs (eds), *Max Weber: Political Writings*. Cambridge: Cambridge University Press, 1994/19.

9 In fact there is never such a thing as entirely 'single' causation, so by this we are simply indicating that it makes sense for certain purposes to focus primarily on a particularly powerful causal mechanism.

10 Jeffrey Alexander's cultural sociology, which has itself focused on current affairs, has done a great deal to illuminate the power of cultural ideas and processes to shift the course of social relations. His work has covered such current affairs processes as Watergate, Egypt's version of the 'Arab Spring', and the cultural performances and effects behind Barack Obama's electoral victories. See, for example, 'Three Models of Culture and Society Relations: Toward an Analysis of Watergate', in J. Alexander, *Action and its Environments: Towards a New Synthesis*. New York, NY: Columbia University Press, 1988, pp. 153–74; J. Alexander, *The Performance of Politics: Obama's Victory and the Democratic Struggle for Power*. Oxford: Oxford University Press, 2010; and J. Alexander, *Performative Revolution in Egypt: An Essay in Cultural Power*. London: Bloomsbury Academic, 2011.

11 Nicos Mouzelis, emeritus professor at the London School of Economics, who has bequeathed a valuable legacy to social analysis through his sustained insistence that attention to hierarchies be brought back into sociological theory, makes a related distinction between ordinary, micro, actors and, less ordinary, *macro actors*. Macro actors, says Mouzelis, are those powerful, institutionally privileged, actors whose actions can have consequences for many people across time and space. He differentiates between collective macro actors, such as businesses or political parties, and what he calls mega-actors, who are individuals one can identify as possessing the kind of power that can lead to the broad consequences he indicates. See Nicos Mouzelis, *Back to Sociological Theory: The Construction of Social Orders*. London: Macmillan, 1991, pp. 34–41, 106–7.

12 See Ian Kershaw, 'Working Towards the Führer: Reflections on the Nature of the Hitler Dictatorship', in Christian Leitz (ed.), *The Third Reich*. London: Blackwell, 1999, pp. 231–52; and Ian Kershaw, *The Nazi Dictatorship. Problems and Perspectives of Interpretation*, 5th edn. London: Edward Arnold, 1989.

13 On this and allied themes, see the recent volume, *On Critique: A Sociology of Emancipation*. Cambridge, MA: Polity Press, 2011[2009], from the French sociologist and social theorist, Luc Boltanski, especially pages 33–7, 108. Also see Bryan Turner and Simon Susen, *The Spirit of Luc Boltanski*. London and New York: Anthem Press, 2014.

14 See Simon Head, *Mindless: Why Smarter Machines are Making Dumber Humans*. New York: Basic Books, 2014.

15 See, for example, James Meek's excellent article, 'It's the Moral Thing to Do' (Review of *Breaking Bad*), *London Review of Books* 35(1), 3 January 2013, 7–9.

16 The ideas in this section benefitted from a lecture given by the Austrian media scholar, Rainer Winter, 'The Formation of Transnational Serial Cultures: Research on Complex Television in the Digital Age of Global Culture Industries', at the Institute of Culture and Society, University of Western Sydney, 3 April 2014. Some of these ideas can be found in R. Winter, '"All Happy Families": The Sopranos und die Kultur des Fernsehens im 21 Jahrhundert', in

R. Blanchet, K. Köhler, T. Smid and J. Zutavern (eds), *Serielle Formen. Von den fruhen Film-Serials zu aktuellen Quality-TV- und Online-Serien.* Marburg, 2011, pp. 153–74. See also Meek, ibid.; and David Bordwell and Kristin Thompson, *Film Art*, 4th edn; international edn. New York: McGraw Hill, 1993, particularly ch. 3, 'Narrative as Formal System', pp. 64–101.

17 See the audience-based research of Martin Scott I mentioned in the Preface, 'The Mediation of Distant Suffering: An Empirical Contribution beyond Television News Texts', *Media, Culture and Society* 36(1), 2014, 3–19. Scott argues that documentaries and other forms of more extended factual programming manage to involve audiences in more complex emotional and action-oriented engagements with the material. While his specific argument is that priority should therefore be given to 'the appearance of distant others in programming outside of the news', his position has interesting overlaps with the kind of audience amalgamation of different sources that I am advocating.

18 See J. Alexander, 'Cultural Pragmatics: Social Performance between Ritual and Strategy', in J. Alexander, B. Giesen and J. Mast (eds), *Social Performance: Symbolic Action, Cultural Pragmatics, and Ritual.* Cambridge: Cambridge University Press, 2006, pp. 29–90.

19 In an influential article in the *American Journal of Sociology*, Mustafa Emirbayer, and Ann Mische, draw on phenomenology, pragmatism and a wide range of empirical sociological studies to conceptualize actors' subjective orientation to their social context in terms of three different temporalities. Actors, they say, can primarily be oriented to the past, the present or the future (they label these as the iterative, the practical-evaluative and the projective and provide a nuanced discussion of each), while in any particular instance the three 'chords' will co-exist and interweave within the consciousness of the actor, as they do in Birgitte's case in this example taken from *Borgen* (her knowledge of what has gone on in the past is indexed, not least, by the documents from Amnesty and Human Rights Watch). The addition of the idea of a contextual field allows us to think more precisely about the elements from each temporal sphere that enter into these subjective moments. See Mustafa Emirbayer and Ann Mische, 'What Is Agency?' *American Journal of Sociology* 103(4), 1998, 962–1023.

20 Erving Goffman's theatrical or dramaturgical conception of the social world in *The Presentation of Self in Everyday Life.* New York: Doubleday Anchor, 1959, makes a distinction between those public or semi-public moments when we are 'front stage', available for others to see, interact with and judge, and those more private moments when we are 'back stage', where the pressures on us to perform are relaxed. Examples of the management of these two types of moment, including the skills involved in keeping each in their appropriate place, and in making transitions between them during the course of a day, abound in this episode of *Borgen*, as they do in everyday life. The character of a political drama, which in this way parallels the political memoir written after retirement, is such that it draws attention to this intermingling of the two worlds in the lives of public figures. Access to private moments of interior reflection and uncertainty can often illuminate politicians' perceived relationship to contextual fields in much more revealing terms than their public performances.

21 William Booth, Abigail Hauslohner and Michael Birnbaum, 'Egypt Orders Arrests of Muslim Brotherhood Leaders as Interim President Takes Office', *Washington Post*, 4 July 2013.

22 See, for example, Liz Sly, 'Backing Egypt's Generals, Saudi Arabia Promises Financial Support', *Washington Post*, 20 August 2013.

23 Jason Koutsoukis, 'Army Stranglehold too Firm to be Dislodged by Change of Government', *Sydney Morning Herald*, 8 July 2013.

24 See endnote 6, above.

25 Such questions are usually referred to as *counter-factuals*, and asking them can be particularly revealing if one wants to consider what might have happened if one or two specific factors were removed from a causal sequence. The answer to these questions can shed a good deal of light on the relative significance or insignificance of those factors.

26 See for example, the work of the literary critic and academic, Matt McGuire, who is also the author of crime novels exploring the realities of post-conflict Northern Ireland. McGuire's insights into the distinctive contribution literature can make to an understanding of social and political issues have enriched my own thinking, most strikingly in a lecture given at the Centre for Writing and Society, University of Western Sydney, Friday 12 April 2013, 'The Thriller and Transitional Justice: David Park's *The Truth*'. See also Matt McGuire, 'Twenty-First Century Northern Irish Poetry', in Paddy Lyons and Alison Younger (eds), *No Country for Old Men: Fresh Perspectives on Irish Literature*, Berlin: Peter Lang, 2009, 87–102.

27 See the points made about 'macro actors' and 'mega actors' in endnote 11, above; and see the parallel substantive argument in George C. Edwards III, *The Strategic President: Persuasion and Opportunity in Presidential Leadership*. Princeton: Princeton University Press, 2009, and in his *Overreach: Leadership in the Obama Presidency*. Princeton: Princeton University Press, 2012.

28 As noted in endnote 32 in chapter 2, the phrase 'skilled and competent actor' is associated with the tradition of ethnomethodology in social theory. This school of thought and research is a reaction against the idea of the behaviour of social actors being entirely the result of their social circumstances, with the idea that their behaviour is somehow structurally determined in all its aspects. In order to counter such ideas, ethnomethodology – the study of the everyday life skills, or methodologies, of ordinary folk – shines a light on the deeply layered knowledgeability of actors and the complex, and often tacit, skills they deploy when drawing on just the right aspects of knowledge and applying them in just the right way when confronted by novel, unfolding situations. For the classic statement of ethnomethodology see Harold Garfinkel, *Studies in Ethnomethodology*. Englewood Cliffs, NJ: Prentice Hill, 1967; and also see Heritage, 'Harold Garfinkel', in Stones (ed.), *Key Sociological Thinkers*, pp. 209–23.

29 This is a distinction identified and developed in Stones, 2005.

30 Such internalization of ways of behaving typically involves a sophisticated awareness of social norms, of conceptions of what is and isn't appropriate behaviour. As such, it includes aspects of basic etiquette, and, more broadly, any aspect of what Erving Goffman characterized as 'situational propriety'. See endnote 20, above, and see also Goffman, *Relations in Public*. Harmondsworth: Penguin, 1972; Philip Manning, *Erving Goffman and Modern Sociology*. Cambridge, MA: Polity Press, 1992; and Greg Smith, *Erving Goffman*. London: Routledge, 2006.

31 See Bourdieu, *Outline of a Theory of Practice*. Cambridge: Cambridge University Press, 1977/72; and also William Sewell Jr., 'A Theory of Structure: Duality, Agency and Transformations', *American Journal of Sociology* 98, 1992, 1–29; and Stones, *Structuration Theory*, pp. 67–9, 87–9.

32 This is a point made strongly and lucidly by Sewell Jr., 'A Theory of Structure', pp. 7–8, although it is already there in Bourdieu's work. It provides a point of connection with the structuralist and post-structuralist traditions of social theory with its emphasis on the level of socio-cultural meaning that circulates within discourses that are produced and mediated by individuals and organizations, but which have a life that is much more powerful than these. Cultural discourses should be thought of as an aspect of the contextual field in which social actors exist, grow, think and act, and for many issues we will want to pay close attention to the points at which actors and such discursive external forces meet, and to what happens at such points. The structuralist and post-structuralist traditions are associated with writers such as Roland Barthes, Michel Foucault, Jacques Derrida, Ernesto Laclau, Chantal Mouffe and Stuart Hall. Also see the reference to Foucault's understanding of discourses in the endnote 25 in chapter 2. For clear introductions to various aspects of this work, complementing the references provided in the endnote mentioned, see David Howarth, *Discourse*. Buckingham: Open University Press, 2000; Michèle Barrett, 'Stuart Hall', in Stones (ed.), *Key Sociological Thinkers*, pp. 293–310; and John Sturrock, *Structuralism*, 2nd edn. Oxford: Basil Blackwell, 2003.

33 This is to emphasize a point at the heart of Stones, *Structuration Theory*, (e.g. p. 5) which is that the moment of understanding what is going on in the interior worlds of actors – the moment of *verstehen* or hermeneutics (see n. 12, ch. 2) – needs to be combined with an awareness of how those worlds are linked to, embedded in, their structural context. I refer to this as the 'structural-hermeneutic' core at the heart of structuration theory.

34 For a magisterial account of such a process see Ewa Morawska, *Insecure Prosperity: Small Town Jews in Industrial America 1890-1940*. Princeton: Princeton University Press, 1996.

35 The reflections of the political theorist and historian of ideas, Quentin Skinner, are fascinating on this topic of 'reconstruction of context', not least because they are theoretically sophisticated at the same time as bearing the marks of sustained, impressive, practical engagements in interpretation. Skinner interprets the works of political theorists such as Hobbes and Machiavelli, through locating the intentions of these writers within the intellectual milieu of the political and historical context in which their writings would be read. See, for example, '"Social Meaning" and the Explanation of Social Action', in James Tully (ed.), *Meaning and Context: Quentin Skinner and His Critics*. Cambridge, MA: Polity Press, 1988, pp. 79–96.

36 A variety of work influenced by the phenomenological tradition illuminates, in their slightly different ways, the significance of the shifts in the ways we see things as we subtly change our focus from one set of tasks or concerns to another. The German philosopher and sociologist Jürgen Habermas has discussed this, in the second volume of his *Theory of Communicative Action: vol. 2. Lifeworld and System: A Critique of Functionalist Reason.* Cambridge, MA: Polity Press, 1987, pp. 122–3, in terms of shifting 'contexts of relevance', which are attendant upon the way we, or the group of people we are involved with, approach a topic. For illustrative examples and applications of Habermas's argument on these points see Stones, *Sociological Reasoning*, pp. 49–55. The ethnomethodological tradition, which we've already mentioned, is informed by the phenomenological sociology of Alfred Schutz, who wrote about the generally unrecognized skills required for actors to align the 'congruency of their systems of relevance'. On this see, John Heritage, *Garfinkel and Ethnomethodology.* Cambridge, MA: Polity Press, 1984, ch. 3, 'The Phenomenological Input', pp. 37–58. And, finally, the French theorists, Luc Boltanski and Laurent Thévenot, have shown in their book *On Justification.* Princeton: Princeton University Press, 2006/1991, how actors, in a series of phenomenological gestalt shifts, can switch between different normative frameworks and principles of justice within different social settings, and often in the very same social setting, accompanying shifts in how a given situation is defined.

37   See Stones, *Structuration Theory*, on active agency, pp. 100–9.

38   The symbolic interactionist tradition of social theory provides incisive tools for the analysis of many aspects of interaction, or joint actions. For a comprehensive, chapter-long, introduction to this approach see Hans Joas and Wolfgang Knöbl, *Social Theory: Twenty Introductory Lectures.* Cambridge: Cambridge University Press, 2009, ch. 6, 'interpretive Approaches (1) Symbolic Interactionism', pp. 123–49; and for an authorititative collection of statements and articles from this tradition, see Ken Plummer (ed.), *Symbolic Interactionism: Foundations and History,* vols 1 and 2. Aldershot: Edward Elgar, 1991. See Susie Scott, *Making Sense of Everyday Life.* Cambridge, MA: Polity Press, 2009, which is strongly influenced by this approach, for a lively indication of how such micro-sociologies enable us to suddenly notice things that have long been part and parcel of our experience of social life.

39   This is what Luc Boltanski, *On Critique, A Sociology of Emancipation.* Cambridge, MA: Polity Press, 2011/2009, refers to as a 'reality test', in that Grozin's presentation of himself as normatively committed to democracy and the rule of law (his 'truth' claim) is here subjected to scrutiny.

Chapter 4

1   On this point, see Chapter 2, including table 1 on the three different types of objectivity. The three meanings of the term 'objective' listed there refer to the categories of methodology, ontology and epistemology. The strategy I am discussing here is related to the *methodological* meaning of objectivity. I'm advocating a pragmatic methodological strategy – a strategy concerned with how best to investigate the social world depending on one's goals. Such a strategy has no need to deny, and in our case would not want to deny, that the subjective dimension is just as real as the elements we've labelled objective. This point, that both are seen as having an objective reality, is an *ontological* one. Finally, accepting the methodological strategy of just focusing on objective elements at certain points in the analysis, and tying this together with a belief in an objective reality, is entirely compatible with an acceptance that any researcher will also bring a subjective standpoint to the investigation. We need to acknowledge that different observers would, for example, approach a methodological strategy of focusing on objective aspects of reality in different ways, from a variety of perspectives and with varying purposes in mind. All of this would affect which parts of objective reality were selected as worthy of interest. However, any elements those observers identified as 'objective', would be contestable as more or less valid or invalid. That is, knowledge of objective elements in the world can be more or less 'objective' in the *epistemological sense* of the word, which concerns itself with the quality of knowledge. Epistemological objectivity is concerned with such things as the provision of substantiated evidence to back up whatever claims are made about the objective elements that have been identified and selected.

2 Adapting a notion from the celebrated Princeton anthropologist, Clifford Geertz. See '"From the Native's Point of View": On the Nature of Anthropological Knowledge', in Clifford Geertz, *Local Knowledge: Further Essays in Interpretive Anthropology.* New York: Basic Books, 1983, pp. 55–70.

3 This section draws from Rob Stones 'Causality, Contextual Frames and International Migration: Combining Strong Structuration Theory, Critical Realism and Textual Analysis', *IMI Working Papers,* International Migration Institute, University of Oxford, paper 62, November 2012.

4 See Stones, *Sociological Reasoning*, pp. 74–8 and *passim*, and Stones, 'Causality, Contextual Frames and International Migration', for earlier expressions of these points.

5 David Nakamura and Rosalind S. Helderman, 'Senate Begins Floor Debate on Immigration Reform Bill', *Washington Post,* Saturday 8 June 2013, p. A3.

6 David Nakamura, 'Obama Renews Push for Immigration Bill', *Washington Post,* Wednesday 12 June 2013, p. A2.

7 This point can be brought out clearly by comparing the level of detail regarding these policy areas provided in the *Bangkok Post* account with the much more complex typifications of these policy areas given in the policy networks and state theory literature. See, for example, Martin Smith, *Pressure, Power and Policy: State Autonomy and Policy Networks in Britain and the United States.* Hemel Hempstead: Harvester Wheatsheaf, 1993; and, for an account that draws out many of the key theoretical issues involved in grasping the complexity of power relations between state and societal agencies, see Bob Jessop, *State Power: A Strategic-Relational Approach.* Cambridge, MA: Polity Press, 2008.

8 Charles Richardson, 'Compare and Contrast: Protests in Ukraine and Thailand', *Crikey,* 3 December 2013.

9 Henry Meyer and Scott Rose, 'Putin Battles Europe for Ukraine, Ex-Soviet States', *Sydney Morning Herald*, 6 December 2013 (original publication: *Washington Post*).

10 R. Emmott, B. Lewis and S. Rao (editing by G. Jones), 'Factbox: Facts about Ukraine's Ties with Russia and Europe', *Reuters*, Friday, 22 November 2013. http://www.reuters.com/article/2013/11/22/us-eu-russia-ukraine-factbox-idUSBRE9AL0LQ20131122 (last accessed 22 April 2014).

11 Ukraine Profile, BBC News Website, 25 November 2013. http://www.bbc.co.uk/news/world-europe-18018002 (last accessed 24 April 2014).

12 The following section draws heavily on Rob Stones, 'Social Theory and Current Affairs: A Framework for Greater Intellectual Engagement', *British Journal of Sociology*, 65(2), 2014, 293–316.

13 On binary oppositions and other aspects of the construction of meaning as characterized in structuralism and post-structuralism see Madan Sarup, *An Introductory Guide to Post-structuralism and Postmodernism*. London: Harvester Wheatsheaf, 1988; Howarth, *Discourse*, 2000; and Sturrock, *Structuralism*, 2003.

14 Norman Fairclough, *Media Discourse*. London: Edward Arnold, 1995, see pp. 125–49 on identity and social relations within media texts.

15 Clifford Geertz, *Works and Lives: The Anthropologist as Author*. Cambridge, MA: Polity Press, 1989, p. 79.

16 Roland Barthes, 'The Reality Effect in Descriptions', in L. Furst (ed.), *Realism*. London: Longman, 1992, pp. 135–41.

17 The analysis was initially written for the article in the *British Journal of Sociology* referenced above, which was submitted in November 2012.

Chapter 5

1 For a lucid, basic understanding of the workings of the financial markets leading up to the Global Financial Crisis, see the skilful, factual account by the novelist John Lanchester, *Whoops: Why Everyone Owes Everyone and No One can Pay*. London: Penguin, 2010. But also, see the review of the book by Howard Davies, the Chair of the Financial Services Authority (FSA) from 1997 to 2003, in the *Guardian*, 23 January 2010, which points to the need to also develop the same kind of sophisticated understanding of regulatory regimes in order to think effectively about preventive strategies that are embedded in real-world complexities.

2 See endnote 10, chapter 3, for references to Alexander's work.

3 See Wright Mills, *The Sociological Imagination*, 2000.

4 Fergal Keane, *Letter to Daniel: Dispatches from the Heart*. London: Penguin, 1996, p. 226.

5 Ibid., p. 150.

6 Ibid., p. 226.

7 Ibid., p. 228.

8 Ibid., p. 229.

9 Ibid.

10 Ibid., pp. 230–1.

11 On the power and significance of cultural processes, see Jeffrey C. Alexander, *The Meanings of Social Life: A Cultural Sociology*. New York, NY: Oxford University Press, 2003; Alexander, *The Performance of Politics*; and Jeffrey C. Alexander and Bernadette N. Jaworsky, *Obama Power*. Malden, MA: Polity Press, 2014.

12 Keane, *Letter to Daniel*, p. 230.

13 Ibid., p. 227.

14 The classical sociologist, Max Weber, noted the tension between morality as pure principle, or 'the politics of conviction', on the one hand, and morality as needing to adapt itself to concerns with real-world consequences – what he called the 'politics of responsibility' – on the other hand. See Weber's 'The Profession and Vocation of Politics', in P. Lassman and R. Speirs (eds), *Max Weber: Political Writings*. For more general literature on related issues see, Stephen Mulhall and Adam Swift's lucid volume, *Liberals and Communitarians*. Oxford: Blackwell, 1992; C. Farrelly, *An Introduction to Contemporary Political Theory*. London: Sage, 2004; and Michael Sandel, *Justice: What's The Right Thing to Do?*. New York: Farrar, Straus and Giroux, 2009.

15 See Emirbayer and Mische, "What Is Agency?" *American Journal of Sociology*.

16 See endnote 13.

17 See Adam and Groves, *Future Matters: Action, Knowledge, Ethics*, 2007, and Adam, 'Future Matters: Challenges for Social Theory and Social Inquiry', *Cultura e Comunicaizione* 1: 47–55.

18 The following section draws heavily on Rob Stones and Ake Tangsupvattana, 'Social Theory, Current Affairs, and Thailand's Political Turmoil: Seeing Beyond Reds vs. Yellows', *Journal of Political Power* 5(2), August 2012, 217–38.

19 It is important to pay close attention to the textual and rhetorical forms in which news and current affairs pieces present their claims to knowledge. Bill Nichols, *Representing Reality: Issues and Concepts in Documentary*. Bloomington and Indianapolis: Indiana University Press, 1991, pp. 32–75, outlines five dominant forms available to documentary makers. These are the Expository; the Observational; the Interactive; the Reflexive; and the Performative. See Stella Bruzzi, *New Documentary: A Critical Introduction*. London and New York: Routledge, 2000, pp. 1–3, for a critical discussion of Nichols's perspective on these forms. For a discussion of the accounts of the Thai conflict discussed here, within an academic article making a parallel general case for stronger links between social theory and news and current affairs, see Stones, 'Social Theory and Current Affairs', *British Journal of Sociology*, 2014.

20 Pasuk Phongpaichit and Baker, C., *Thaksin*, 2nd expanded ed. Chiang Mai: Silkworm Books, 2009, p. 237.

21 See David Beetham and Kevin Boyle, *Introducing Democracy: 80 Questions and Answers.* Cambridge, MA: Polity Press, 1995, pp. 31–3 and *passim*; Somchai Phatharathananunth, *Civil Society and Democratization: Social Movements in Northeast Thailand.* Copenhagen: Nordic Institute of Asian Studies Press, 2002, p. 126ff.

22 Oliver Pye and Wolfram Schaffar, 'The 2006 Anti-Thaksin Movement in Thailand: An Analysis', *Journal of Contemporary Asia* 38(1), 2008, 38–61. See pages 40–4; and see Stones and Ake, 'Social Theory, Current Affairs, and Thailand's Political Turmoil', 2012, for a more extensive chronicling of the academic literature relevant to this case.

23 This is not to imply that all the resistance was democratically motivated – this was certainly not the case, as future events were to roundly demonstrate – but large segments of it probably were, and, at the very least, the interests of the forces involved can be made better sense of when they are positioned around these socio-structural domains and not simply around the domain of electoral democracy.

24 For example, Ukrist Pathmanand, 'A Different Coup D'État?' *Journal of Contemporary Asia* 38(1), 2008, 124–42; see pp. 130–3; cf. Alexander, *The Meanings of Social Life*, pp. 155–77.

25 Alexander's work on cultural processes is invaluable in understanding the relative autonomy that such processes can gain from other institutional and organizational dynamics, and the links between this autonomy and the power that cultural processes manage to harness in particular times and places.

26 Dominic Hughes, 'Scandal Hit Mid Staffs "Faces Being Dissolved"', BBC News website, 28 February 2013. http://www.bbc.co.uk/news/health-21624407 (last accessed 20 June 2014).

27 The notion of a 'binary opposition', in which texts are organized in terms of a major division between different sets of meanings (often with one pole of the division rendered as positive and the other as negative) attached to different groups, is a central focus of structuralist and post-structuralist analysis. These theoretical approaches are the repository of a wealth of enduring insights about how texts of all kinds manage to construct and convey meaning. See endnote 13, chapter 4 for references, and also see Ernesto Laclau and Chantal Mouffe, *Hegemony and Socialist Strategy.* London: Verso, 1985.

28 Duncan Campbell and Denis Meikle, 'Mid Staffs Report Calls for Sweeping Changes to Improve Patient Safety', *The Guardian*, Wednesday 6 February 2013. http://www.theguardian.com/society/2013/feb/06/mid-staffordshire-report-sweeing-changes (last accessed 21 August 2014).

29 In other words – in the disciplined way of thinking we've been insisting upon – we are talking about the *explanandum* or 'phenomenon-to-be-explained'.

30 Campbell and Meikle, 'Mid Staffs Report', 6 February 2013.

31 Ibid.

32 The eminent Polish sociologist, Zygmunt Bauman, has written powerfully about the relationship between spatial distance and moral inoculation within bureaucracies. See his *Modernity and the Holocaust.* Cambridge, MA: Polity Press, 1989.

33 The Mid Staffordshire NHS Foundation Trust Public Inquiry, Chaired by Robert Francis QC, *Report of the Mid Staffordshire NHS Foundation Trust Public Inquiry*, HC 947. London: The Stationery Office, February 2013, volume 1, paragraph 2.215–8, p. 197.

34 Ibid., volume 1, paragraph 2.214, p. 198.

35 Ibid., volume 1, paragraph 2.220, p. 198.

36 Ibid., volume 1, paragraph 2.224, p. 199.

37 Ibid.

38 On the concept of an 'independent causal force or influence', and the difference between this and 'irresistible causal forces' see Rob Stones, *Structuration Theory*, pp. 109–15.

39 *Report of the Mid Staffordshire NHS Foundation Trust Public Inquiry*, volume 1, paragraphs 2.222 and 2.223, pp. 198–9.

40 See endnote 6, chapter 3, for actors' 'hierarchy or purposes' see Giddens, *New Rules of Sociological Method*, 2nd edn, pp. 84, 89–91. On the parallel notion of the 'ordering of concerns' see Archer, *Being Human*, pp. 230–41; and *The internal Conversation*.

41 *Report of the Mid Staffordshire NHS Foundation Trust Public Inquiry*, volume 1, pp. 198–9.

42 Ibid., volume 1, paragraph 2.237, pp. 210–2.

43 Charlie Cooper, 'Mid Staffs Nursing Chief Says: I'm Not to Blame', *Independent*, 23 July 2013, p. 23.

44 See Nicos Mouzelis, *Back to Sociological Theory*, pp. 34–41, 106–7.

45 Andrew Sparrow, 'Sir David Nicholson: I'm Accountable, But Only a Bit. The Main Points From the NHS Head's Evidence on The Mid Staffordshire Hospital Trust Scandal', *theguardian.com*, Wednesday 6 March 2013. http://www.theguardian.com/society/2013/mar/05/sir-david-nicholson-nhs-mid-staffs (last accessed 21 August 2014).

Bibliography

Adam, B. (2010), 'Future Matters: Challenges for Social Theory and Social Inquiry', *Cultura e Comunicaizione* 1: 47–55, online: www.pic-ais.it/upload/rte/Rivista_online_PicAis_aprile2010_N1.pdf

Adam, B. and Groves, C. (2007), *Future Matters: Action, Knowledge, Ethics*. Leiden: Brill Books.

Alexander, J. C. (1988), 'Three Models of Culture and Society Relations: Toward an Analysis of Watergate', in J. Alexander, *Action and its Environments: Towards a New Synthesis*. New York, NY: Columbia University Press.

—(2003), *The Meanings of Social Life: A Cultural Sociology*. New York, NY: Oxford University Press.

—(2006), 'Cultural Pragmatics: Social Performance between Ritual and Strategy', in J. Alexander, B. Giesen, and J. Mast (eds), *Social Performance: Symbolic Action, Cultural Pragmatics, and Ritual*. Cambridge: Cambridge University Press.

—(2010), *The Performance of Politics: Obama's Victory and the Democratic Struggle for Power*. Oxford: Oxford University Press.

—(2011), *Performative Revolution in Egypt: An Essay in Cultural Power*. London: Bloomsbury Academic.

Alexander, J. C. and Jaworsky, B. N. (2014), *Obama Power*. Malden, MA: Polity Press.

Anon (2009), 'Burma "Protected by its Powerful Neighbours"', *Bangkok Post*, 13 August.

Archer, M. (2000), *Being Human: The Problem of Agency*. Cambridge: Cambridge University Press.

—(2004), *The Internal Conversation: Mediating Between Structure and Agency*. Cambridge: Cambridge University Press.

Barrett, M. (2008), 'Stuart Hall', in R. Stones (ed.), *Key Sociological Thinkers*, 2nd edn. London: Palgrave Macmillan.

Barth, L. (2008), 'Michel Foucault', in R. Stones (ed.), *Key Sociological Thinkers*, 2nd edn. London: Palgrave Macmillan.

Barthes, R. (1992), 'The Reality Effect in Descriptions', in L. Furst (ed.), *Realism*. London: Longman.

Bauman, Z. (1989), *Modernity and the Holocaust*. Cambridge, MA: Polity Press.

BBC News Website (2013), 'Ukraine Profile', 25 November. http://www.bbc.co.uk/news/world-europe-18018002 (last accessed 24 April 2014).

Beach, A. (2011), 'Return to Tahrir Square: Egypt Erupts in Protest', *Independent*, 9 July.

Beetham, D. and Boyle, K. (1995), *Introducing Democracy: 80 Questions and Answers*. Cambridge, MA: Polity Press.

Berger, P. and Luckmann, T. (1967[1966]), *The Social Construction of Reality: A Treatise in the Sociology of Knowledge*. London: Penguin Books.

Bhaskar, R. (1979), *The Possibility of Naturalism: A Philosophical Critique of the Contemporary Human Sciences*. Brighton: Harvester Wheatsheaf.

Boltanski, L. (1999), *Distant Suffering: Morality, Media and Politics*. Cambridge: Cambridge University Press.

—(2011[2009]), *On Critique: A Sociology of Emancipation*. Cambridge, MA: Polity Press.

Boltanski, L. and Thévenot, L. (2006[1991]), *On Justification*. Princeton: Princeton University Press.

Booth, W., Hauslohner, A. and Birnbaum, M. (2013), 'Egypt Orders Arrests of Muslim Brotherhood Leaders as Interim President Takes Office', *Washington Post*, 4 July.

Bordwell, D. and Thompson, K. (1993), *Film Art*, 4th edn; international edn. New York: McGraw Hill.

Bourdieu, P. (1977[1972]), *Outline of a Theory of Practice*. Cambridge: Cambridge University Press.

—(1984[1979]), *Distinction: A Social Critique of the Judgement of Taste*. London: Routledge.

—(1990[1980]), *The Logic of Practice*. Cambridge, MA: Polity Press.

—(1998[1996]), *On Television and Journalism*. London: Pluto Press.

—(2000[1997]), *Pascalian Meditations*. Cambridge, MA: Polity Press.

Bruzzi, S. (2000), *New Documentary: A Critical Introduction*. London and New York: Routledge.

Campbell, D. and Meikle, D. (2013), 'Mid Staffs Report Calls for Sweeping Changes to Improve Patient Safety', *The Guardian*, Wednesday 6 February. http://www.theguardian.com/society/2013/feb/06/mid-staffordshire-report-sweeing-changes (last accessed 21 August 2014).

Carey, P. (1989), *Oscar and Lucinda*. London: Faber & Faber.

Chouliaraki, L. (2006), *The Spectatorship of Suffering*. London: Sage.

Coman, J. (2013), 'How Germany Rode the Storm: Progressive Business and Labour Principles Underpin Europe's Economic Giant', *The Guardian Weekly*, 7–13 June, pp. 1 and 8.

Cooper, C. (2013), 'Mid Staffs Nursing Chief Says: I'm Not to Blame', *Independent*, 23 July, p. 23.

Davies, H. (2010), 'Book Review of John Lanchester, *Whoops: Why Everyone Owes Everyone and No One can Pay*', *Guardian*, 23 January.

De Botton, A. (2014), *The News: A User's Manual*. London: Hamish Hamilton, pp. 99–100.

Djerf-Pierre, M., Ekström, M. and Johansson, B. (2013), 'Policy Failure or Moral Scandal? Political Accountability, Journalism and New Public Management', *Media, Culture & Society* 35(8): 960–76.

Edwards III, G. C. (2009), *The Strategic President: Persuasion and Opportunity in Presidential Leadership*. Princeton: Princeton University Press.

—(2012), *Overreach: Leadership in the Obama Presidency*. Princeton: Princeton University Press.

Emirbayer, M. and Mische, A. (1998), 'What Is Agency?' *American Journal of Sociology* 103(4): 962–1023.

Emmott, R., Lewis, B. and Rao, S. (editing by Jones, G.) (2013), 'Factbox: Facts about Ukraine's Ties with Russia and Europe', Reuters, US Edition, Friday, 22 November, 8.34am EST. http://www.reuters.com/article/2013/11/22/us-eu-russia-ukraine-factbox-idUSBRE9AL0LQ20131122 (last accessed 22 April 2014).

Entman, R. M. (1993), 'Framing: Towards Clarification of a Fractured Paradigm', Journal of Communication 43(4): 51–8.

—(1996), 'Reporting Environmental Policy Debate: The Real Media Biases', Harvard International Journal of Press/Politics 1: 77–92.

Fairclough, N. (1995), Media Discourse. London: Edward Arnold, 1995.

—(2003), Analysing Discourse; Textual Analysis for Social Research. New York: Routledge.

Farrelly, C. (2004), An Introduction to Contemporary Political Theory. London: Sage.

Francis, R. (2013), Report of the Mid Staffordshire NHS Foundation Trust Public Inquiry, HC 947. London: The Stationery Office, February, volume 1.

Garfinkel, H. (1967), Studies in Ethnomethodology. Englewood Cliffs, NJ: Prentice Hill.

Geertz, C. (1983), '"From the Native's Point of View": On the Nature of Anthropological Knowledge', in C. Geertz, Local Knowledge: Further Essays in Interpretive Anthropology. New York: Basic Books.

—(1989), Works and Lives: The Anthropologist as Author. Cambridge, MA: Polity Press.

Giddens, A. (1976), New Rules of Sociological Method: A Positive Critique of Interpretative Sociologies. London: Hutchinson.

—(1984), The Constitution of Society. Cambridge, MA: Polity Press.

—(1993[1976]), New Rules of Sociological Method, 2nd edn. Cambridge, MA: Polity Press.

—(1996), 'Functionalism: Aprés La Lutte', in A. Giddens, In Defence of Sociology: Essays, Interpretations and Rejoinders. Cambridge, MA: Polity Press.

Goffman, E. (1959), The Presentation of Self in Everyday Life. New York: Doubleday Anchor.

—(1967), Interaction Ritual: Essays on Face-to-Face Behavior. New York: Anchor.

—(1971), Relations in Public: Microstudies of the Public Order. New York: Basic Books.

Habermas, J. (1987), Theory of Communicative Action: vol. 2. Lifeworld and System: A Critique of Functionalist Reason. Cambridge, MA: Polity Press.

Head, S. (2014), Mindless: Why Smarter Machines are Making Dumber Humans. New York: Basic Books.

Heritage, J. (1984), Garfinkel and Ethnomethodology. Cambridge, MA: Polity Press.

—(2008), 'Harold Garfinkel', in R. Stones (ed.), Key Sociological Thinkers, 2nd edn. London: Palgrave Macmillan.

Howarth, D. (2000), Discourse. Buckingham: Open University Press.

Hughes, D. (2013), 'Scandal Hit Mid Staffs 'Faces Being Dissolved', BBC News Website, 28 February. http://www.bbc.co.uk/news/health-21624407 (last accessed 20 June 2014).

Ishiguro, K. (1989), Remains of the Day. London: Faber & Faber.

Iyengar, S. (1994), *Is Anyone Responsible? How Television Frames Political Issues*. Chicago: University of Chicago Press.

Jessop, B. (2008), 'Karl Marx', in R. Stones (ed.), *Key Sociological Thinkers*, 2nd edn. London: Palgrave Macmillan.

—(2008), *State Power. A Strategic-Relational Approach*. Cambridge, MA: Polity Press.

Joas, H. and Knöbl, W. (2009[2004]), *Social Theory: Twenty Introductory Lectures*. Cambridge: Cambridge University Press.

Kalberg, S. (1994), *Max Weber's Comparative Historical Sociology*. Cambridge, MA: Polity Press.

Kalman, M. (2011), 'Netanyahu May be Forced to Destroy Settlers' Homes', *The Independent*, Saturday 23 July.

Keane, F. (1996), 'A Letter from Africa', in F. Keane, *Letter to Daniel: Dispatches from the Heart*. London: BBC Books/Penguin Books.

—(1996), *Season of Blood: A Rwandan Journey*. London: Penguin Books.

Kershaw, I. (1989), *The Nazi Dictatorship. Problems and Perspectives of Interpretation*, 5th edn. London: Edward Arnold.

—(1999), 'Working Towards the Führer: Reflections on the Nature of the Hitler Dictatorship', in Christian Leitz (ed.), *The Third Reich*. London: Blackwell.

Koutsoukis, J. (2013), 'Army Stranglehold too Firm to be Dislodged by Change of Government', *Sydney Morning Herald*, 8 July.

Kuypers, J. (2010), 'Framing Analysis from a Rhetorical Perspective', in P. D'Angelo and J. Kuypers (eds), *Doing News Framing Analysis: Empirical and Theoretical Perspectives*. London: Routledge.

Laclau, E. and Mouffe, C. (1985), *Hegemony and Socialist Strategy*. London: Verso.

Lanchester, J. (2010), *Whoops: Why Everyone Owes Everyone and No One Can Pay*. London: Penguin.

Manning, P. (1992), *Erving Goffman and Modern Sociology*. Cambridge, MA: Polity Press.

Marx, K. and Engels, F. (1962), *Marx and Engels Selected Works*, vol. 1. Moscow: Foreign Languages Publishing House.

Maton, K. (2008), 'Habitus', in M. Grenfall (ed.), *Pierre Bourdieu: Key Concepts*. Stocksfield: Acumen.

McGuire, M. (2009), 'Twenty-First Century Northern Irish Poetry', in Paddy Lyons and Alison Younger (eds), *No Country for Old Men: Fresh Perspectives on Irish Literatur*. Berlin: Peter Lang.

—(2013), 'The Thriller and Transitional Justice: David Park's *The Truth*'. The Centre for Writing and Society: University of Western Sydney, 12 April.

McLellan, D. (ed.) (1971), *The Thought of Karl Marx: An Introduction*. London: Macmillan.

Meek, J. (2013), 'It's the Moral Thing to Do' (Review of *Breaking Bad*), *London Review of Books* 35(1), 3 January, 7–9.

Merton, R. K. (1968), 'Manifest and Latent Functions', in R. K. Merton, *Social Theory and Social Structure*, enlarged edn. New York: Free Press.

Meyer, H. and Rose, S. (2013), 'Putin Battles Europe for Ukraine, Ex-Soviet States', *Sydney Morning Herald*, 6 December 2013 (original publication: *Washington Post*).

Mills, C. W. (2000[1959]), *The Sociological Imagination (Fortieth Anniversary Edition)*. Oxford: Oxford University Press.

Morawska, E. (1996), *Insecure Prosperity: Small Town Jews in Industrial America 1890-1940*. Princeton: Princeton University Press.

Morley, D. (1999), 'Finding Out about the World from Television News: Some Problems', in J. Gripsrud (ed.), *Television and Common Knowledge*. London: Routledge.

Morrison, K. (1995), *Marx, Durkheim, Weber: Formations of Modern Social Thought*. London: Sage.

Mouzelis, N. (1991), *Back to Sociological Theory: The Construction of Social Orders*. London: Macmillan.

Mulhall, S. and Swift, A. (1992), *Liberals and Communitarians*. Oxford: Blackwell.

Nakamura, D. (2013), 'Obama Renews Push for Immigration Bill', *Washington Post*, Wednesday 12 June, p. A2.

Nakamura, D. and Helderman, R. S. (2013), 'Senate Begins Floor Debate on Immigration Reform Bill', *Washington Post*, Saturday 8 June, p. A3.

Nichols, B. (1991), *Representing Reality: Issues and Concepts in Documentary*. Bloomington and Indianapolis: Indiana University Press.

O'Reilly, K. (2012), *International Migration and Social Theory*. London: Palgrave Macmillan.

Outhwaite, W. (1986), *Understanding Social Life: The Method Called Verstehen*, 2nd edn. Lewes: Jean Stroud.

Pasuk Phongpaichit and Baker, C. (2009), *Thaksin*, 2nd expanded edn. Chiang Mai: Silkworm Books.

Philo, G. and Berry, M. (2011), *More Bad News from Israel*. London: Pluto Press.

Plummer, K. (ed.) (1991), *Symbolic Interactionism: Foundations and History*, vols 1 and 2. Aldershot: Edward Elgar.

Postman, N. (1987[first published 1985]), *Amusing Ourselves to Death: Public Discourse in the Age of Showbusiness*. London: Methuen.

Postman, N. and Powers, S. (2007), *How to Watch TV News*, rev. edn. London: Penguin Books.

Potter, J. and Wetherell, M. (1987), *Discourse Analysis and Social Psychology*. London: Sage.

Pye, O. and Schaffar, W. (2008), 'The 2006 Anti-Thaksin Movement in Thailand: An Analysis', *Journal of Contemporary Asia* 38(1): 38–61.

Richardson, C. (2013), 'Compare and Contrast: Protests in Ukraine and Thailand', *Crikey*, 3 December.

Robbins, D. (2000), *Bourdieu & Culture*. London: Sage.

Sandel, M. (2009), *Justice: What's The Right Thing to Do?*. New York: Farrar, Straus and Giroux.

Sarup, M. (1988), *An Introductory Guide to Post-structuralism and Postmodernism*. London: Harvester Wheatsheaf.

Sayer, A. (1992), *Method in Social Science; A Realist Approach*, 2nd edn. London: Routledge.

—(2000), *Realism and Social Science*. London: Sage.

—(2005), *The Moral Significance of Class*. Cambridge: Cambridge University Press.

—(2011), *Why Things Matter to People: Social Science, Values and Ethical Life*. Cambridge: Cambridge University Press.

Schrøder, K. C. and Phillips, L. (2007), 'Complexifying Media Power: A Study of the Interplay between Media and Audience Discourses on Politics', *Media, Culture & Society* 29(6): 890–915.

Scott, M. (2014), 'The Mediation of Distant Suffering: An Empirical Contribution beyond Television News Texts', *Media, Culture and Society* 36(1), January, 3–19.

Scott, S. (2009), *Making Sense of Everyday Life.* Cambridge, MA: Polity Press.

Sewell Jr., W. (1992), 'A Theory of Structure: Duality, Agency and Transformations', *American Journal of Sociology* 98: 1–29.

Skinner, Q. (1988), '"Social Meaning" and the Explanation of Social Action', in James Tully (ed.), *Meaning and Context: Quentin Skinner and His Critics.* Cambridge, MA: Polity Press.

Sly, L. (2013), 'Backing Egypt's Generals, Saudi Arabia Promises Financial Support', *Washington Post*, 20 August.

Smith, D. (1987), *The Everyday World as Problematic: A Feminist Sociology.* Boston: Northeastern University Press.

Smith, G. (2006), *Erving Goffman.* London: Routledge.

Smith, M. (1993), *Pressure, Power and Policy: State Autonomy and Policy Networks in Britain and the United States.* Hemel Hempstead: Harvester Wheatsheaf.

Somchai Phatharathananunth (2002), *Civil Society and Democratization: Social Movements in Northeast Thailand.* Copenhagen: Nordic Institute of Asian Studies Press.

Sparrow, A. (2013), 'Sir David Nicholson: I'm Accountable, But Only a Bit. The Main Points From the NHS Head's Evidence on The Mid Staffordshire Hospital Trust Scandal', *theguardian.com*, Wednesday 6 March. http://www.theguardian.com/society/2013/mar/05/sir-david-nicholson-nhs-mid-staffs (last accessed 21 August 2014).

Stones, R. (1991), 'Strategic Context Analysis: A New Research Strategy for Structuration Theory', *Sociology* 25(3): 673–95.

—(1996), *Sociological Reasoning.* London: Palgrave Macmillan.

—(2002), 'Social Theory, Documentary Film and Distant Others: Simplicity and Subversion in "The Good Woman of Bangkok"', *European Journal of Cultural Studies* 5(2): 217–37.

—(2005), *Structuration Theory.* London: Palgrave Macmillan.

—(2006), 'Habitus', in John Scott (ed.), *Sociology: The Key Concepts.* Abingdon: Routledge.

—(2012), 'Causality, Contextual Frames and International Migration: Combining Strong Structuration Theory, Critical Realism and Textual Analysis', *IMI Working Papers*, International Migration Institute, University of Oxford, paper 62, November.

—(2014), 'Social Theory and Current Affairs: A Framework for Greater Intellectual Engagement', *British Journal of Sociology* 65(2): 293–316.

Stones, R. and Ake Tangsupvattana (2012), 'Social Theory, Current Affairs, and Thailand's Political Turmoil: Seeing Beyond Reds vs. Yellows', *Journal of Political Power* 5(2), August, 217–38.

Street, J. (2001), *Mass Media, Politics and Democracy.* London: Palgrave Macmillan, 2001.

Sturrock, J. (2003), *Structuralism*, 2nd edn. Oxford: Basil Blackwell.

Turner, B. and Susen, S. (2014), *The Spirit of Luc Boltanski*. London and New York: Anthem Press.

Ukrist Pathmanand (2008), 'A Different Coup D'État?' *Journal of Contemporary Asia*, 38(1): 124–42.

Wacquant, L. (2008), 'Pierre Bourdieu', in R. Stones (ed.), *Key Sociological Thinkers*, 2nd edn. London: Palgrave Macmillan.

Warnke, G. (1987), *Gadamer: Hermeneutics, Tradition and Reason*. Cambridge, MA: Polity Press.

Weber, M. (1989[1919]), 'Science as a Vocation', in P. Lassman and I. Velody with H. Martins (eds), *Max Weber's 'Science as a Vocation'*. London: Unwin Hyman.

—(1994[1919]), 'The Profession and Vocation of Politics', in P. Lassman and R. Speirs (eds), *Max Weber: Political Writings*. Cambridge: Cambridge University Press.

Widerberg, K. (2008), 'Dorothy Smith', in R. Stones (ed.), *Key Sociological Thinkers*, 2nd edn. London: Palgrave Macmillan.

Williams, R. (2008), 'Erving Goffman', in R. Stones (ed.), *Key Sociological Thinkers*, 2nd edn. London: Palgrave Macmillan.

Winter, R. (2011), '"All Happy Families": The Sopranos und die Kultur des Fernsehens im 21 Jahrhundert', in R. Blanchet, K. Köhler, T. Smid and J. Zutavern (eds), *Serielle Formen. Von den fruhen Film-Serials zu aktuellen Quality-TV- und Online-Serien*. Marburg: Schüren Verlag.

—(2014), 'The Formation of Transnational Serial Cultures: Research on Complex Television in the Digital Age of Global Culture Industries', The Institute of Culture and Society, University of Western Sydney, 3 April.

Wolfsfeld, G. (2011), *Making Sense of Media and Politics: Five Principles in Political Communication*. London: Routledge.

Young, I. M. (2011), *Responsibility for Justice*. Oxford: Oxford University Press.

Index

www.ingramcontent.com/pod-product-compliance
Lightning Source LLC
Chambersburg PA
CBHW062024270326
41929CB00014B/2307